DIRECTED BY GOD

DIRECTED *by* GOD

JEWISHNESS *in* CONTEMPORARY ISRAELI FILM *and* TELEVISION

YARON PELEG

UNIVERSITY OF TEXAS PRESS
Austin

Printed in the United States of America
First edition, 2016

♾ The paper used in this book meets the minimum requirements of ANSI/NISO Z39.48-1992 (R1997) (Permanence of Paper).

LIBRARY OF CONGRESS CATALOGING-IN-PUBLICATION DATA
Names: Peleg, Yaron, author.
Title: Directed by god : Jewishness in contemporary Israeli film and television / Yaron Peleg.
Description: First edition. | Austin : University of Texas Press, 2016. | Includes bibliographical references and index.
Identifiers: LCCN 2015046846 | ISBN 978-1-4773-0950-6 (cloth : alk. paper) | ISBN 978-1-4773-0951-3 (pbk. : alk. paper) | ISBN 978-1-4773-0952-0 (library e-book) | ISBN 978-1-4773-0953-7 (nonlibrary e-book)
Subjects: LCSH: Jews in motion pictures. | Motion pictures—Israel—History. | Jews—Identity. | Israel—In motion pictures. | Motion pictures—Social aspects—Israel. | Zionism in motion pictures.
Classification: LCC PN1995.9.J46 P45 2016 | DDC 791.43/6529924—dc23
LC record available at http://lccn.loc.gov/2015046846

doi:10.7560/309506

This book is dedicated to my parents, Sadie and Uri Peleg,
who taught me humility and common sense.

CONTENTS

PREFACE AND ACKNOWLEDGMENTS ix

A NOTE ON TRANSLITERATION xi

INTRODUCTION 1

CHAPTER 1

JEWISH AND HUMAN:
IMAGES OF ORTHODOX JEWS 23

CHAPTER 2

JEWISH AND ISRAELI:
IMAGES OF MIZRAHI JEWS 53

CHAPTER 3

JEWISH AND FANATIC:
IMAGES OF RELIGIOUS ZIONISTS 81

CHAPTER 4

JEWISH AND POPULAR:
IMAGES OF RELIGION ON TV 105

AFTERWORD 135

NOTES 145

BIBLIOGRAPHY 175

FILMOGRAPHY 183

INDEX 185

PREFACE *and* ACKNOWLEDGMENTS

This book began in a small academic conference that I organized at the University of Cambridge in the spring of 2012. While I had only a vague sense about the increasing expression of Jewish religiosity in contemporary Israeli media before convening the conference, the phenomenon seemed painfully obvious by its end. Of course, the writing had been on screens, so to speak, long before then, but the conference's concentrated references to this growing religiosity suddenly turned it into a glaring pattern. Moreover, it seemed that no one was talking about this development, especially the unprecedented number of recent films and television programs apparently preoccupied with present-day Jewish religious concerns. What had once been immured in segregated religious communities began to be increasingly displayed in public. The advent of religious discourse in Israeli politics has long been noticed, but the cultural development that eventually followed it has rarely been acknowledged. This book attempts to remedy that omission by describing how Israeli national society has been redefining its relationship to the religion that inspired its very creation but that it has always sought to ignore, if not suppress.

I want to thank my friend and colleague Eran Kaplan, who remains my strongest inspiration and most constructive critic and whose meticulous reading of an early version of this book made it undoubtedly better. Two blissful summers as the guest of Middlebury College's School of Hebrew, under the inspiring guidance of my friend and colleague Vardit Ringvald, gave me the time and peace of mind to write much of it, for which I am grateful.

A NOTE *on* TRANSLITERATION

Since modern Hebrew does not differentiate between ayin and alef or khet and chaf, one spelling is used for each of these pairs throughout: *a* for either ayin or alef and *ch* for either khet or chaf. A hamza, "ʾ", is used to denote a glottal stop, as in "*Haʾaretz*."

DIRECTED BY GOD

INTRODUCTION

This book makes a claim and a suggestion. The claim is that a century after its establishment as a secular, Jewish national entity, the State of Israel at the dawn of Zionism's second century is becoming increasingly more religious in many important ways. The suggestion this book makes is that one of the most vivid testimonies of this ironic metamorphosis can be found in the history of the country's visual media—Israeli films and television programs.

ZIONISM AND JEWISH RELIGION

In 1958 David Ben-Gurion famously asked the Jewish sages of his day to help him define "who is a Jew," as he put it.[1] Israel's first prime minister must have known that his quest was impractical, but he still engaged in an exercise that characterized the state's foundational era when such grand questions loomed large and urgent. He was also motivated by specific political reasons. The replies he received were not political, however. They were varied and fascinating, and expressed a wide range of perceptions about the nature of a category that will likely remain elusive forever. None of them solved Ben-Gurion's immediate problem, and he eventually sidetracked it by seeking a practical political solution, as was his wont.

One of the most interesting aspects of this episode was the fact that it even arose, although this was probably inevitable in a country that was founded in the name of an ancient religion but wished at the same time to be modern and secular. Ben-Gurion's inquiry articulated that paradox in a rare moment of clarity, and the kind of political solution he eventually devised to avoid its explosive nature has come to characterize Israeli politics ever since. It was perhaps possible to be more decisive during the heady days of state building, when the secular spirit that animated Jewish nationalism reigned almost supremely. But this was not the way the state's founders chose to negotiate its religious character, preferring instead to build consensus by leaving the matter unresolved.

Wrapped into this episode and the way it unfolded was the question, somewhat old even then, about the nature of a Jewish existence severed from religion. Suggestions for such an existence had abounded since the nineteenth century. Jewish nationalism was only one of several ideas that were cultivated at the time to solve the so-called Jewish problem, and one of the least practical ones, as well as one of the least likely to materialize. The more sensible ideas tried to leverage post-biblical Jewish history and not work against it, like Zionism did. While Zionism tried to reverse history by reestablishing a Jewish polity, other Jewish thinkers tried to modernize some of the rich spiritual and intellectual legacies of Judaism and fit them to the secular age. Instead of uprooting and moving millions of people to a faraway and half-imagined land, these intellectuals suggested something that sounded far more practical—using Judaism as philosophy, not as religion; using the power of its ideas rather than its praxis.

The ideas of Asher Ginsberg, better known as Ahad Ha'am, about Judaism as a culture or civilization made much more sense given the history and conditions of Jews at the time. Choosing cultural politics rather than state politics, Ginsberg advocated the creation of a spiritual culture that would be informed by Jewish wisdom and heritage but not governed by it. Skeptical of Zionism as an all-encompassing national and territorial solution, Ginsberg did think that a small Jewish community in the land of Israel could potentially inspire and maintain the kind of Jewish spiritual revival he believed in. A Jewish entity of this kind would not uphold Jewish law but rather renew it in the spirit of modernism and become a model and example for Jews elsewhere.[2]

A Jewish secularism based on an acknowledgment of the depth and breadth of Jewish spiritual and intellectual traditions was also something the poet Haim Nahman Bialik strongly believed in. For much of his later life Bialik worked toward that goal, first by what he called *kinus*, that is, collating, editing, and reinterpreting important works of Jewish genius and reintroducing them to contemporary, secular Jewish readers. Although he realized that much of this literature would have little practical use for modern readers, he did not think that the new national community in Eretz Yisrael could be Jewish in any meaningful sense without knowledge of what he termed The Bookcase[3]—in other words, a historical Jewish canon. Bialik also believed that the Jewish holiday calendar, especially the Sabbath, was equally important in shaping the new national community in the spirit—not practice—of Judaism, and he laid great emphasis on upholding these traditions as a way to shape such a spiritual-Zionist community. Both these efforts had limited influence on the development of Hebrew nationalism in Bialik's lifetime and beyond, although, as we shall see, they eventually resurfaced and have gained new traction in the last few decades.

A. D. Gordon's so-called religion of labor was another powerful modern idea that combined old Jewish traditions, especially Hasidism and Kabbalah, with contemporary philosophical ideas that were inspired by thinkers like Leo Tolstoy and Friedrich Nietzsche. Gordon himself practiced what he preached, immigrating to Palestine in 1904 to work as a simple farmhand. He regarded labor as personally and communally redemptive rather than nationally instrumental. Gordon was more concerned with individual than with political praxis. He hoped that behavioral change would inspire an internal spiritual transformation: working the land would literally and figuratively ground Jews and make them into a new and more holistic community. Hasidism and Kabbalah provided Gordon with a traditional Jewish context for his modern, romantic idea of individual agency, the idea that one person *can* make a difference and act on the universe. Although the traditions and practices of Kabbalah and Hasidism approach the matter very differently, they both emphasize individual initiative and a personal search for truth, Hasidism through devotion and Kabbalah through mysticism. During the formation of the early Yishuv in Palestine, Gordon's ideas resonated deeply with young Zionist pioneers, whose kibbutz invention had several quasi-religious aspects.[4]

In many respects, then, Ben-Gurion's question tried to summarize almost a century of such quandaries, which the establishment of a Jewish state was supposed to settle once and for all. It was not surprising that an answer could not be found. Realizing the weightiness of this question even as they knew the magnitude of their own revolution, early Zionist leaders preferred to leave it open to be shaped and molded by the forces of history. This book looks at these forces of history, at the changing nature of Zionism, by observing the ways Judaism and Jewishness are reflected in Israeli films and television programs, which provide an authentic vehicle for the reflection of cultural trends, as I explain below.

The book examines the paradox of Zionism as a national movement that is both Jewish and secular, and looks at the development and changes in this precarious admixture since the middle of the twentieth century. The following chapters examine the challenges to the secular nature of

Zionism by looking at the way Israeli films and television programs have reflected or projected different kinds of Judaisms or expressions of Jewish religiosity since the establishment of Israel in 1948 as part of the state's national culture. These projections can be divided into three different strands of expressions of Jewish religiosity that have developed in Israel since the mid-1900s: Ashkenazi, Mizrahi, and national. Ashkenazi religiosity refers to the evolution of the image of Ashkenazi Orthodox Jews in Israeli popular culture and the migration of this strand from the margins to the center. Mizrahi religiosity refers to the development of what is called *masortiyut*, or traditionalism, a less strict form of Jewishness practiced by many Mizrahim in Israel, which was one of the earliest forms of Jewish religiosity that was legitimized and tolerated by secular Israeli culture. National Judaism refers to the rise of political Judaism, usually identified today with the settler community, primarily in the West Bank. These three strands or iterations of Jewish religiosity as part of contemporary Israeli culture challenge the secularity of Jewish nationalism as conceived by early Zionist thinkers, developed in Yishuv culture, and sanctioned by the early state in its cultivation and promotion of statism, or *mamlachtiyut*.[5]

CURRENT SCHOLARSHIP

Despite the paradoxical nature of Zionism as a secular Jewish national movement, or perhaps because of it, religiosity has always been at the forefront of Israeli public life in various ways. For the first half of the country's history, attempts to keep religiosity out of public life were remarkable, as the nascent Israeli state tried to suppress Jewish religiosity as part of its efforts to forge a new national, secular Jewish society.[6] For the second part of its sixty-odd years, the potent return of religiosity is noteworthy, as the rise of Likud to power in 1977 and the end of Labor's twenty-nine-year-old statist hegemony ushered in a new era of greater official tolerance toward Jewish religious values and growing attempts to promote them publicly. Two decades later, at the dawn of the twenty-first century, we are experiencing an unprecedented surge in the political and cultural expressions of Jewish religiosity in Israeli public life. Throughout this time, the divide between the secular and the religious in Israel has been one of the central fault lines defining Israeli culture.[7]

It is not surprising, then, that academic studies devoted to these various aspects are plentiful—too numerous to discuss in detail here. Nonetheless, it is worth noting a few representative studies in each of the four following categories: the separation between state and Jewish law, Kulturkampf as a political issue, and the settlers, as well as Mizrahi religiosity. Studies that provide a historical assessment of these phenomena over time are not so common; I will turn to them at the end of the following literary survey.

STATE AND JEWISH LAW

The tension between *medina* (state) and *halakha* (Jewish law) can be found in studies that examine the place of religion within civil society in Israel and consider this issue from a politico-philosophical perspective. While there were many thinkers who pondered this issue in depth, beginning with the spiritual founder of religious Zionism, Rabbi Abraham Yitzhak Hacohen Kook, the most well known and influential contributor to this inquiry in Israeli culture at large was probably Professor Yeshayahu Leibowitz, an accomplished scientist and public intellectual. Earlier in his life, through his involvement in politics, Leibowitz worked toward a synthesis between the Israeli state as a secular political entity and *halakha*, which he perceived as the essence of Judaism. But eventually, especially after the occupation of the Palestinian territories in 1967, Leibowitz abandoned these efforts and became progressively more convinced that a secular Jewish state was an oxymoron. In his 1975 book *Judaism, the Jewish People and the State of Israel* (Yahadut, am yehudi umedinat Yisra'el), Leibowitz explains that a Jewish state that ignores the moral dictates of the Jewish religion cannot be considered Jewish in any meaningful way. In other words, Leibowitz believed that for a state to be regarded as Jewish, it must practice and preach *halakha*, a reality he himself thought nigh impossible.[8]

At the same time, Leibowitz did not write much on the subject after his 1975 book, instead confining his critique to frequent appearances in public and in the media.[9] He became one of the harshest and most prophetic critics of the problematic nature of investing a state, which is an essentially secular entity, with holiness, or sanctity. Leibowitz considered it nothing less than sacrilege (חילול השם). He compared it to Sabbateanism, the much-maligned seventeenth-century heretical Jewish messianic movement led by Shabtai Zvi, and warned of similar tendencies in religious Zionism, especially after 1967. On other occasions, he pointed to similarities between German National Socialists and the national religious in Israel, whose relationship to religion was similar in his mind to the Nazis' relationship to socialism.

A less harsh critic, although one who identified with Leibowitz's views in many ways, was the prominent scholar and modern Jewish thinker Avi Ravitzky. Unlike Leibowitz, Ravitzky attempted to reconcile Jewish religiosity with Jewish nationalism. He published several studies that examined these issues. In his 1993 book *Messianism, Zionism, and Jewish Religious Radicalism*, Ravitzky looked at the various ways in which ultra-Orthodox Jewish groups accommodated the creation of a sovereign Jewish state, while still waiting for the messiah to arrive.[10] But his more germane publications for this discussion were published under the aegis of the Israel Institute for Democracy, an organization established in 1991 to provide in-depth analyses by various experts aimed at strengthening democratic principles. In addition to several edited essay collections, Ravitzky composed for the institute three main studies on questions of *halakha umedina*—Jewish law and the state: the 2000 *Religious and Secular Jews in Israel: A Kulturkampf?*,[11] the 1998 *Religion and State in Jewish Thought*,[12] and the 2004 *Is a Halakhic State Possible?*[13] Unlike Leibowitz, Ravitzky is no Jeremiah. He has generally refrained from admonishments, leaving the tension between state and Jewish law to the interplay between men and history. Although his scholarly examinations of the issue provide a learned Jewish context for this paradox, he is alive to the possibility of a compromise that might be struck at some point in the future between the demands of Jewish law and the demands of Jewish nationalism.

KULTURKAMPF

The tensions between the secular and the religious in Israel are often referred to as Kulturkampf after its original use in late nineteenth-century Prussian politics and Bismarck's attempts at separating state and church. Plenty of studies have been devoted to describing the contours and various manifestations of this culture war in Israeli public life, from the Sabbath wars in early Tel Aviv in the 1920s to its radicalization after the mass immigration from the former Soviet Union. Almost every social history of Israel written since 1948 includes this aspect as part of its discussion of life in Israel. Two works form symbolic bookends to this discussion. First, Maoz Azaryahu's study *Tel Aviv: Mythography of a City* describes the early civic battles over the Jewish nature of the first Hebrew city.[14] Conflicts over the public expression of traditional Jewish values, like keeping the Sabbath or serving kosher food, raged in the city from its very first days. These conflicts are still going on today, as evidenced by their latest iteration, sparked after the High Court issued new directives in 2014 curbing commercial activity in the city on the Sabbath.[15]

The other book is a study by Guy Ben-Porat, *Between State and Synagogue: The Secularization of Contemporary Israel*, which looks at the growing divide between the secular and the religious in Israel in the 2000s.[16] Ben-Porat notes the growing lack of communication between these two extremes. If, as Azaryahu tells us, the beginning of the Yishuv saw serious attempts to reach some modus vivendi by bridging the gap between more traditionally minded Jews and those who wished to lead secular lives, at the dawn of Zionism's second century the two sides do not seem able to or interested in communication or compromise. As the state becomes ever more beholden to the radical Jewish factions that run it politically, the private lives of secular individuals become progressively more disconnected from that official culture as well as what it represents, says Ben-Porat.

SETTLERS

The settlers have steadily received attention since their rise into political prominence in the 1980s, following their settlement of the territories captured in the 1967 war. One of the first major works that focused attention on them as a national phenomenon was not an academic work, but rather a more reflective study—Amos Oz's 1982 collection of essays, *In the Land of Israel*.[17] Oz writes about a variety of issues, bending his ear, as it were, to the people's murmurings so as to gauge the zeitgeist. These essays are valuable because they provide one of the first indirect exposures to their political agenda, delivered in their own words, since they were recorded by an attuned and keen observer who was also a revered author. As such, the essays were quite prophetic, even if the radical messages they contained were dismissed at the time as the mad ravings of a quirky minority.

In the years since then, numerous studies have been devoted to the settlers. Most of them focus on the political aspects of the movement and the dangers it poses. Few studies, however, have attempted to go beyond some of the obvious political consequences of the settlers' ascendancy to examine the threat of their religious agenda to Israeli civic society. Among such studies, two are worth mentioning. The first is Idith Zertal and Akiva Eldar's monumental and groundbreaking 2007 study *Lords of the Lands*, which was the first attempt to evaluate the settlement project in an encompassing and synoptic manner and to offer an assessment of the fundamental ways in which it has changed Zionism.[18] Expansive and bold, *Lords of the Land* presents a full picture of the extraordinary success of the settlement project—a resounding political triumph that has expanded to other parts of Israeli society and has already bent it in various ways to its messianic agenda.

The second study is Gideon Aran's 2013 *Kookism*, on the ideological origins of Gush Emunim, the Block of the Faithful. The book is based on Aran's doctoral thesis, written in the early 1980s, and it is precisely the lag of three decades from the time of its composition to its publication that lends it power. Aran spent about two years between 1975 and 1978 with the founding group of West Bank settlers, and his firsthand account of their fledgling project makes us privy to the hesitant beginnings of what would later become a phenomenal success. In the words of the divinity scholar Tomer Persiko, "The book describes a picture which has since vanished and conveys an early innocence marred by the painful knowledge of what came later on." At the same time, he continues, "Rarely do we get the chance to witness the formative stages of a religious movement, especially a movement of such import."[19] Thus, the thirty-year gap between the initial research and its publication allows us to see the momentous change that the settlers wrought on Zionist ideology. If the Zionists labored to bring Jews back into history and turn them into active agents, authors of their own fate, the settlers seem bent on returning to the imperatives of divine history set in the Hebrew Bible. Reality to them is nothing but the revealed wishes of God. All one has to do is look hard in order to understand it.[20]

MIZRAHI RELIGIOSITY

Although attention to the religious affiliation of Mizrahim in Israel increased after the Likud's rise to power in 1977, it was primarily the ascendancy of the Sephardi-Orthodox political party, SHAS, in the 1980s that brought it into greater focus.[21] The party's very raison d'être was to leverage the electoral power of Mizrahi voters and use it to help advance them materially, socially, and politically—benefits the Likud did not appear to deliver. Whether SHAS ultimately benefited Mizrahim or not remains debatable.[22] What cannot be disputed is the fact that it reformulated Mizrahi religiosity and developed it in new directions. One of the most comprehensive recent studies of these changes is Nissim Leon's *Soft Orthodoxy* (Harediyut raka), in which he looks at the changing patterns of Mizrahi religiosity in the last few decades.[23] Unlike many who have focused on SHAS, Leon is not concerned primarily with the politics of this extraordinarily successful movement.[24] As a social anthropologist, he examines the metamorphosis of Mizrahi religious practices in Israel in general, of which SHAS is only one component.

Leon's 2010 study is the culmination of several years of research into various aspects of this issue. The most valuable contribution of his study lies in its attempt to account for the general shift in Mizrahi religiosity and the unique way it has incorporated and interpreted Ashkenazi orthodoxy. Pushed by the socialist secularism of Israeli statism, Mizrahim were also pulled by Ashkenazi orthodoxy, writes Leon. While they resented the first, the second lured them with an Israeli religiosity that would replace their own form of traditionalism, which had been devastated by immigration.[25] But if Ashkenazi orthodoxy tends to be insular, it became much less so for those Mizrahim who adopted and adapted it (hence the book's title, *Soft Orthodoxy*). The important aspect of Leon's analysis for this book is the seductive effect of soft Mizrahi orthodoxy. Unlike their exclusive Ashkenazi colleagues, Orthodox Mizrahim easily mingle in existing communities and consequently tend to have a greater impact on the secular society in which they are embedded.

But while such focused examinations are plentiful, studies that try to consider the religious metamorphosis of Israeli society over a longer period of time are fewer in number. Observations of these small and disparate changes to the so-called status quo, which in Israel refers to the relations between the secular and the religious, take place mostly in the media—newspapers and, increasingly, the Internet. Yet, because of the short and scattered nature of media items, as well as their inherently brief lifespan, such observations leave only faint trails that are not easily picked up again. Even now, with the advent of the Internet, which has in fact lengthened the shelf life of online newspaper articles, such news items tend to be evanescent, lost in an ever-growing ocean of data. One of the aims of this study is to connect the dots between such observations and provide a more permanent map, as it were, a map that shows the cumulative effect of these temporal notices in a more permanent way.

Even a casual reader of the Israeli press cannot help but notice the number of articles that appear regularly and with increasing frequency concerning the heightened level of religious aspects or sensibilities in Israeli public life: articles about the growing presence of religious soldiers and officers in the IDF (Israel Defense Forces); political articles concerning nationalist-religious legislation in the Knesset, various government policies concerning religious education programs in state schools, segregated urban developments of Orthodox towns; articles about lifestyle choices such as the segregation of the sexes in public places or public transportation; articles about growing religious intolerance toward non-Jewish minorities and even nonobservant Jews; articles concerning more general issues such as the cultivation of Jewish ethics and the development of secular seminaries that reinterpret Jewish rabbinical traditions; and statistical reports on the numbers of Israelis who believe in God and demographic changes in the ratio of religious to secular populations.[26]

Rather than surveying Israeli daily press items concerning these issues, this book looks at visual fiction—Israeli films and television programs—as a medium that is inspired indirectly by such trends and incorporates them more holistically.

WHY FILMS AND TELEVISION?

Literary critics often examine belles lettres as documents that contain various historical, social, or cultural facts about their societies, and use fiction as a cultural anthropological record. Though fictional, books can nevertheless capture historical moments and reveal a complex set of aspects about the societies that write and read them. The makeup and nature of political or cultural hegemony; relationships between people, classes, or minorities; economic patterns; and even dress, architecture, and etiquette are all embedded in fiction in one way or another. In addition to content, literary style can provide another historical record. Drama, novels, and short stories can be of cultural anthropological value, pointing to economic and social developments and the changes in cultural consumption they entail. In my last book, for instance, I examined the short story as an expression of a fragmented and impatient age in Israel in the 1990s.[27] In this book I propose to apply a similar principle to the study of feature films and television drama series. In other words, I wish to look at films and TV programs as if they were fictional texts, without neglecting, of course, their visual aspects as well.

As John Weakland writes, "Feature films are cultural products by definition."[28] But, he asks, what might their contribution to cultural anthropology be? Unlike documentary films, feature films—and this applies to television drama as well—are records of culture. While documentary films try to record concrete realities, feature films create fictional realities. The anthropologically minded film critic does not, therefore, examine the projected reality as an objective one, but as an image of a made-up reality that nevertheless reflects elements from the real world that are likely to both influence and explain human behavior. Consequently, film images need to be studied with filmmakers, audiences, and other aspects in mind.

We regularly evaluate films according to various criteria. We look at films from social or moral perspectives, we consider them in relation to reality, and we pay attention to their aesthetics, among many other considerations. Our anthropological interest in films as cultural products should be guided by what Weakland calls our specific viewing angle and an awareness of the selective process.[29] Very often, that viewing angle means the various ways films' content relates to real life, a consideration that raises several questions about the relations of films to their cultural sources, about the cultural function and influence of films, and about the way films shed light on more general patterns.

My aim in this book is to consider the visual works I selected for study along these guidelines, with two special emphases. The first emphasis is on Jewish masculinity. The second emphasis is on questions of morality. The study of gender, and especially Jewish masculinity, has been one of the most fruitful categories of inquiry into the origin and development of Zionism. Based on various studies about New Hebraism such as Daniel Boyarin's studies on modern Jewish masculinity, for example, this book looks at the legacy of this cultural innovation after Israel's independence and the expressions it received in the culture, particularly with respect to religious imagery. The study is based on the premise that the New Jew or New Hebrew in Zionism, epitomized by the image of the pioneer, was developed primarily against images of so-called diasporic Judaism, epitomized by the bearded and frocked Jewish men of the Eastern European *shtetl*. The study therefore assumes that the continued references to that negative source of influence after Zionism's triumph yield valuable historical insights. Put differently, the book proposes to examine what happened to Zionism's negation of exile—the animosity it felt toward the Eastern European traditional Jewish society that gave birth to it—when the alternative it set up against it, the State of Israel, succeeded so well and went from strength to strength.[30] The films and TV series examined in the following chapters ponder this question and look at some of the ways secular Israeli culture has processed and reflected on its religious heritage, a dialectics that is visibly negotiated through masculine categories and imagery.

I also wish to determine the moral stance of films and television programs toward the Jewish religion and Jewish religious practices in Israel in the on-screen private and public lives of characters. I want to examine the selected works in this book from a historical perspective and understand what has changed in the way Israeli society views religion and religious practices over the years, determine how these changes came about, and identify the values assigned to these changes. As is well known and widely accepted, "In projecting structured images of human behavior, social interaction and the nature of the world, fictional films in contemporary society are analogues in nature and structural significance to the stories, myths, rituals and ceremonies in primitive societies."[31] By looking at the way Judaism and Jewishness are (and have been) created, dealt with, related to, and projected on screens in Israel for over half a century, I hope to show some of the changes these images underwent during that time and the meaning this might have for Israel and beyond.

Finally, I examine visual culture and not prose, as I have in the past, primarily because it has become a clearer and more focused gauge of Israeli national culture. Since the early 1990s, modern Hebrew literature has been losing the cultural centrality it had enjoyed since the nineteenth century, first in Eastern Europe and later in Israel. Modern Hebrew literature birthed and nurtured modern Hebrew culture and was the origin for much of what later became Israeli culture, which it influenced and sustained throughout the twentieth century.[32] But as the hold of Zionist ideology waned toward the end of the 1980s and the beginning of the 1990s; as Israel opened to outside influences; as it became more capitalistic and developed other media, especially television, the culture changed apace. Since the early 1990s Israelis have not raised their eyes in admiration toward a select few writers and poets, those who until that time had been understood as seers.[33]

What literary critic Gershon Shaked called the Zionist meta-narrative has by and large ceased to inform the works of Israeli writers since the 1990s—certainly not to the extent it did before.[34] That is, the light that automatically went on in readers' minds when they opened a modern Hebrew work, the light that prompted them to think of its symbolic significance in the context of Jewish or Zionist history, as author Amalia Kahana-Carmon once wrote, was disconnected.[35] This stands to reason, of course, as the country had matured by that time and was less anxious about melting the pot, as it were, and creating a homogenous, native Israeli culture out of the multitudes of its various immigrants. It was probably also less able to do so in a postmodern age, which later came to be known as a post-Zionist age as well.[36] The country also grew in size, making space for more writers, who in turn catered to various and growing communities with diverse interests. Israeli literature might have boomed, as Alan Mintz noted, but it was no longer as consensual or as interested in some of the grand national questions of yore.[37]

The cultural space that was left behind by the diminution of the written word was taken up by the ascendancy of the visual image, which has moved toward center stage and attracted more public and critical attention since the 1990s.[38] This was not unique to Israel, of course, but a global phenomenon. It does not mean that Israelis stopped reading books, either. It only means that since the last decade of the twentieth century they began to regroup—to the extent that they regrouped at all—increasingly more around a visual rather than a textual campfire.

Yet another reason for the increased communal relevance of films in Israel relates to the special structure or nature of Israeli film production. Since the Israeli film market is relatively small and few films are viable commercially, most of them are supported by public money that is doled out based on assessed merit. A script's worth is determined by elected arts councils, which often consider the greater communal value or national interest of scripts that are submitted for their evaluation. This is both reasonable and unsurprising. But it also makes films prime candidates for the kind of examination this book offers: most of the funded films in Israel engage with the grand national issues that books used to engage with.[39]

If this is true for films, it is even more so for TV programs, which not only are communal artistic projects but also necessitate a greater consensus during the production process. In Israel, television programs, unlike films, are also beholden to commercial concerns, as in other capitalist markets. The ability of TV programs to innovate, then, and take artistic risks, is limited in comparison to Israeli films. Because of these constraints, though, television programs can be considered a more genuine reflection of cultural trends. By a peculiar coincidence, and somewhat contrary to these arguments, Israeli TV programs with considerable religious content are both innovative and popular. Their introduction of new themes and their visual representation of hitherto unrepresented religious communities have so far met with interest and enthusiasm by a majority of viewers. This is yet another manifestation of the phenomenon this book examines.

I should perhaps also note why this book does not consider religious imagery in other national cinemas and why it does not probe the remarkable ability of the cinematic medium to capture and comment on religious or spiritual experience in general. The cinema of Iran, for instance, to name one of the most interesting and developed cinemas in the Middle East, has dealt with the increasing religiosity of Iranian culture after the 1979 Islamic revolution with astuteness and sophistication. Iranian cinema, not unlike cinema in Israel, tried to incorporate religion as well as criticize and resist it, as Nacim Pak-Shiraz has shown us.[40] Similarly, films like Avishai Sivan's 2010 *The Wonderer* (Hamshotet) use the cinematic medium as a vehicle or platform for expressing spirituality in ways that are not available to other art forms, as Dan Chyutin notes.[41] Such considerations would have undoubtedly enriched this study. But they would also be taking away from the purpose of this book, which is to examine a specific issue—religious representation—in a specific visual corpus—Israeli film and television—over a specific period of time—1960s to 2010s—in order to gauge the changes in it as a reflection of similar changes in Israeli culture itself.

The comparative aspect of this study is, therefore, folded into its very premise. That premise posits that Zionism began as a national Jewish ideology that was fundamentally anticlerical.[42] Over time and because of various factors—some of them political, like the continued emergency situation in Israel and the political radicalization that accompanied it, others demographic, like the growth of the religious sector in Israel—religious elements penetrated public life in Israel more and more. By adopting a historical perspective that follows gradual changes in the frequency and kind of visual religious imagery over time, this study aims to show the extent to which Israeli culture has changed in this regard.

HISTORICAL OVERVIEW

Indeed, the overall pattern that emerges from the films examined in this study is that Jewish Israeli society has been undergoing a slow but increasingly discernible "religification" in the last few decades—so much so, in fact, that the Hebrew Language Academy has coined a neologism to describe it: הדתה.[43] The most obvious reason for this shift has been the identity crisis Zionism has been experiencing since 1967, which has been most eloquently articulated by the new historians and by some of the post-Zionist thinkers who followed them.

Much has been written about the so-called new historians. Their importance for our discussion is the very fact that from the 1980s onward they reexamined much of the received Zionist historiography and changed hitherto common perceptions of it. What historians like Simha Flapan, Benny Morris, Tom Segev, and Baruch Kimmerling did was to reassess Zionist historiography from a more dispassionate and critical perspective. Flapan's 1987 *The Birth of Israel: Myths and Realities* was a critical examination of the Arab-Israeli conflict that tried to differentiate between the inherent justice and value of Zionism and some of the problematic ways it was implemented.[44] This was the ameliorative impetus behind all of the new historians' writings. Such was Benny Morris's well-known 1988 *The Birth of the Palestinian Refugee Problem, 1947–1949*;[45] Tom Segev's important histories about the birth of Israel, the legacy of the Holocaust in Israel, the British Mandate, and the 1967 war;[46] and Baruch Kimmerling's 1993 *Palestinians: The Making of a People*,[47] as well as his 2001 *The Invention and Decline of Israeliness: State, Society, and the Military*.[48]

All of these new historians were blamed at various times for undermining Zionism.[49] But their critiques were motivated, among other things, by a desire to change Israeli society for the better. They wrote in the name of the early modernist ethics of Zionism against Israel's intoxication with power after 1967. As such, these historians represent an evolutionary stage in the development of Israeli historiography and in the country's very consciousness—its psychological perception of itself, if one may define it so.[50] That is, the perceptive change, which the new historians noted and represented, lifted the tight ideological lid of Zionism and enabled a freer expression of differing ideologies that have long been pent up. One of the most powerful of these ideological forces was the inherently religious element of Zionism, whose presence in the country's life since the 1980s has increased with the growth of its two biggest religious communities, the ultra-Orthodox and the national religious, or settler, communities. Moreover, these demographic changes have obvious political corollaries that play into well-established traditions set long before religious voters became a political force.[51]

A much newer change—one not surprising given these demographics—was the increasing visibility of religious expressions in the last two decades of the twentieth century in popular music, film, and television. These mediums, which in the past were the purview of secular Zionist culture and were fervently developed to establish and promote it as an alternative to Jewish traditional-religious expressions, seem increasingly more attentive to the role of Judaism in Israeli society today.

Given the secular nature of Zionist ideology and its strong religious antipathy, it is not surprising that in the first decades of the state Israeli popular culture made very little mention of religion or religiosity in its various entertainment mediums. The terms "popular culture" and "entertainment" should perhaps be qualified when we talk about the early decades of the state. Israeli culture, just like the state itself, was a new invention that developed over time based on various guiding principles, most importantly an elite that steered the process. Despite this Soviet-sounding description, this was probably a necessary stage without which the state would never have come into existence.[52] As the country grew and developed, both the heavy hand as well as the artifice that went along with it subsided, and what we call today the politics of representation has been diffused in ways that resemble similar patterns in other countries, primarily in the West. But this was a slow and often turbulent process, and it needs to be taken into account when we speak about "popular culture" and "entertainment" as part of it.

Consequently, the two key factors that controlled the representation of religiosity in the country's popular culture in the beginning were both the antireligious sentiment that animated Zionism and the controlled manufacture of Israeli culture at large. The upshot of both was that almost none of the relatively few films that were made in Israel in the first decades after statehood even dealt with the subject.[53] But, to the extent that they did, representation in those films can be divided into two kinds. The first and more obvious of the two is the patronizing and dismissive portrayal of religious Judaism—usually the ultra-Orthodox community—as a bizarre sect, a comical and pathetic historical relic whose dismal present state justifies its relegation to the dustbin of history and the ascendancy of a different kind of Jewishness: national Jewishness. The second and less obvious reference to religiosity included the ritual practices of Sephardi, or Mizrahi, Jews, those who immigrated to Israel from Muslim countries in the first decades of statehood. Many of the films that depicted those practices belonged to the Bourekas film genre, ethnic comedies that were very popular during the 1970s and 1980s and that exhibit Mizrahi Jews in their "traditional Jewish habitat," as it were. Boosting Mizrahim as bone fide Jews to an Ashkenazi culture that thought of them as Arabs, many Bourekas films spend considerable screen time showing these so-called Arabs as legitimate Jews who know their prayer book, attend synagogue, and (especially) observe the Sabbath.[54]

Both representations can be labeled "anthropological," although both had very different rationales. The initial portrayal of the Orthodox community was mainly as a curiosity, an odd relic of a bygone world that deserved pity more than anything else. It was a vulgarization of Ashkenazi Jewish folklore that was milked for amusement at the expense of its subject. The presentation of the Sephardi, or Mizrahi, Jewish religiosity was much more sympathetic, although the dynamics in most of the Bourekas films clearly point to filmmakers' expectations that the religious antics of the older generation portrayed in them will eventually die out and disappear.

Again, until the ascendancy of the settler community in the late 1980s, Mizrahi Jewishness was almost the only legitimate expression of religiosity in Israel's body culture—a holistic religiosity that received a special label, "traditionalism," that rendered it more palatable to the generally antireligious hegemonic culture.[55]

Neither of these portrayals—the Orthodox and the Mizrahi—dealt with, examined, or used religion artistically in any deep and serious way. Such portrayals were simple records, albeit tendentious, of negligible social phenomena that they either rejected, in the first case, or reluctantly embraced, in the second. Curiously, the only serious engagement with religiosity in Israeli cinema prior to the 2000s involved Christian imagery. Films like Judd Ne'eman's 1984 *The Silver Platter* (Magash hakesef), Amos Gutman's 1988 *Himmo King of Jerusalem* (Himmo melech yerushalayim) and his 1992 *Amazing Grace* (Chesed mufla), and perhaps most notably

Assi Dayan's 1993 film *Life according to Agfa* (Hachayim al pi agfa) all play with Christian ideals of sacrifice and martyrdom.[56]

The first film that can be said to engage much more seriously and earnestly with Judaism, certainly politically, is Joseph Cedar's 2000 *Time of Favor* (Ha-hesder). That film marked the dawn of what can perhaps be called a religious age in Israeli visual culture and signaled a notable increase in the number of films dealing more seriously with the culture's secular legacy. Both *Time of Favor* and Cedar's subsequent film, *Campfire* (Medurat hashevet), from 2004, focus for the first time on Israel's growing settler community. Cedar's films focus on a large and influential Israeli religious community that was practically absent from cinema until then; but they also represent one of the first serious attempts to offer an artistic interpretation not just of religiosity but especially of its politicization, and a willingness to deal head-on with the religious threat to the country's former way of life. A film such as *Time of Favor* not only acknowledges for the first time the existence of sizable religious communities in Israel but also alerts viewers to the fact they are no longer content with remaining marginal; they have clear and definite plans to inherit Zionism as we know it.

Not all of the post-2000 films that dealt with religion focused on politics. Other kinds of religious films, like the 2003 *Ushpizin* (dir. Gidi Dar), dealt more artistically with the intrinsic value of Judaism as a philosophy and a way of life. *Ushpizin* was a religious project in a way; its writer and main actor, Shuli Rand, is a *ba'al tshuva*, a secular man who found God and became ultra-Orthodox. Rand, who is a gifted, multifaceted artist, got permission from his rabbi to make the film as a way to reach out to secular Israelis, to show them the good face of religion and perhaps even return them to the faith.

Ushpizin can be said to belong to the politics of identity genre, which informed a number of Israeli films throughout the 1990s, primarily about Mizrahim, whereas films like the 2007 *My Father My Lord* (Chufshat kayitz; dir. David Volach) exhibit a genuine interest in the Orthodox community from the outside, as it were.[57] *Ushpizin* had a real proselytizing agenda in that it sought to dispel persistent negative images of the ultra-Orthodox community. *My Father My Lord*, on the other hand, was neither a branding nor an image film, neither a political accusation nor an anthropological study. In fact, while the story derives its dramatic meaning from the religious environment it depicts, it transcends its ostensible particularity to become universal. Herein lies its innovation. The fact that the Orthodox community is used as a background to a universal story about family relations marked a significant difference in the place, role, and attitude of Israeli culture toward religious themes and its various religious communities. It is certainly a far cry from early parodies of Orthodox Judaism, like the 1976 *Kuni Leml in Tel Aviv* (dir. Joel Silberg), and it is a measure of the culture's acceptance of the ultra-Orthodox Jewish way of life as part of what might be considered Israeli Jewish life in general.

This change is perhaps most obvious from some of the most recent portrayals of religiosity in Israeli visual culture in films like the 2012 *God's Neighbors* (Ha'mashgichim; dir. Meny Yaesh) and *Fill the Void* (Lemaleh et hechalal; dir. Rama Burstein), from the same year. Both films received high critical acclaim and won various awards. Both also continue Israel's impressive cinematic output of the first decade of the twenty-first century, with international hits such as *Yossi and Jagger* (dir. Eytan Fox, 2002), *Walk on Water* (Lalechet al hamayim; dir. Eytan Fox, 2004), *Beaufort* (dir. Joseph Cedar, 2007), and *Waltz with Bashir* (dir. Ari Folman, 2008). It should be noted that the more recent films, *God's Neighbors* and *Fill the Void*, look at the intricacies of religious life in Israel as opposed to focusing on the army and the conflict with the Arab world, like the other international hits listed above.

Finally, reference should also be made to television programs, which are perhaps a better gauge of popular trends, especially television series that are more commercial in nature and are made more strictly for profit. Television series began being produced in earnest in Israel with the deregulation of the TV industry in the early 1990s.[58] But it was not until the late 2000s that a major, and popular, series based on a religious theme was created. Although only one season was produced of the 2007 *A Touch Away* (Merhak negi'a), it was a runaway hit that attracted a great number of fans and considerable Internet chatter. The show is still remembered as a groundbreaking program for the direct, genuine, and, significantly, sexy way it broached the relationship between a fiercely secular Russian immigrant and his young Orthodox neighbor.

The 2008 series *Srugim* (literally meaning "knitted," referring to the knitted skullcaps worn by men in the national religious movement) is another recent television series with a significant religious component. *Srugim* takes place in an almost exclusively religious environment, into which secular people wander only rarely. This enormously successful series has had several successful seasons to date. The popularity of the show derives not only from its resemblance to the well-known and well-loved American television series *Sex and the City* (with sex being conspicuously absent yet very much present, of course), but also from its ability to present an anthropological view of "the religious" by focusing on their exotic dating rituals. In addition to the good drama that viewers were served every week, the show also acquainted viewers with an artistically underrepresented sector of the Israeli public. Surprisingly, although the national religious, as they are called in Israel, have been politically central since the 1980s, they have been seldom represented in films and TV. That they are increasingly being shown, as this study demonstrates, is a significant testimony to dramatic and ongoing changes in Israeli society.

At the same time, the religious transformation, even revolution, that Israeli television has been undergoing since the 2000s with respect to the representation of Jewish religious themes should also be carefully considered in light of the deliberate efforts of the Avi Chai Foundation to influence this discourse in Israel. The US-based foundation has been active since the 1990s in supporting various educational and cultural initiatives in Israel designed to bridge the gap between the secular and the religious, as the foundation puts it, and to introduce Jewish traditional themes into Israeli popular culture, primarily through the arts. Toward that end it has been generously financing adult educational initiatives, musical productions, and, since the 2000s, television programming.[59] Such blatant and external interference in national culture merits serious consideration and needs to be acknowledged in discussing the "religification" phenomenon on television. What makes this even more interesting is the genuine popularity of the produced shows, which further complicates the picture and makes it even more difficult to evaluate.

Chapter 1, "Jewish and Human: Images of Orthodox Jews," looks at the metamorphosis of the images of Jewish Ashkenazi religiosity as it was known in Eastern Europe and against which secular national Jewishness developed. The chapter looks at eight films that span half a century and follows the changes that images of Haredi Jewish men have undergone—from the ridiculous to the real and finally to the sympathetic. The chapter begins with the Kuni Leml trilogy (1966, dir. Israel Becker; 1976 and 1983, dir. Joel Silberg), about the adventures of a hapless and pathetic Orthodox groom. It continues with the 1972 stylized historical religious drama *I Love You, Rosa* (Ani ohev otach, Rosa; dir. Moshe Mizrahi); the 1990 *The Appointed* (Hameyu'ad; dir. Daniel Wachsmann), about religious mysticism; and the 1999 drama *Kadosh* (dir. Amos Gitai), about the plight of Haredi women under the yoke of a harsh religious patriarchy. The chapter ends with two films that bring images of Haredi men closer to modern audiences by presenting them as complex and loving humans: the 2003 romantic comedy *Ushpizin* (The guests; dir. Gidi Dar) and the 2009 gay Haredi drama *Eyes Wide Open* (Einayim petuchoth; dir. Haim Tabakman).

Chapter 2, "Jewish and Israeli: Images of Mizrahi Jews," looks at the creation of a unique Israeli Judaism out of the various religious practices of Mizrahi Jews during the immigration waves of the 1950s and 1960s. The chapter examines the Israelification of "Arab" Jews by means of familiarizing audiences with their Jewish difference and by sanctioning these differences as one of the earliest forms of Jewish religiosity (*masortiyut*) accepted by the state, which shunned other forms of Jewish religiosity, primarily orthodoxy. The chapter also looks at the concurrent usurpation of Ashkenazi masculinity, symbolized by the image of the New Hebrew, by a Mizrahi masculinity unencumbered by religious anxiety. The chapter examines several films that chart the development of these images, from frivolous and exotic in various Bourekas films like the 1964 *Sallah Shabati* (dir. Ephraim Kishon) through identity politics films of the 1990s like the 1990 *Shuroo* (dir. Savi Gabizon), the 1993 *Sh'chur* (Black magic; dir. Shmuel Hasfari), the 1995 *Lovesick on Nana Street* (Chole ahava Beshikun gimel; dir. Savi Gabizon), and the shorter *Shuli's Guy* (Habachur shel Shuli; dir. Doron Tsabari), from 1997, which begin to deal more complexly with Mizrahi imagery. The chapter continues with the 2008 *Shiva* (Seven days; dir. Ronit Elkabetz and Shlomi Elkabetz). Finally, *God's Neighbors* brings together religiosity and Mizrahi masculinity in more harmonious, if problematic, ways.

Chapter 3, "Jewish and Fanatic: Images of Religious Zionists," investigates the infiltration of religion into Israeli politics by following the rise of the settler movement in two Joseph Cedar films: the 2000 *Time of Favor* and the 2004 *Campfire*. The chapter focuses on the settlers' interpretation of the image of the New Hebrew and the infusion of this old Zionist symbol with religious elements that change but also preserve the impetus that gave rise to it in the first place, that is, the Zionists' historical claim to the land of Israel. The chapter concludes with a brief mention of two additional films, *Waltz with Bashir* and *Beaufort*, whose characterization of Israeli men, especially soldiers, accentuates some of the changes in the representation of Israeli masculinity observed in *Time of Favor* and *Campfire*.

Chapter 4, "Jewish and Popular: Images of Religion on TV," begins by looking at early television shows like *A Touch Away* and *Srugim*, which popularized Cedar's more controversial images and made them into familiar and beloved household images. The chapter then examines the ubiquity of religious imagery in contemporary Israeli television and the various ways it is incorporated into programming today by analyzing three representative shows—*Shtisel* (2013), *Urim Vetumim* (2011), and *Hasamba 3rd Generation* (Hasamba dor shalosh, 2010–2013). Some of this imagery is engineered by external forces, such as the Avi Chai Foundation. Some of it is symbolic and pays homage to the religious as a way to acknowledge their increased participation and visibility in the culture. Yet other parts of this imagery are less consciously wrought, reflecting instead the natural growth of various religious communities in Israel and their increased acceptance by the culture.

The study concludes with an assessment of the erosion of the secular aspects of Zionism since its establishment as the latest, and perhaps not so unexpected, iteration of Jewish nationalism.

CHAPTER 1

JEWISH *and* HUMAN: IMAGES *of* ORTHODOX JEWS

Although Zionism was developed as a secular national movement, many of its founders and early practitioners came from traditional Jewish and religious backgrounds. Indeed, Jewish secularism hardly existed anywhere in the world before the rise of Zionism. But while the nature of Zionism as a particularist European movement was shaped in many ways by the religious legacy of its founders and practitioners, that legacy was ultimately used to create a distinctly secular movement in the Yishuv and then the young Israeli state.

Zionist culture, which was greatly influenced by the civic religion of European bourgeois nationalism, also developed as a reaction against Jewish traditional life and religious practices in Eastern Europe.[1] Zionism preserved the secular liberalism of the Haskala, the Jewish Enlightenment, but it was also inspired by the great social reform movements of the time, such as socialism and communism, which were decidedly antireligious. When it was later transferred to Palestine and developed there, the movement continued to be animated by the antireligious sentiments of its early thinkers, a sentiment that eventually also comprised part of an animosity that came to be known in modern Hebrew culture as the "negation of exile" (*shlilat hagola*). Moreover, the Zionist notion of negation of exile was premised on the differentiation between traditional—which usually meant Ashkenazi religious Jewishness—and the new Hebraism, which was cultivated in the Palestinian Yishuv.[2] On the one hand, the image of the New Hebrew or New Jew that developed in Palestine during the 1930s and 1940s was inspired by European national models. On the other hand, some of its traits, like overt masculinity and aggression, were a reaction against stereotypical images of Jews in the European anti-Semitic imagination as feminine and weak, among other aspersions. Indeed, it is another commonplace notion that the perceived differences between the two—the old, diasporic, Ashkenazi Jewishness, and its converse image of Palestinian New Hebraism—

were often gendered. Traditional, religious Judaism was cast as feminine and inferior, while the new, secular Judaism in its Zionist iteration was cast as masculine and superior.[3]

The negative imagery of religious Judaism in Israeli culture, cinema included, has been fairly common and has been examined in several studies.[4] For the most part, these images were limited to caricatures of Orthodox Jews, who were easy to identify and mock. After the ultimate triumph of Zionism in 1948, the ridicule of Orthodox Judaism in popular Israeli culture also served as a simplistic and vulgar justification of Zionist ideology. The 1966 musical comedy *Two Kuni Leml* (dir. Israel Becker) and its two sequels, the 1976 *Kuni Leml in Tel Aviv* and the 1983 *Kuni Leml in Cairo* (both by dir. Joel Silberg), which will be discussed first in this chapter, epitomize the patronizing attitude of the Zionist establishment and its culture toward this relic of its Eastern European tradition, a mutilated avatar of its religious past.[5] This attitude not only distinguished the state's view of Ashkenazi orthodoxy but also characterized in general its opinion of all the immigrants it ingathered after independence, who were expected to adopt the tenets of Yishuv culture.[6] The wish to homogenize these disparate immigrant groups—mostly Holocaust survivors and non-Ashkenazi Jews—into a unified national culture in accordance with statist policies was the origin of the longstanding Israeli penchant for ethnic humor, which characterized its popular culture in the decades after the 1967 war.[7]

During the 1960s, 1970s, and 1980s, many popular films, especially comedies, were predicated on the differences between immigrant groups, especially Ashkenazi and Mizrahi Jews; that is, Jewish immigrants from Europe and Jewish immigrants from the Levant. Much has been written about the chief cinematic genre that promulgated this kind of humor, the so-called Bourekas films, which continue to attract popular and academic attention and remain contentious to this very day.[8] But while Bourekas films negotiated the relationship between the absorbing, veteran Ashkenazi establishment and immigrants from various Arab or Muslim countries, a subcategory of that genre included ethnic comedies of a slightly different kind, which focused more exclusively on Ashkenazi culture and trafficked in various images of the Jewish *shtetl*.[9] The reasons for the appearance of such films, sometimes labeled the gefilte-fish genre,[10] are not clear and may include a nostalgia for a bygone Jewish world that vanished cataclysmically in the Holocaust, a greater willingness to deal with that old world by a culture whose earlier hostility toward it was assuaged by the pivotal trial of Adolph Eichmann in 1961, or perhaps a desire to capitalize on the enormous success of the Ur–ethnic comedy *Sallah Shabati* (1964).

In comparison to the plethora of Bourekas films produced during the state's first thirty years, so-called gefilte-fish films were few and far between. The Kuni Leml trilogy, therefore, stands apart as one of the subgenre's most visible examples. So much so, in fact, that the mocking images of Orthodox Jewry it depicted became etched in the popular Israeli imagination and reverberated in the culture for decades to come. The first film in the trilogy, *Two Kuni Leml*, was a cinematic adaption of a popular Yiddish play by Abraham Goldfaden, a musical comedy involving mistaken identity and the attempts of a young *schlemiel*—a stuttering, limping yeshiva youth—to find a wife.[11] When the film was released in 1966, it became an instant hit, despite what seem today like low production values and a theatrical, noncinematic look.[12] This may in fact explain some of its attraction to an Israeli public that was more theatrically educated and less cinematically sophisticated.[13] Another attraction was the cast, which included an impressive list of well-known and well-liked stage actors as well as the unforgettable debut of the young and fresh-faced singer-actor Mike Burstein, who played the two grooms and delivered several of the musical's best-loved hit songs.[14]

Although the Jewish society depicted in the film is not the kind of Orthodox Jewish society familiar to us today—which is in fact a new phenomenon in Jewish history[15]—the community described in it is decidedly traditional, guided by a religious calendar that marks time and regulates daily life. Yet unlike maskilic literature, which was full of scathing depictions of the decrepitude of *shtetl* life, sharp critiques that were meant to enlighten readers and encourage them to change, *Two Kuni Leml* is a relic, a stylized fossil of a bygone era that lacks any corrective agenda. The film preserves *shtetl* life, even if the society it depicts no longer exists, wiped completely off the face of the earth and lost in the Holocaust. Nostalgia, then, is precisely the point. If we look closely and put aside the rich theatrical performances of the avuncular men and matronly women, whose distinct Eastern European accents and familiar antics remind (Ashkenazi) viewers of their own family, we are left with an unflattering image of the *shtetl* as a sort of axiom.

In many respects, this is the same *shtetl* audiences could see in the slightly earlier American musical, *Fiddler on the Roof* (1964), a vibrant Jewish community that is celebrated with vim and verve and sweetened by catchy tunes. But even if the public in America and Israel regarded both shows with more than a modicum of nostalgia, the different cultural contexts meant a different reception as well. For reasons particular to the USA and probably also to the history of the North American Jewish community, *Fiddler on the Roof* remained the longest running Broadway show for ten years after it opened. The most memorable part of *Two Kuni Leml*, on the other hand, apart from one song, is the image of the film's hero as an Orthodox clown. Burstein's Kuni Leml is guileless and sweet, but he is also a stuttering dimwit, a small and nervous creature who is outsmarted at every turn. This made for excellent comedy, but it also fixed the image of orthodoxy in the Israeli imagination for the next forty years as a pathetic holdover from a maligned Jewish diasporic past.[16] That this was so, despite Mr. Burstein's formidable acting and singing abilities, says something about the culture that preserved it as such. No doubt his image resonated with a society that was ready to accept it and find proof in his performance of its own preconceived notions of Jewish orthodoxy.[17]

For all of these reasons, *Two Kuni Leml* is less interesting for our discussion, belonging as it does to the old Yiddish theatrical tradition and to the faint echoes of its post-Holocaust nostalgia more than to authentic, modern Israeli culture. The second film in the trilogy, *Kuni Leml in Tel Aviv*, as its name suggests, is much more contemporary, a genuine product of its time that can be positioned squarely within the ethnic-comic tradition of Israeli cinema. Made ten years after the first film, *Kuni Leml in Tel Aviv* re-creates the original story and transposes it to modern Tel Aviv. The plot involves a competition between two twin brothers, played again by Mike Burstein in a reprisal of his original role. One brother is a dashing, secular songwriter who is dating a non-Jewish girl, Marilyn (Mandy Rice-Davies). The other brother is a naive and slow-witted yeshiva student. The twins' American Orthodox grandfather promises $5 million to the first grandchild to make aliyah to Israel and marry a nice Jewish girl by year's end. The film follows the brothers' race for those millions and for the girls they love.

Kuni Leml in Tel Aviv has done away with *shtetl* society, remnants of which can be seen only in the opening scene in New York City, during the grandfather's eightieth birthday party, replete with Jewish familial sentimentality, traditional food, and songs. The rest of the film takes place in Israel, where the twins immediately try to fulfill the conditions of the wager. The mockery and derision of Orthodox society in the film takes three forms: the flouting of *halakha*, the parody of Orthodox conduct, and the censure of Orthodox society as potentially corrupt and violent. The fact that none of these depictions seem deliberately critical, but appear rather to be used for cheap comic affect, is all the more telling.

Jewish religious law, *halakha*, is flouted right away, on the trip to Israel. The Orthodox twin finds himself seated next to his brother's non-Jewish girlfriend, Marilyn, who is traveling to Israel to join her boyfriend, convert to Judaism, and marry him. It is during the flight that Kuni, the religious brother, falls in love with his secular brother's girlfriend, whom he pursues throughout the film until he finally succeeds in wooing her away from his brother, Muni. After partaking of his dinner, a pot of *cholent* he brings with him on the plane, the young yeshiva student falls asleep on Marilyn's bosom and, like Lysander in Shakespeare's *A Midsummer Night's Dream*, wakes up deeply in love with the "shiksa," as Marilyn is often referred to in the film. Even if the stricture of *isur negi'a*, the prohibition against physical contact between unmarried people, may not have been observed then as strictly as it is today, the possibility of something like that happening in real life is highly unlikely. Yet the religious young man is completely unbothered by it upon waking up, smirking like a horny fool.

Worse still, when later on in the film he is studying at a yeshiva in Jerusalem, Kuni suddenly bursts into a song of love to Marilyn, whose face appears before him superimposed on the open pages of the Talmud. Young men will often think of sex. This is one of the chief urges that the study of Torah, especially at a younger age, is meant to curb. Yet here, in this scene, Kuni happily thinks of his love, who floats on top of the hallowed Hebrew script in all her non-Jewish glory. That the young man is aware that he needs to hide his desire is evident from the careful glances he throws at the sentries, which stand behind him on order from his rabbi. Yet to himself and in the midst of his holy occupation, he fantasizes unabashedly about Marilyn the shiksa, to whom he croons such lines as, "For you I shall wait seven years, even more, like Jacob waited for Rachel," and finishes off the song with the following scandalous line: "Out of the pages of midrash, she appears like a flash, Marilyn Jones" (בין דפי המדרש / היא נראית כמו ממש / מרילין ג'ונס). The notion, as well as its visualization in this scene, is halakhically shocking. If the film were released today, it would likely arouse a significant protest from the religious community, which is now much more powerful and which rejects far more trivial challenges from Israeli secular society to its religious practices.[18]

The antics of the ultra-Orthodox community make up some of the film's most comical moments. I already mentioned the pot of *cholent*, which Kuni brings with him on the plane to Israel, and that even Marilyn, who is eager to become Jewish, cannot easily abide: as he opens the lid during lunch, both the smell and the sight of this brown and gloopy Ashkenazi stew take Marilyn aback. The portrayal of the religious as unsophisticated primitives who are unfamiliar with the refined culture of the Western bourgeoisie continues in the airport in Israel, where Kuni is met by a delegation of men from the yeshiva of his destination. Dressed in their Haredi garb, the men surround Kuni as he emerges from the terminal, pushing a luggage cart with his pot of *cholent* in it. Their happiness at seeing the grandson of their yeshiva's chief benefactor is translated into the film's first dance number, a stylized Hasidic frolic that is performed in the airport's parking lot.

What looks like a typical wedding dance, which we can see for instance at the wedding that concludes the first Kuni Leml film, is taken here out of its usual ritualistic context. This is not unusual in the context of the genre's conventions, as musicals are predicated on this kind of artificiality. Moreover, dance is not alien to Hasidic society either, which stresses merrymaking. Still, given the seriousness with which religious society tends to take itself—unlike the self-deprecation of traditional Eastern European society—and considering the prominent role Kuni has in the dance, hanging stubbornly on to his *cholent* pot as he flails rhythmically about, the dancing Hasidim look farcical indeed. The long screen time given to their dance accentuates their oddness, prolonging the spectators' wondering gaze upon what looks like a curiously fascinating native dance for tourists.

Finally, the corruption and violence of Haredi society is suggested at various junctures in the film. First, the rabbi is eager to wed his daughter to the grandson of his wealthy benefactor, and uses force to do so, irrespective of their obvious and mutual dislike for each other. After both clearly tell him they are not interested in each other, he sends several of his thugs to force Kuni to comply. He instructs his men to follow the young man around, and when Kuni escapes to Tel Aviv to see Marilyn, they pursue him and literally kidnap him and take him back to Jerusalem. If up to that point the rabbi enjoyed a semblance of "cuteness," which he earned earlier in the film in his dancing role, even if it was at his own expense, his mafiosi handling of Kuni strips him of it fairly quickly.

Throughout the film, Haredi society is ridiculed, mocked, derided, and completely discounted—treated as one big joke. In one of the most farcical moments in the film, Kuni walks through a Tel Aviv neighborhood followed by a group of children, with whom he has a singing exchange that would sound quite unrealistic today. Surrounding him with great curiosity, the children keep asking him to explain who and especially what he is. "Mister," they ask, "why are you wearing this funny hat? Mister, why do you have a funny coat? Mister, why do you have such funny earlocks?" Kuni might well have been one of those natives brought back to Europe by various explorers as a curiosity to be gawked at. Yet this moment of "othering" does not seem unreasonable in a film that is premised on the oddness of these strange Jewish Orthodox "creatures." They are so obviously unfamiliar, so out of place in contemporary, secular, modern Israel that such questions seem reasonable.

Even in the context of the ethnic comedic genre and subgenre it belongs to, the depiction of Haredim is mercilessly negative in the film. Contrary to the economy of ethnic stereotyping, they enjoy neither a moment of grace nor an ounce of mercy. As such, they rank far below Mizrahi characters, who despite their problematic portrayals in many Bourekas films as backward and primitive at least end up on top, compensated for their disadvantage in life by a triumph on screen. A similar advantage is not given to the ultra-Orthodox in this and for a long time in other films that followed it.

The discussion of the Kuni Leml trilogy should perhaps be concluded with a consideration of Kuni's image as a man, or more accurately, his a-masculine image in the context of those times. The Kuni Leml films were made during the apogee of native Israeli masculinity, which evolved from Zionism's early New Hebrew man into the soldier-citizen of the decades prior to and after the 1967 war. In popular culture this image was reproduced again and again, first and foremost in popular music, especially in songs by the various army entertainment troupes that proliferated at the time and that were the engine of Israeli popular music during that era.[19] Many of these songs, as in many other modern national cultures, promulgated tropes of a comely and chaste boy-man, innocent and good, who bravely goes into battle to defend his country, regarding the possibility of death for its glory as a privilege and an apt expression of his worth. A possible origin of this metamorphosis and an important impetus for its development and cultivation in Israel might have been Nathan Alterman's celebrated sacrificial poem "The Silver Platter." The 1947 poem, which envisions Israel's birth as an independent country at the end of a long, bloody war, sanctifies the moment by focusing on two young people, a young man and a young woman, who march slowly before the nation, tired and soiled by the terrible battle, saying, "We are the silver platter on which the Jewish state was given."[20]

Alterman's poem emphasizes the battle readiness of the young people, a representation that continued to be cultivated in the decades that followed, no doubt because of Israel's escalating conflict with its Arab neighbors. Eventually, as these aspects were repeated in countless popular songs, this soldierly image was burnished in more serious songs like "How Shall I Bless?" (Ma averech) and vulgarized into the sort of clichés found in popular songs like "He Is Only a Tank-Man" (Hu pashut shiryoner).

"How Shall I Bless?," by the Navy Troupe, gives a hallowed expression to these masculine traits, focusing on the tragedy inherent in young Israeli manhood. The song recounts the stages of a young Israeli man's life, from birth through childhood and eventually to his death as a young man on the battlefield. The notion of sanctity bestowed on the young Spartan's life is conveyed through a line that repeats at the head of each stanza: "How shall I bless him, asked the angel?" Thus, the child in the song is blessed with eyes to see and a heart to feel, with feet to dance, an ear for music, and a love of nature and humanity. The young man is blessed so that his hands, which formerly picked flowers, will now be able to handle steel, so that his dancing feet will now be able to march, and so that his musical ear will enable him to obey his commanders. The song ends with the angel's inability to bless the man anymore, since he is now dead, presumably on the battlefield. He is now an angel himself.

A YouTube search for this song will bring up a dramatic image that opens with members of the troupe dressed in navy white and poised like a Greek chorus at the edge of a cliff overlooking an expansive valley, probably the Jordan or Hulla.[21] As they begin to sing, the camera pans over the valley in all its natural glory. The beautiful land becomes a visual representation of its supreme value for the young man's life, as well as a picture of the very altar on which he was sacrificed. The extreme long-shot pan is interspersed with a montage of baby boys, toddlers, young men, and soldiers—wholesome and smiling avatars of the man in the song. The great power of this clip comes not only from the beautiful tune and angelic voices of the singers, especially the sweet voice of the incomparable Rivka Zohar, the soloist, but also from the pictures of the vigorous, handsome men who will soon be plucked, as the song intimates, and die at the height of their blossoming promise.

The tank-man song, which was written for and performed by the Armored Corps Troupe, presents a more vulgar image of Israeli military manhood. The song distills the image of Israeli manhood into a tall, blue-eyed, broad-shouldered, smiling, attractive young man of few words, confident but naive. And while he is irresistible to women, his true love is his country; women who fancy him must wander far south, where they will find him manning his tank and protecting the country's borders. A quick YouTube search for the song will bring up a droll clip of it, with nine attractive female members of the troupe performing the fluffy number in what looks today like an odd combination of burlesque and militarism that characterized army entertainment troupes at the time (though not just in Israel, of course).[22]

These kinds of images, manipulative in their way, were replicated on screen as well, even in films that were somewhat critical of the Israeli hero worship and its Spartan-like cult of the military, such as the 1969 *Siege* (Matzor; dir. Gilberto Tofano).[23] Written by one of Israel's chief enfants terribles at the time, the iconoclastic writer and commentator Dan Ben-Amotz, the film worshipped the soldier-hero even as it emphasized the heavy toll that such idolatry takes on the people who are left behind, primarily war widows. While the film focuses on Tamar (Gila Almagor), the widow of a 1967 war hero, and favors her attempts to go on with her life and even date men after her husband's death, it nonetheless places the dead husband as well as his living incarnation, his commander (Yoram Ga'on), on a pedestal. This kind of image persisted in the culture for decades. Again, some films openly celebrated this image, like the 1977 *Mivtza Yonatan*, aka *Operation Thunderbolt* (dir. Menahem Golan), which was based on the Israeli 1976 Entebbe rescue operation. Other films, like the 1982 *Repeat Dive* (Tzlila chozeret; dir. Shimon Dotan), dealt more realistically with the personal lives of navy commandos, but nevertheless promoted their elite status as combat soldiers.

Against such powerful imagery, Kuni Leml's manhood is not only wanting, it is practically nonexistent. Both of his Jewish American iterations look like jokes next to images of the brave young men that proliferated in the popular Israel imagination at the time. If the secular Burstein enjoys a bit of American urbanity and sophistication—with his attractive English girlfriend, his nice cars, and the expensive hotels he frequents—the religious Burstein is more boy than man. He is scrawny and gawky, and his awkward behavior with women—both his childish rejection of the rabbi's daughter and the equally awkward way he flirts with Marilyn—make him seem barely eighteen. In one of the most unconvincing scenes in the film, Kuni and Marilyn, sitting in her Tel Aviv hotel room, read a book of Jewish law together, the *Shulchan aruch*, the well-known sixteenth-century Code of Jewish Law. Silly joke aside, the jejune Mr. Burstein looks almost like a child next to the more mature Marilyn. The scene certainly provides another opportunity to poke fun at the unsexy religious. But it fails to convince viewers that the adolescent Kuni is manly in any way, even if Marilyn does jump up and kiss him at the end of the lesson.[24]

This, then, was the representational form Orthodox men took in most Israeli films until the very end of the century. If they were not ridiculed, they were at best exoticized, as in films like the 1972 *I Love You, Rosa* (Ani ohev otach, Roza; dir. Moshe Mizrahi) and in some ways also in the 1990 *The Appointed* (Hameyu'ad; dir. Daniel Wachsmann). In Mizrahi's film, the love story between a widow, Rosa (Michal Bat-Adam), and her husband's younger brother, Nissim (Gabi Utterman), unfolds against the traditions of the old Sephardi Yishuv in Jerusalem at the beginning of the 1920s. Dressed in billowing robes and fancy headdresses, wondering through the narrow, winding streets of Jerusalem, the film's traditional Jewish characters look decidedly biblical. The very drama is exotic, as it revolves around the biblical levirate law: Nissim needs to publicly release his brother's wife from her obligation to marry him, but instead the two fall in love. The fact that Nissim is still underage makes their connection initially impossible, a hurdle they overcome with the passage of time. Despite the high artistic quality of the film, which competed for the foreign Oscar, it does not qualify as a historical drama, with its depiction of Rosa's independence and rebelliousness, which add modern, feminist elements to the story. And although the representation of non-Ashkenazi Jewishness is decidedly more respectful than the prevalent Bourekas imagery of the time, in the last analysis, the film is a quaint and nostalgic look at the imagined simplicity and innocence of traditional Jewish life in a bygone era.

The Appointed is quite different, predicting some of the trends that would characterize cinematic representations of Jewish religiosity toward the end of the millennium and beyond. Shmaya Ben-David (Shuli Rand), the son of a well-known Galilean kabbalist, leaves his religious community to become a performing magician. His meeting with a mysterious young woman, Oshra (Ronit Elkabetz), who apparently possesses supernatural powers, has a deep effect on him, which angers emissaries from his religious community: they demand that he return to the faith and lead their community after his father's death. Eventually Shmaya does so, but he continues to be torn between the burden of the special healing powers he inherited from his father and his love for the "evil" Oshra. His thuggish handlers try to prevent him from seeing Oshra, who finally torches the Torah ark in the synagogue Shmaya is locked up in, setting fire to her lover rather than allow him to be imprisoned by religion.

Faith is a central issue in a film that makes a rather obvious analogy between magic tricks and miracles. The refuge Shmaya finds in legerdemain as a defiant reaction to his father's kabbalistic shamanism is abandoned when he assumes his father's role as leader of the small religious community. Although Shmaya is reluctant to do this at first, it turns out that he is more successful as a shaman than he was as a magician. While his stage act was nothing more than trickery, he seems to possess real healing powers once he returns to his old religious community and assumes his dynastic role as a kabbalist healer. At the same time, the more comfortable he becomes in his new role, the more he incorporates into it aspects from his former life as a showman. He takes his healing show on the road, as it were, recording audiocassettes of his sermons for sale, traveling farther afield, and gradually forming a well-oiled organization designed to bring him more money and power.

All this while, however, Shmaya's attraction to Oshra remains powerful, and the two try to meet repeatedly, only to be forcefully separated and kept apart by Shmaya's handlers. For Oshra is regarded by the religious community as a Lilith of sorts, a devil-woman who represents an earthly love that threatens to lure their leader away. Indeed, Oshra's mysterious ability to set objects on fire by the power of her thoughts becomes a visual metaphor for the passion she and Shmaya have for each other, the fire of their romantic love. In the end, it is this fire that consumes Shmaya, who is unable to extricate himself from the clutches of a religion he may not have meant to embrace so totally.

The Appointed remains one of the few films to explore the supernatural in Israeli cinema. But unlike Shuli Rand's later film, the 2003 *Ushpizin*, it does not extend its investigation much beyond a curiosity. Its exploration of the power of faith in contemporary Israeli society is limited. To the extent that it does probe the topic, the film may perhaps be an allegory of the growing tensions between the religious and the secular in Israel at that time, during the ascendancy of the Mizrahi religious party, SHAS, and the growing visibility of the Babah phenomenon that accompanied it.

Babahs are Jewish spiritual leaders who for the most part adhere to mystical traditions, primarily Kabbalah. In Israel, they are associated with Jewish Mizrahi traditions, mainly Moroccan, where they have been part of the culture for centuries. Their involvement in Israeli politics became controversial after the rise of SHAS to prominence, because leaders of the party routinely consulted them on political matters. Secular Israelis considered this a problematic mixing of religion and politics. The fact that the Babahs were mystics made it all the more suspect.[25] *The Appointed*, rather presciently, gives expression to these anxieties by portraying a small and isolated community of superstitious believers. The community is heavy-handedly ruled by several violent men who derive their power from the group members' simple belief in the supernatural powers of Shmaya. These men do believe that Shmaya has special powers, but they take advantage of the simpler folk by cynically maximizing Shmaya's appeal and influence to augment their own.

Yet the film's stance toward religious devotion remains conflicted, unresolved. *The Appointed* often makes clear that Shmaya is indeed a miracle worker, that he has otherworldly powers. At the same time, it also presents his followers as superstitious. Shmaya's first inkling that he possesses some kind of extrasensory abilities is revealed to him when he unintentionally, absentmindedly almost, cures a mute baby; the baby begins to cry for the first time in his life after Shmaya puts his hand on his head and blesses him. Until that time, Shmaya was a regular magician, a trickster. Now, suddenly, he begins to understand the extent and meaning of the powers he inherited from his father—which he also uses for ill, not just for good. When a community member doubts his suitability as a leader and his father's heir, Shmaya puts a curse on him that visibly makes his detractor unwell. Similarly, when Shmaya is asked to speak to a gathering of believers, he chooses instead to tear up pieces from the challah in front of him and throw them into the crowd. As the frenzied believers reach out their hands to catch the tossed pieces of bread, Shmaya laughs derisively at their foolishness.

Ultimately, then, *The Appointed* presents religion as a force for good while it warns against the excesses of religious belief and religious devotion. A decade later, with the continued growth of the Orthodox community, the portrayal of religious Jews began to take on more sinister forms in films like *Kadosh* (dir. Amos Gitai, 1999), for instance, which is discussed below. Because of Zionism's ideological aversion to religion and because religious Israelis were few and powerless, for many years they were an easy target for ridicule, especially in comedies, which used their unusual appearance and distinct way of life to great comic effect. The contrasting portrayals of Haredi Jews and Mizrahim in Israeli films reflect fairly accurately the differences in the size and presence of the two communities. Neither group was represented very well politically. But because Mizrahim were more numerous, comprising more than half the population by the late 1980s, before the mass Russian immigration, the interest and willingness of the culture at large to absorb them was greater. Both the proliferation and popularity of the Bourekas film genre and its narrative structure reflect this. Most Bourekas comedies ended happily with a wedding between the Mizrahi and Ashkenazi characters as a kind of artificial solution to the more serious, real-life problems of Mizrahim in Israel.[26] Haredim did not receive the same kind of cinematic attention because they were negligible—discounted, a completely marginal community.

It is only since the mid-1980s that the ultra-Orthodox have grown in number and increased their power over Israeli politics. And it was not until the mid-1990s, with the explosive growth of the Mizrahi religious party, SHAS, that the power and presence of Haredim in Israel began to attract the culture's attention for the first time in earnest. Historically speaking, Amos Gitai was one of the first directors to take note of the Haredi community, dedicating an entire film to them, their society, and their way of life. His 1999 film *Kadosh* tells the story of two Haredi women who are both frustrated in their intimate lives with their men, for different reasons. Rivka (Yael Abecassis) has been married to Meir (Yoram Hattab) for ten years, and their inability to have children overshadows their love until it finally tears them apart. Malka (Meital Barda) loves a young man who left the religious community and became secular. Eventually, she agrees to marry another man, Yossef (Uri Klauzner), a violent ignoramus who makes her miserable. The film ends with Rivka's suicide and Malka's probable abandonment of her husband and community.

A remarkable aspect of *Kadosh*, comparatively speaking, is its attempt to portray religious characters as real, living, breathing people and not caricatures. *Kadosh* contains painful and at times excruciatingly intimate scenes from the lives of the characters that populate it, which lets viewers into their innermost sanctums—their living rooms, their dining rooms, and finally also into their bedrooms. As opposed to Kuni, whom we never get to know as a real person and who remains a cipher that stands for a whole community, *Kadosh* familiarizes us with an array of different characters from an "authentic" Orthodox community. Each of the main characters in the film is a distinct person, a rounded character. In the history of religious imagery on Israeli screens, *Kadosh* is, therefore, an important milestone.

Gitai's distinct cinematic style certainly contributes to the importance of the film; his long, slow shots are great vehicles for intimacy, patiently acquainting viewers with their subjects. Thus, the film opens on a morning in the bedroom of Rivka and Meir, who are shown in the most natural way, sleeping, getting up, praying, and even making love briefly. Like the omniscient narrator in literature, the psychology of the cinematic shot, its head-on, intimate point of view, is clearly designed to take viewers in, familiarize them with the characters, and consequently make the characters likable. When Meir gets up quietly, trying not to wake his wife, and slowly prepares to pray, the protracted screen time spent on following him getting dressed, wrapping the prayer shawl around him, and then binding on the leather straps of his phylacteries inevitably endears him to viewers. He appears sensitive, earnest, well meaning, and most of all, genuinely observant. Even for nonreligious viewers, such a direct correlation between belief and practice commands respect. This kind of seriousness in the treatment of Orthodox Jewish life distinguishes Gitai's film throughout.

But as the opening scene continues to unfold, the refreshing realism begins to paint a different picture. Things do not seem quite right; Meir does not leave the room to pray, but stays inside the small space, performing the ritual standing close to his sleeping wife's bed, spatially crowding her. This seems a bit odd, as he tries to keep very quiet the whole time. Stranger still are his attempts to wake her up afterward without taking off his prayer shawl or phylacteries. Fully dressed in his ritualistic regalia, he gets into their bed, and when she has awoken, the two begin to make love. The tender smiles, the gentle touches leave no doubt that the two love and respect each other. But even at this early stage, the place of religion and religious practice in their lives seems problematic, excessive, unhealthy. Ritual ob-

FIGURE 1.1
Yael Abecassis and Yoram Hattab as an Orthodox couple in **Kadosh** *(1999).*

jects, religious artifacts, are literally invading their most intimate spaces and get into their bed, foreshadowing things to come.

The sense of confinement, even entrapment, continues in the next scene, which takes place at the synagogue. We see Rivka and another young woman, Malka, looking at the praying men through the *mechitza*, the screen that divides the men's from the women's section. As the wooden divide fills the screen, it creates a background against which the two women are shot from a close distance as they talk about Malka's chances of getting married, hinting at one of the young men on the other side as a possible match. At this point in the story, we do not know why Malka is so opposed to the match and seems averse to marriage in principle. But without even knowing that she is in love with the ineligible Yaacov (Sami Huri), who left religion and their community some time ago, we sense an uncomfortable feeling of constraint and repression. The extreme close-up of the two women's faces and the latticed screen behind them make it look as if the two were in jail.

It soon becomes clear that this is precisely the situation in which both women find themselves, although for different reasons. Rivka is happy to be intimate with her husband, whom she loves very much. Although the two are often seen close together on-screen, they are also painfully reminded that this intimacy is for naught, as they are barren; they do not have children yet after ten years of marriage. Without the ability to have children, marriage has no purpose according to *halakha* and is therefore useless, even sinful. Yet the film constantly highlights this paradox by bringing the two together, creating a mounting pressure that eventually explodes with their separation and Rivka's suicide. In one of the most heartbreaking scenes in the film, Rivka initiates a very tender love session with Meir. But because she has her period, and menstruating women are forbidden to their husbands according to Jewish law, she has to stop at some point. Religion, says the film, has once again thwarted love and has come between two people.

Malka, on the other hand, suffers from the opposite problem. We understand why she does not want to marry anyone when we see her meet Yaacov at the store where she works. As opposed to the opening scene, in which Rivka and Meir, the loving husband and wife, were comfortably snug in their little room, Malka and Yaacov stand in a large space that has a big window onto the street. Although no one looks on or comes in, Malka is anxious someone would and cannot express the obvious desire she feels for Yaacov, whom she knows she cannot marry as long as she stays in the community. Both scenes, with Rivka and Meir and Malka and Yaacov, express in inverse ways the infiltration of religion and orthodox society into the privacy of people's lives and the serious problems this creates. When Malka later marries the violent Yossef, her desire to get away from him, to be as far away as possible from him, continues this dynamic.

The performance of the men in the film is generally rigid and unnatural, perhaps because some of the things they say sound extremely harsh and even incredulous to secular ears. It would be no surprise to learn, then, that these men comprise a stiff religious patriarchy, from the fire and brimstone rabbi (Yussuf Abu-Warda) to the thuggish Yossef and even down to Rivka's husband, Meir, who eventually succumbs to the community's pressure and agrees to divorce his beloved wife. When Meir asks for advice about his marriage, the rabbi, who is played by an Arab actor, strongly advises him to divorce her. "A Jewish woman's only purpose is to have babies," he says to the troubled Meir. "Raising Jewish children!" he says. "This is the only way we'd be able to beat them, the heathens who control this state." This ugly statement is visually highlighted later on when Yossef rapes his wife Malka on their wedding night, ramming into her with animal passion and without any regard for her distress.

So while *Kadosh* is certainly more realistic than silly comedies like the Kuni Leml films and creates a much more authentic and well-rounded picture of Orthodox people, it does so with a very clear purpose: to criticize the Jewish Orthodox society harshly. The film asks, what or who is *kadosh*, meaning "holy" in Hebrew. The answer is implied. The film may portray a holy community, as traditional Judaism often refers to Jewish communities in general, but there is absolutely nothing holy about it. The opposite is true. The community is shown as a backward and primitive religious sect that opposes the basic rights of humans, especially women. What is falsely perceived as holy in the film, Jewish law, is seen as standing in the way of real holiness—human dignity.

While the religious men and women in *Kadosh* are much more sympathetic than religious images in many previous films, religion itself appears very negatively in the film. Jewish religion in *Kadosh* is shown as oppressive, dark, unenlightened, and cruel. It is an iron rule of rigid laws, a rule that seems unconcerned with the mental well-being or spiritual comfort of individuals. Kuni and his other cinematic religious peers may have looked like idiots, but their religious belief never seemed sinister or problematic or even threatening. *Kadosh* changes this dynamic. The film treats religious individuals with great care but has no sympathy for religion itself, which it represents as a jail.

The question then arises as to the place *Kadosh* occupies in the developmental trajectory discussed here. Why go into such trouble and make such a negative film about Orthodox society, especially when there was little chance that any member of that society would ever see the film?[27] The accepted conceit is that any works of art, especially narrative forms of art like films, are made with the hope of making viewers reflect on the issues they raise and perhaps even do something about them. The answer to this question lies in the changes that the Orthodox society has undergone in the decades that preceded the film and to which it seems to be responding.

At the end of the 1990s, the size, place, and presence of the Orthodox community in Israel was changing dramatically from previous decades, moving from the social periphery closer to the center. Ultra-Orthodox religious parties have always been part of the Israeli political scene, but it was not until the mid-1990s and the growth of the Mizrahi religious party, SHAS, that they became a force to reckon with. These changes had already begun in the early 1980s and relate for the most part to Labor's momentous 1977 electoral defeat and the consequent ascendancy of the more conservative, right-wing Likud Party. Likud was more willing to include religious parties in government coalitions and happier, for ideological reasons and not just for cold political calculations, to promote them and cater to their demands.[28]

The readiness of Likud to include religious parties in coalition governments certainly improved the status of the ultra-Orthodox, benefiting them financially and helping their community prosper and grow. But the biggest change in the political dynamic between the secular and the religious in Israel occurred when SHAS combined religion and ethnicity as a political agenda in the mid-1980s. Utilizing the political conservatism of

Mizrahim in Israel as well as their religious traditionalism, SHAS offered a combination that promised the best solution for their nagging social, economic, and political disenfranchisement. The ingenuity of the invention was handsomely rewarded in the elections of 1996, when the twelve-year-old party nearly doubled its seats in the Knesset, from six to ten, and then did it again four years later when it jumped to seventeen seats. Many of the reasons for this impressive growth are not germane to this study. What is important to note, though, is the curious metamorphosis of Mizrahi religiosity under SHAS, which mixed the folksier Mizrahi religiosity with Ashkenazi orthodoxy to create a powerful native Israeli hybrid. The chief attraction of SHAS was a "democratic" inclusivity that did away with the dynastic exclusivity of Ashkenazi orthodoxy, primarily Hasidism, and opened Haredi Judaism up for anyone who cared to join, primarily by setting up subsidized educational frameworks.[29]

For secular, liberal, left-leaning, and Western-identified Israelis these developments were alarming. SHAS presented a heightened threat; the religious danger it posed for the secular Israeli state was augmented by its Mizrahi aspects, which further undermined the European orientation of the teetering old hegemony. The fusion of two reactionary forces, orthodoxy and orientalism (Mizrahiyut), was frightening. The casting of an Arab actor, Yussuf Abu-Warda, in the role of the barbarous rabbi in *Kadosh*, then, can be seen as an expression of this anxiety and a symbolic representation of the film's concern. While this casting decision may well have originated in Gitai's liberal tendencies and his wish to break with ethnic stereotyping, it nevertheless becomes part of the negative image of religiosity in the film. The rabbi's dark complexion and sinister "Arab" look stand as a visual impression of the dark religion he represents and whose harshness is clearly expressed by the damning sentiments that come out of his mouth. It is worth noting that the brutish Yossef also looks Mizrahi, adding to the association the film makes between the violent nature of the character he plays and his non-Ashkenazi look.[30]

Both the rabbi and Yossef, then, represent dark forces that threaten the Israeli body culture metaphorically and literally. *Kadosh* indicts them as such. As a result of the rabbi's unbending instruction to Meir to divorce his wife, Rivka is made to leave the house. Away from her beloved husband she slowly withers, cast in a desolate room somewhere, lonely and sad. When she returns to him at the end of the film and climbs into his bed to make love to him for the last time, it is in order to commit suicide in his arms, becoming an Orthodox Juliet who is unwilling to go on living without her Romeo. After Rivka's death, and after her own husband violently beats her, Malka decides not to follow her friend to the grave. Although the ending of the film is ambiguous, her visit to the cemetery on the Mount of Olives without her head covering, framed against the view of Jerusalem, indicates that she may have chosen to leave her oppressive community and join her former lover on the outside.

The differences between the Kuni Leml trilogy and *Kadosh* illustrate the changed place and importance of religion and religiosity in Israeli, Jewish culture toward the end of the twentieth century. The irreverent comedies of the earlier years were indicative of the marginality of the Orthodox in Israeli culture and their existence as a curio. The poignant critique of *Kadosh* conveys a sense of real threat to secular Israel from growing internal religious forces. The menacing religious patriarchy in *Kadosh* is the visualization of a secular nightmare.

But the expansion of the Orthodox community in Israel also produced positive images. With time, it also took on more variegated forms that aptly expressed the growing religious community and its increasing complexity. The rate of change was slow at first, as it took almost two decades: from 1983, when the last film in the Kuni Leml trilogy was released, to 1999, when *Kadosh* came out. The initial direction of change was predictable as well, as can be seen in *Kadosh*. For it was not surprising that a society that had discounted orthodoxy for so many years would be taken aback when it suddenly realized that it could no longer afford to do so.

Eventually, and probably inevitably, the growing religious community began to produce its own image-makers, who could present personal versions of who they were without mediation. Joseph Cedar was probably the first to do so with his 2000 film *Time of Favor* (about the settler community), which is discussed later in the book. Four years after that, Shuli Rand became the first Orthodox filmmaker to come out with a film that dealt with the maligned Ashkenazi Orthodox community. His 2003 runaway hit *Ushpizin* is a religious romantic comedy (!) that takes place in an ultra-Orthodox community in Jerusalem and tells the story of a humble, righteous, and loving married couple, Moshe and Mali Bellanga, whose poverty is embittered by their inability to have children. Structured like a Hasidic tale, the story takes place at the time of the Festival of Tabernacles (Sukkot), during which Moshe and Mali are put to a series of difficult tests. At the end of the film, having withstood their trials and proved their belief in God, the loving couple is rewarded with a child, a baby boy.

Ushpizin, like most films belonging to what can be called the new religious cinema since the 2000s, was a religious project; its writer and main actor, Shuli Rand, is a *ba'al tshuva*, a secular man who returned to the faith and became ultra-Orthodox. Rand got permission from his rabbi to make the film as a way to reach out to secular Israelis. He probably did not think the film would swell the size of his community with a rush of secular moviegoers, who would clamor for a religious return to the faith. Rather, the film's Hasidic elements as well as its more modern romantic sensibilities were used to paint a more positive picture of his community for a generally hostile secular Israeli public. The Hasidic elements present a neat and attractive tale and seem like a genuine expression of his sincere faith, while the love story appeals to secular viewers. For *Ushpizin* is also a romantic comedy, one of the most popular of all cinematic genres. The only difference is the religious context and the charming component of "miracles" in which the naive couple believes and which the film medium renders so well.[31]

Early on in the story, after he fails to scrape money together for the approaching holiday, Moshe wonders aimlessly in the streets of his neighborhood. Everyone around him hurries to and fro, busy with preparations for the holiday. But having been shamed out of the house by his wife, who scolded him for not providing for them, he feels no part of the excitement around him and walks about despondently. But things are about to change, for the righteous are always rewarded, and Moshe and his wife Mali are about to have a miracle. The notion that something unusual is about to happen is hinted at by the slightly slowed motion of the street scene: the walking men, with their earlocks and long coats flapping ever so slowly about, the Breslov Hasidic missionaries jumping dreamily up and down on the roof of their mitzvah-mobile, and above all the sound of a shofar blowing tremulously in the offing and a haze that shrouds everything as if the *shechina*, the presence of God, were slowly coming down from on high.

Finding his way to a small park, Moshe sits glumly on a bench overlooking the holy city of Jerusalem, and, like the true Hasid he is, begins to pray to God, pouring out his heart. Significantly, it is not the most identifiable view of Jerusalem, with the Temple Mount and the mosques on top of it, but a more neutral, "Jewish" vista of the city. All Moshe is asking for is a miracle, and indeed, as he does so, the film cuts to a nearby office, where we see two religious charity workers from Moshe's community wondering what to do with an excess of $1,000 they were left with and no one to give it to. "Pick a number," the older of the two says, pointing to a ledger with the names of charity cases the community supports. The next scene is an adeptly parallel-edited sequence that cuts between the praying Moshe, his wife, who also sits at home and prays, and the slowly counting charity worker, who goes down the list in his ledger and stops at Moshe Bellanga's name just as the very man finishes his supplication for a miracle with a fervent cry that bursts out of the depth of his aching heart.

This expertly rendered scene is a good example of the power of the

FIGURE 1.2
Shuli Rand as a Breslov Hasid in **Ushpizin** *(2003).*

cinematic medium to manipulate images. It is hard to think of a secular filmmaker who would be able to create such a wonderfully naive picture that conveys religious faith with an innocence so convincing. For even the most hardened of secular hearts cannot but rejoice with the destitute couple, whose goodness and honesty are rewarded so handsomely and in such a timely manner. Rand's innovation here is to harness the art of filmmaking to convey religious faith in a way that would be believed and accepted by secular outsiders. *Ushpizin* was targeted at cinematically sophisticated secular viewers and not made for internal religious consumption; thus, the better the film, the more palatable its religious message.

This is probably also why the film was made as a romantic comedy, which focuses on the love between Moshe and Mali. Neither character fits Hollywood's common aesthetic ideals of romantic heroes, as they are nearly middle aged, not especially good looking, out of shape, and dressed very shabbily. But that also allows the film to cater to two sensibilities at once: the modern comedic-romantic sensibility as well as the Hasidic one, which ties suffering and need to heavenly rewards. The miracle, however, comes at a cost. As soon as the ecstatic couple manages to put together a beautiful *sukkah* and decorate it lavishly in time for the holiday, they are put to a series of additional tests that take the form of two guests, the *ushpizin* of the film's title.[32]

The two guests are escaped criminals who decide to extend their weekend furlough and skip jail. Looking for a place to hide, the two remember their old friend Moshe, who was a criminal too before he mended his ways and found God, and they repair to his *sukkah*. The return of his repressed past in the guise of his former gang members presents Moshe and his wife with a formidable trial, which they must endure during the seven days of the holiday, and which lasts until film's end. The hardened criminal guests abuse their hospitality, disrespect the holiday, and behave in ways that shame Moshe and Mali and finally tear them apart, at least temporarily. But it is because of this separation and Moshe's unwillingness to divorce his beloved wife, despite their childless union, that the two are blessed at the very end with a baby boy.

The identity of the *ushpizin*, or guests, is perhaps the least convincing aspect of the film, because it implies a connection between secularity and criminality: the two gangsters are the only secular characters in the entire film. Moreover, the guests' portrayal as criminal Mizrahi types is exaggerated to the point of absurdity. They are dark, ugly, aggressive, rude, uncouth, and downright stupid. Moreover, in a curious disregard for the traditionalism that is usually associated with Mizrahim, they seem to lack even the most basic knowledge of Jewish customs.[33] Their role, aside from trying Moshe, also serves to highlight the differences between the animal he used to be and the holy man he has become after his rebirth as an Orthodox Jew. But the film misuses some of these masculine cultural tropes, undermining another one of its goals, to masculinize Moshe by making him sound slightly Mizrahi and therefore less Ashkenazi and "diasporic." In other words, while the film strips the obvious Mizrahi masculine types—the two criminals—from any vestige of Judaism, it gives the religious Moshe subtle Mizrahi traits in order to establish his masculinity and delineate it over and against the geeky and diasporic Ashkenazi image most of his sect members have in the popular Israeli imagination.[34]

Ushpizin is an interesting film not only because it is good art but also because it is the first major film about the ultra-Orthodox made by a member of that group. As such, it tells the story of a unique community, one that is radically different from general Israeli society. While the film certainly wishes to acquaint secular viewers with this milieu, it does not have an integrative agenda and makes no claims other than to ask viewers to recognize the community as different but legitimate. In the name of contemporary multiculturalism, the film's religious community wishes to be seen as equal to other communities in a postmodern, post-Zionist Israel. While the film remains sectarian in the way it depicts the exclusive ways of the sect, it demands equality of representation and consideration as part of the new mosaic called modern Israeli society. This is certainly different from the suspicion with which the Orthodox community was held by the general Israeli public until then, as well as from the reluctance of the Israeli ultra-Orthodox to acknowledge the State of Israel.

The existence of these cultural exchanges was also made possible by the fact that, like most if not all filmmakers who have made films about the religious in Israel since 2000, Shuli Rand, the creator of *Ushpizin*, has not always been religious.[35] This is true of the three other so-called religious directors, whose films will be discussed later: Joseph Cedar and his various films, Meny Yaesh and his film *God's Neighbors* (2012), and Rama Burstein and her film *Fill the Void* (2012). The story of each of these filmmakers is different, but common to them all is a great familiarity with the secular world, the cultural codes of which they have internalized and taken with them into their religious or Orthodox communities.[36] Their cinematic projects are, presumably, based on the Western, liberal, and even romantic belief in the power of art to influence and change society. This would also account for the special dispensation both Rand and Burstein received from their rabbis to produce their films in the first place, and their attempt, especially Burstein's, to limit the involvement of non-Orthodox crew members in her film's production.[37] In this respect, one of Israel's most celebrated filmmakers, Uri Zohar, who became Orthodox after a fervent and brilliant film career in the 1970s, is an exception. Zohar became completely silent after his conversion and has hardly used his prodigious artistic talents at all since then.

Indeed, the massive expansion of the Orthodox community in Israel at the turn of the twenty-first century makes it ever more difficult to keep it apart from the rest of Israeli society, as some members of that community and its leaders may wish. One fascinating result of the increasingly porous divisions between the Orthodox and the rest of Israeli society has been the emergence of filmmakers who straddle both communities, like Rand and Burstein. A concurrent and perhaps even more intriguing phenomenon has been an increase in the number of filmmakers who operate within the exclusive and hermetic Orthodox community. The growing body of works by these Orthodox filmmakers is made for internal consumption only and is strictly divided according to gender, with men directors making action films by, with, and for men, and women directors making more educational films by, with, and for women.[38] These productions do not circulate outside the Orthodox community and are relevant to this study mostly as a phenomenon that can attest to the general changes the Orthodox community is undergoing as well as to the power of the cinematic medium. The adoption of such a secular art form, formerly forbidden by most Orthodox rabbis, signifies the growing acculturation of the Orthodox community to Israeli life. Yet because Orthodox filmmaking is so tightly controlled and remains insular, it does not yet engage in a significant dialogue with the outside world.

The last film discussed in this chapter is the 2009 gay Orthodox drama *Eyes Wide Open* (Einayim petuchoth; dir. Haim Tabakman), a passionate story about the attraction between a married Orthodox butcher and a young Orthodox man who shows up on his doorstep one day, becomes his helper at the store, and wakes in him hidden life forces. "Gay drama" may perhaps be an overstatement, because the film does not necessarily promote or advocate a relationship between the two men. On the other hand, neither does it paint the Orthodox society as a dark and backward community that oppresses the individuality and true identity of its members to the extent one would perhaps expect. In 2009, that would have been retrograde, too close to the heavy hand of *Kadosh* and too far from the nuanced sophistication of films like *Ushpizin*. But although the film has many obvious gay components, ultimately the attraction between the two men is used more as a modernizing device of Orthodox society than a critique of it.

Meat, or flesh, is one of the main and obvious metaphors in this film, most of which takes place in or around the butcher shop of the protagonist, Aharon (Zohar Shtrauss), a thirty-year-old man with a wife, Rivka (Tinkerbell), and four small children. At the beginning of the film, Aharon breaks into the locked butcher store—he must have forgotten the key—in order to take it over from his recently deceased father, Menachem Fleischman. We later surmise that Aharon's forceful entry into the "house of flesh" is subconsciously symbolic. Unlike his father, whose name literally means consoler (Menachem) of flesh (Fleischman), Aharon will not be happy to continue appeasing his own flesh and will eventually succumb to and embrace his carnality. His spirit of defiance is underscored by his gathering and throwing out with disgust the meat that had rotted inside the store during the shiva, the week of mourning for his father. Aharon is cleaning house, clearing the dead meat away and readying himself for a new life by posting a "help wanted" sign on the door.

An opportunity to seize this new life soon materializes in the shape of a fetching young man, Ezri (Ran Danker), who bursts into the butcher shop one evening looking for shelter from the pouring rain. The first hint at his sexuality, besides his sensual good looks, comes when he dejectedly mutters, "I've come for you" to another man on the other side of a cell phone he borrows from Aharon. Spontaneously, Aharon invites him to stay the night in the empty room above the butcher shop before he leaves to go home. Over the course of the next few days the two develop a silent closeness until Aharon offers Ezri a job as his helper. Nothing physical transpires between them, but it is obvious that Aharon is strangely attracted to Ezri, whom he follows around the neighborhood and begins to suspect of being drawn to men. Yet despite his suspicion, and likely because of it, Aharon continues to employ the young man. Ezri's leave to remain in Aharon's life is cinematically symbolized by a complementary scene to the earlier one of Aharon breaking into the butcher shop. When Ezri returns to the store one day he uses his key to easily enter the "house of flesh." That which Aharon struggled for and used force to gain access to, Ezri enters as a matter of fact.

Pretty quickly the two men develop a friendship, which they celebrate one Friday by swimming in a mountain spring outside Jerusalem. The idea is suggested by Ezri, who in Orthodox terms is a troublemaker, as we slowly learn. He was thrown out of a yeshiva in another city, Safed, for immoral behavior, and his attempts to connect with a local yeshiva student, who was probably a former lover, are predictably frowned upon. But Aharon does not seem concerned and feels alive for the first time in a long while in his presence. Although he is reluctant to go into the spring at first, and does not take off his underwear until he is in the water, he is positively giddy later on during the Sabbath meal at his house, to which he invites Ezri. He sings loudly, bangs on the table, and seems to generally enjoy himself for the first time in a film that up to that point showed him as gloomy and withdrawn.

But although Aharon is powerfully drawn to Ezri, he initially refuses to consummate the connection, rejoicing in Ezri's presence as a wonderful opportunity to exercise his power of abstention, resist the evil urge, and purify his sinful soul through suffering. Soon, however, he breaks down and succumbs to his desire, and the two begin a torrid affair. At first no one suspects anything unusual about their relationship, but as time passes and the two men get closer, people begin to talk. Rumors of Ezri's former exploits eventually reach the community, and despite the favored position Aharon enjoys in it, he is asked to let Ezri go. He is visited by members of the community's "modesty police," who threaten him, and he is then asked by his rabbi to do the same. His wife notices the change in him too and is anxious about its meaning for their future life together.

Predictably, the film does not end well. Since Aharon is unwilling to leave either Ezri or religion, it cannot be otherwise. When Ezri finally departs, giving in to mounting pressures, the despondent Aharon goes back to the mountain spring where he was first "baptized" into his true self. In a heartfelt gesture toward his lost lover, he takes his clothes off completely before going into the water and immersing himself ritualistically as one does in a mikveh, a Jewish ritual bath. The film ends ambivalently during one of those dips, from which Aharon does not emerge. Is he lingering underwater or committing suicide, drowning himself from sorrow?

Unlike *Kadosh*, *Eyes Wide Open* is not an antireligious film. As its name suggests, Aharon's eyes are open, and he is also willing to stand up to his community and stick by his lover without abandoning his religious way of life, and in some ways, even his family. Thus, it is a very unusual film about religion. Ostensibly, it shares the Western, bourgeois liberalism of *Kadosh* in its critical attitude toward religion. Homophobia replaces male chauvinism in the film and religious patriarchy is the focus of critique. But it would be too easy to accuse the Orthodox community in *Eyes Wide Open* of homophobia, and quite beside the point, too. Most if not all religions censure homosexuality, or at least did so until very recently, especially fundamentalist sects like the one shown in the film.

Eyes Wide Open attempts something rather more sophisticated. Under the pretense of an antireligious film that caters to clichéd views of orthodoxy as backward and primitive, it actually attempts to show it in a much more positive light. It comes as no surprise that Aharon's society does not accept his homosexual relationship. The film would have been inauthentic were it otherwise, for this is the Jewish Orthodox reality. But in various ways, the film presents orthodoxy as tolerant to a degree and as a system that allows it members, to some extent, a measure of freedom and individuality. It does so through the casting, in its attentive portrayal of Aharon as well as that of his relationship with Ezri, and finally by its depiction of a moderate religious establishment.

The first and most visually obvious element that denotes these changes is the casting of Ran Danker as the object of desire in the film. Most love stories, whether poetic, literary, or cinematic, cast attractive young people in the role of lovers. When the convention is ignored, it is usually done for a specific reason. In *Ushpizin*, for instance, the homeliness of the married lovers is an important part of the film's religious message, as good looks would have obscured their inner worth, for which they are rewarded at the end. *Eyes Wide Open* plays with these conventions. Aharon cannot be too good looking or stand out because his character is that of an ordinary member of a religious community, an Orthodox Everyman. Ezri's good looks, on the other hand, function as a narrative device, a dramatic motivation.

More importantly, even if Ezri's religious credentials are doubted by his community, viewers see him as an attractive young man. In the history of Haredi visual imagery, this is unusual and noteworthy. The secular gaze is usually trained on signs of Haredi difference: clothes, facial hair, ritual artifacts, customs. Haredi people are seldom openly objectified sexually, as their insistence on modest clothing attests. By presenting Ezri as an attractive lover, *Eyes Wide Open* engages in basic moviemaking, of course. But

FIGURE 1.3
Ran Danker and Zohar Shtrauss as gay Orthodox lovers in ***Eyes Wide Open*** *(2009).*

in the context of the secular culture's relationship with Haredi society, it is an innovation. By associating aestheticism, a central tenet of modern, Western national culture, with a religious community that fundamentally rejects it as worldly and unimportant, the film in effect pulls aestheticism into its cultural sphere. It not only makes Orthodox society "easier on the eyes," as the saying goes, but literally clears a spot in the hairy Orthodox forest, amid the bushy hair that hides men's faces and the wigs that cover woman's heads. It also familiarizes and modernizes orthodoxy by doing so. Here is a society that we can relate to, says the film—a society that at least to some extent operates as we, secular people, do. It responds to beauty and pursues it.

The same principle operates with respect to the homosexual love story. Homosexual and not gay, because the relationship between Aharon and Ezri has many of the characteristics that love relations between men had in earlier, less tolerant periods in history. The prohibitions of the film's Orthodox society against same-sex relationships are similar to ones that obtained in, say, nineteenth-century England. Precisely because the psychological knowledge of the self was advanced enough to acknowledge such tendencies, social conventions and legal restrictions explicitly forbade their mention or practice. Consequently, Aharon and Ezri's relationship is mostly physical, separated from other communal, religious, and even conjugal activities they regularly participate in. But this is precisely why their relationship "works" cinematically. At a time when gay rights have become one of the most definitive measures of a society's liberalism, tolerance, freedom, and legal advancement in the West, the film invites viewers' empathy toward the two men as tragic victims. At the same time, the film also paints Orthodox society as modern in a way.

The tolerant attitude toward homosexuality becomes a measuring stick of the film's Orthodox society. The rabbi stands out in particular in this respect because, even though he is aware of the situation, he gently lets Aharon grapple with it himself and arrive at what he hopes will be the right decision. He mentions it very gently to Aharon on a few occasions, urging him to let Ezri go without scolding, shaming, or threatening him. Moreover, when members of the "modesty police" show up in Aharon's butcher shop to warn him for the second time and start bullying him, the rabbi, who chances in, orders them angrily out. "You are not students of Torah," he scolds them, using one of the worst Orthodox insults, preferring the sinning Aharon to the nominally religious bullies.

In the penultimate scene of the film, after Ezri has left and before Aharon goes to the spring again, he prays silently in his bedroom while his wife, Rivka, sits glumly on her bed reading a prayer book. "Why are you praying, Aharon?" she suddenly asks him. "Where do you want to be?" Rivka is understandably upset, but her question contains not only full acknowledgment but also acceptance, as it still leaves Aharon a choice that denotes a willingness to receive him back if he so wishes. "You need to decide," she insists. "There is nothing to decide," Aharon replies resolutely. "I want to be here. It is only the evil urge in me. Protect me," he pleads with his wife, who takes him into her arms. As the camera pulls back, the two are seen embracing on the bed for a few brief moments like a Madonna and child. More than anything else, Aharon craves mercy. He has already proved that he is not a pawn in the hands of an oppressive religious establishment. He is a self-reflecting autonomous being. Whether he stays or leaves is his own decision. In comparative terms, then, the Orthodox individual has been given a lot of agency in this film. That a solution to the problem is not simple, as the ending proves, cannot be otherwise.

Even if the film does not faithfully reflect the goings-on in most Orthodox communities today, the association it makes between two of the most extreme poles of Israeli society, Western liberalism and fundamentalist Judaism, is telling. It is a reflection of the Israelification of the Orthodox community and its growing need to deal with many of the issues that occupy its "host" secular culture. The opposite is true as well. By virtue of their growing presence in its midst, Israeli society needs to take note of the Orthodox and learn to live with them. The relationship of the two men, then, Aharon and Ezri, symbolizes this meeting quite literally and "gayifies" the Orthodox society. If gay means socially advanced and culturally sophisticated, the maligned image of orthodoxy gains by its selection as the relatively tolerant background for this love story. Orthodox society is presented as neither negligible and ridiculous nor esoteric and exclusive; nor is it primitive and oppressive. *Eyes Wide Open* marks yet another change in the perception of Haredi society, which for the first time is presented as part of the larger Israeli society. The gay love story makes Haredi society look "cooler," but it also challenges that society to grapple with such issues more constructively.

Finally, and quite surprisingly given the history of Jewish-Israeli manhood, by making the protagonists of the film homosexual, the film does not perpetuate images of Orthodox men as weak and effeminate. Rather than create such "diasporic" associations, *Eyes Wide Open* relies on metrosexual rather than homosexual imagery to boost the masculinity of its "gay" characters. In other words, what would have perhaps been interpreted during an earlier era as less masculine—paleness, studiousness, restraint—receives a different take in the film, a metrosexual take. Both Aharon and Ezri are very confident men despite their precarious position as "sinners" in their religious community. Their ability to juggle both worlds, the world of Torah and the world of their forbidden desire, is seen as a strength, a measure of their sophistication and agency as independent individuals. Their so-called metrosexuality resides in their attempt to pursue their own personal happiness despite the invasive demands of their society with a carelessness that is very uncharacteristic of the community-minded Orthodox.

Although the analogy only goes so far, Ezri especially is his "own love object," as Mark Simpson quipped about metrosexuals, for whom pleasure is a sexual preference.[39] His peripatetic lifestyle, his composure, his artistic pursuit of drawing, his somewhat instrumental use of Aharon for sex, and above all his sensual good looks, which he seems aware of and which he cultivates and uses, mark him as metrosexual to a degree. In his free spirit and daring sexuality he is an odd member of a religious community. Yet rather than being perceived as weak, Ezri is perhaps the strongest character in the film. Based on his history and conduct in the film, and notwithstanding his fictionality, he probably survived his affair with Aharon unscathed and moved on to another city, where he likely continued his life undisturbed.

None of this, however, is meant to cast aspersions on the religious community whence Ezri comes. If anything, it portrays the community as part of a natural Israeli background or context that is used for social commentary. Religious society in the film is an authentic canvas upon which the characters are drawn. But the community itself and its "un-Israeli, diasporic" ways are no longer a focus; rather, religiosity is seen as a legitimate and even neutral frame of reference. If anything, the homo- or metro-sexual associations serve to present the Orthodox as contemporary, up-dated, perhaps even sexy. Religion is certainly not ridiculous, as in the Kuni Leml trilogy, nor is it oppressive, as in *Kadosh*. It simply is.

CHAPTER 2

JEWISH *and* ISRAELI: IMAGES *of* MIZRAHI JEWS

As was mentioned in the beginning of the first chapter, Zionism tried to minimize expressions of traditional religiosity in the new Jewish culture it constructed in Palestine. And since most of the founders of Zionism hailed from Eastern Europe, religiosity for them was primarily associated with what they knew back home: Ashkenazi orthodoxy. The roots of Zionist antireligious antagonism go all the way back to the Haskala and its project of acculturating traditional Jewish society in Europe in the spirit of the Age of Reason. The *maskilim* took it upon themselves to bring the old, traditional Jewish establishment into modernity by exposing it to the light of knowledge and reason and minimizing the role of the clerical establishment in everyday Jewish life.

Predictably, the greatest resistance to the Enlightenment came from the religious establishment itself, which stood to lose the most from the proposed reforms. Consequently, much polemical Haskala literature was directed at that establishment, whose antiquated ways were lambasted and ridiculed in countless writings throughout the nineteenth century.[1] Soon enough, and for reasons of convenience as well, the Orthodox came to visually represent the reactionary forces that stood in the way of the Jewish community's modernization, integration, and prosperity—so much so that they probably inspired the famous maskilic injunction, "Be a Jew at home and a man outside."[2] Folded into this phrase was the assumption that there were visual differences between Jews and non-Jews. Not so much physiognomic differences (those would be concocted later on) but for the most part sartorial and behavioral. Integrating into the general, non-Jewish society—fitting in—required eliminating signs of difference, which were to be replaced with visible signs of belonging.[3]

Zionism extended and expanded this concept to the national level. The Zionist call to be "a nation like all other nations" (עם ככל העמים) and its preoccupation with "normalcy" emerged from the same cultural idea. This meant that when it left Europe to begin a new life in Palestine, Zionism took with it across the Mediterranean the old, original prejudice that expressed so well some of its most tortured cultural and political origins. The consequent construction of a native Palestinian Hebraism, particularly Hebrew masculinity, in contradistinction to a diasporic Judaism, as epitomized by Ashkenazi orthodoxy, was referred to earlier. As a result, Yishuv culture at the dawn of Israeli independence in 1948 was probably the first secular Jewish society in Jewish history, that is, the first society that boasted of its Jewish origin—its pedigree, or history—while eliminating any public signs of Jewish religious distinction as a matter of principle and ideology.[4]

As the new Hebrew society in Palestine was fairly homogeneous, too, in terms of both the geographic origin of its members and their Zionist ideology, its antireligious sentiments did not cause serious problems internally, even if the annals of the early Yishuv are dotted with feuds over this issue.[5] The problems began to arise with the influx of millions of Jewish immigrants from around the world after 1948, particularly from the Arab world. Although these immigrants were very different from one another, hailing from Morocco, in western Africa, to Iraq, Yemen, and as far as India, they came to be defined in Israel as Mizrahim, that is, Easterners (*mizraḥ* means "east" in Hebrew), reflecting the reference point of the European founders.[6] Since their history, as well as the circumstances that brought them to Israel, differed from that of European Jews, most of the emigrants from the Islamic world did not share Zionism's anxiety about religion, integrating it fairly naturally into their lives.[7] This difference was one of the first and most painful pangs of absorbing Mizrahim into the new Israeli culture.[8]

The official policy of the state was to fully integrate all immigrants into the newly created Israel. Yet most Mizrahi immigrants stood out not only because of their traditional religiosity but also because many of them seemed like Arabs to members of the Yishuv, who now found themselves in charge of more than a million of these strange newcomers. One of the problems that quickly came to the fore, then, was how to incorporate these so-called Jews, who were both religious and Arab-like, into a socialist state that opposed religiosity in principle and identified with the West.[9]

Israeli films were at first slow to comment on this absorption process, and the cinematic birth of Mizrahi imagery is generally thought to have taken place in 1964 in the well-known comedy *Sallah Shabati* (dir. Ephraim Kishon). The film follows the adventures of Sallah (Haim Topol) and his family after their arrival in Israel, their languishing in a miserable absorption camp (*ma'abara*), and their clever maneuvers to secure public housing, which they manage at the end.[10] Two glaring traits distinguish Sallah as he gets off the plane to begin his new life in Israel: Levantinism and religiosity. Both are exaggerated and ridiculed. Sallah wears mismatching clothes, speaks with a guttural Arab accent, walks funny, and peppers his speech with religious references and expressions.

Much has been written about the negative stereotyping of Sallah as a primitive Arab Jew whose religion only serves to throw him further backward. To summarize this critique: Sallah is mocked and denigrated in the film by a patronizing Ashkenazi establishment. To add insult to injury, his image was penned by an Ashkenazi, the Hungarian-born scriptwriter and film director Ephraim Kishon, and portrayed by another Ashkenazi, actor Haim Topol. But a closer look at Sallah's image reveals surprising similarities to religious gestures, appearance, and traits that are more readily associated with Ashkenazi Judaism. The most immediate source of this similarity is probably the actor Haim Topol himself. Three years later, Topol played Tevye, the main character in the successful 1967 West End version of the musical *Fiddler on the Roof*, in much the same way he played Sallah.[11] That is, Topol played a religious Ashkenazi Jew—Tevye—in the same way he played a Mizrahi Jew—Sallah. Were it not for the actual words each character utters, they could have been identical.[12] As Topol was born in Palestine in 1935, and his exposure to Mizrahi Jews was limited until their arrival in Israel during his teens, could it be that his portrayal of Sallah was based on antireligious stereotypes that circulated in the Yishuv earlier on, stereotypes of Ashkenazi Judaism?

Consider, for example, the indeterminate origin of Sallah's image; he seems to be an amalgam of various Mizrahi types, from Yemen to Iraq to Morocco. This has been one of the critiques leveled at his portrayal. Instead of respecting at least one non-Ashkenazi Jewish community and giving Sallah its identifying cultural traits—this would become de rigueur in the multicultural 1990s—the film presents him as a humiliating mishmash of exotic insignia.[13] But another way to look at his image, aside from its allegory as an immigrant Everyman, as the film itself claims,[14] would be as a Jewish religious Everyman. As such, Sallah may likely epitomize the Zionist fear of the return of an image it has long thought suppressed, that of diasporic, Orthodox Judaism. The Arabizing traits that are added to his image in the film simply update what remain damning *religious* associations in suspicious Zionist eyes.

A nightmarish vision of Sallah's subversive potential can be found in the singing scene in the café, one of the best-loved moments in the film. The slothful Sallah celebrates the birth of his son in the camp's café, drinking and singing with his friends. The party is accidentally witnessed by a pair of Labor Party apparatchiks there to campaign for the upcoming elections. For the onlooking Ashkenazi guests, this scene is the very picture of oriental mayhem: a bunch of adult males, disheveled, dressed in an assortment of mismatching clothes, some of them even wearing pajamas, whiling their time away in a café, singing and dancing irresponsibly instead of working and providing for their families.[15] Even if the joke is ultimately on the party apparatchiks and the corrupt establishment they represent, even if the song quickly caught on and is still known and loved in Israel more than fifty years later, Sallah remains lazy, Arab-looking, and religious. He may be loved—the film was one of the most viewed and highest grossing Israeli films for a long time—but he is still a backward religious Arab-Jew.

The commercial success of *Sallah Shabati* spawned a whole genre of films, mainly comedies, that were based on the tensions between Ashkenazim and Mizrahim in Israel. Labeled Bourekas films, these comedies relied on cheap ethnic humor that stressed difference but always ended happily by trying to bridge it, usually with a wedding between members of the two groups. The weddings expressed the hope in the future of the secular Zionist state, which shall continue marching forward, skipping over, as it were, the "desert generation" of Mizrahi parents, who were considered a historical relic, an appendage that would eventually shrivel and die. This was not a double standard. The founders of the Yishuv developed their own, earlier culture according to similar principles. Zionist pioneers left their parents in Europe precisely because they were deemed a relic of an irrelevant past that could not contribute to the construction of a new and secular Jewish state in Palestine. The problem was, of course, that Mizrahim arrived in Israel with their families in tow.

Dealing with the "desert generation," then, and trying to grapple with their Arabism and religiosity were recurrent themes in many Bourekas films. A strategy that was developed early on, based on the success of *Sallah Shabati*, was to dedicate a lot of screen time to the religious rituals of Mizrahi Jews. Dramatically, such scenes added very little to the plot. But the ethnographic details they contained gradually familiarized viewers with the so-called Mizrahi difference. On the one hand, they served to acculturate Mizrahim as members of the new, secular state. On the other hand, they introduced their Jewishness and legitimized it. The efficacy of the combination was proved by the popularity of the genre. For much of the state's first three decades, ethnic comedies of the Bourekas kind were the only films that were commercially viable.[16]

No doubt the soap-operatic qualities of the films attracted Israeli viewers, who thirsted for popular entertainment venues like TV, which were

FIGURE 2.1
The Sabbath meal in ***Salomonico*** *(1974).*

scant at the time.[17] But the films' unabashed exhibition of Mizrahi religious traditions contributed to their embrace as well. Mizrahi viewers were happy to see their culture—so often disparaged as Arab—publicly celebrated, even if it was often exaggerated and distorted. Ashkenazi viewers tolerated a display of Judaism that was different enough from Ashkenazi Orthodox Judaism and more constructively integrated into everyday life. As a result, Mizrahi religiosity, also known as traditionalism in Israel, became almost the only form of Judaism that was culturally tolerated until the rise of the settler movement in the 1980s.[18]

In the 1974 film *Salomonico* (dir. Alfred Steinhardt), for instance, nearly ten whole minutes are dedicated to the depiction of a Sabbath ceremony. The scene has little to do with the film's drama, which is the story of a poor dockworker who refuses to improve his social standing and move out of his poor but genuine neighborhood, as the rest of his friends did. Hailing from Thessaloniki, Greece, Salomoniko (Reuven Bar-Yotam) is still considered Mizrahi in Israel by virtue of his non-Ashkenazi origin. The film spends a lot of time emphasizing his difference, dwelling on his accent, his Ladinoized Hebrew, and his religiosity. The said Sabbath scene is a veritable anthropological safari into the rituals of Greek Jewry, displaying their different melodies, table setting, table manners, rituals, and foods.

The protracted scene no doubt establishes Salomonico's sense of coziness and comfort in his old, decrepit neighborhood, and justifies his wish to return to it at the end of the film after trying an alienating new (Ashkenazi) suburb. But spending ten dear screen minutes on it still seems exaggerated. One clue to its logic may be found in the behavior of the younger generation around the table, and especially in the presence of a soldier in uniform, all of them Salomonico's children. The lengthy Sabbath meal with all of its rituals does not interest the children much. One of the small boys is late for it, while the oldest daughter asks to be excused the minute she finishes her food so she can go to a party with her classmates. All of this is typical of children that age, but their inclusion in the scene emphasizes the instability of the tradition depicted. From the perspective of statism, ממלכתיות, this is comforting, of course, and sanctioned, too, by the soldier at the table. Soldiers do not usually wear their uniforms to a dinner at home, especially not on the Sabbath. The uniformed presence becomes representative of the state, which legitimizes the manifestation of a Jewish religiosity that it nevertheless does not expect to survive for long.

The Jewifying agenda of Arab Jews in Bourekas films was not confined to folkloric displays of their culture. Often, it was much more literal. The phrase *koolanu yehudim*, "We're all Jews," can frequently be heard in those films, especially when Jews from different ethnic origins meet and try to overcome their differences with this soothing, inclusive statement. Rather than a glib reference, this is a telling glimpse into one of the genre's most important agendas: the construction of a Jewish, Israeli nationality that includes Mizrahim as a legitimate component. Two such important moments of recognition and legitimization occur in the 1970 film *The Policeman* (Ha'shoter Azulai; dir. Ephraim Kishon), about the adventures of a hapless and allegedly dimwitted Mizrahi policeman, Azulai, whose true worth and sagacity are proven by film's end.

The first instance is Azulai's interaction with ultra-Orthodox Jewish demonstrators who threaten the peace one Sabbath by preventing cars from driving through their neighborhood. When the head of the police force sent to disperse the demonstration is about to clash with the rowdy and stone-throwing Orthodox men and drive them away with clubs, Azulai suggests a different method. Given reluctant leave by his doubting superior, who is not eager to use force, Azulai gingerly approaches the angry men and tries to calm them down. The ensuing scene is certainly played for its comic potential, but it is still fascinating. In a battle of memory and wits, Azulai, who is discovered to be a proficient scholar of Jewish scripture, duels with the demonstrators and manages to impress them enough with his knowledge of Torah that they forget their cause and engage enthu-

FIGURE 2.2
Kulna yahud *[We are all Jews (Arabic)]; Shaike Ophir and Joseph Shiloach in* ***The Policeman*** *(1970).*

siastically in the scholarly debate he has initiated. In the meeting between two kinds of Judaisms—the old diasporic, Ashkenazi orthodoxy and Mizrahi traditionalism—the latter has the upper hand. Azulai is shown to be just as Jewish if not more so than the ultra-Orthodox. Yet unlike them, he is not ridiculous and irrational but acts like an agent of the state. As a policeman, he is literally a Jewish peacemaker.

In another scene in the film, Azulai takes his wife to the movies. Although off duty, the overzealous policeman thinks he spots a terrorist when one of the viewers gets up to walk out of the theater in the middle of the film, leaving behind him on the floor a paper package. Azulai jumps the man, yelling "terrorist" loudly. When the police arrive to investigate, it turns out the man is not an Arab terrorist at all but rather a small-time criminal, Amar (Yossef Shiloach), who is well known to the police. Embarrassed, Azulai explains that the man who left the package behind—a few half-empty liquor bottles—looked like an Arab to him because of his dark complexion. "Me, an Arab?" the Arab-looking gangster with the Arab name and accent asks with indignation. The two are then made to reconcile by Azulai's superior, who asks them to shake hands and make up. Facing each other and taking up the central part of the screen, the two then begin to hug, showing their affection toward each other by speaking *Arabic* together—both are Mizrahi Jews whose native tongue is Arabic. They conclude their reconciliation with the reassuring phrase *kulna yahud*, "We're all Jews"—in Arabic, of course.

Beyond the immediate and obvious comic value of showing two Jews reaffirm their identity by using the language of their enemies, their recognition of each other also validates their Mizrahi identity precisely because it is conducted in Arabic. The moment of recognition becomes then a moment of acceptance.

There can be little argument that the images of Mizrahim in *Azulai* are problematic and perpetuate some of their stereotypical characteristics. At the same time, they become part of a growing number of legitimate Jewish-Israeli identities. This was the value and power of many Bourekas films, which rehashed these images over and over again, and by doing so circulated them as legally tendered Jewish-Israeli identities. By the 1970s, Mizrahim were already closely associated in Jewish Israeli culture with traditional Judaism. In fact, they became the only meaningful expression of Jewish religiosity for the majority of a secular society alienated from more fundamental religious minorities, like national religious Jews or ultra-Orthodox Jews.[19]

By the 1990s, however, during the Oslo era, the popular association between religiosity and Mizrahiyut proved an obstacle to the continued integration of Mizrahim and yet another challenge to their inclusion as an integral part of Israeli culture. In other words, the identification of religion with Mizrahiyut, which initially served to acculturate Mizrahim as Jews, began to be perceived as problematic later on for several reasons. First, the heady days of Oslo saw a resurgence of the old secular, statist spirit of yore, a spirit that abated somewhat after the 1977 ascendancy of the more religiously sympathetic Likud. Second, the chance for a final peace with the Arabs temporarily mitigated their negative image in Israeli culture and with it the negative associations of Arabness that were assigned to Mizrahim.[20]

Although the so-called Oslo era lasted for a relatively brief time, from 1993 to 1996 and the assassination of Prime Minister Yitzhak Rabin, the influence it had on the culture was profound and lasted longer. Much of its impact derived from what seemed at the time like an actual and final peace with Israel's Arab enemies, a hope that accompanied the Arab-Israeli conflict from its very beginning. Whether this hope for peace was ever real or just the manipulation of a cynical cultural establishment, as some have argued, it was nevertheless deeply ingrained in Israeli culture by that time.[21] And so when the agreement with the demonized leader of the Palestinians,

Yasser Arafat, was signed in 1993, many Israelis thought it was indeed the beginning of a new epoch in the history of the country.

The consequent or complementary election of a Labor government in 1992, headed by Yitzhak Rabin, created for a brief time the appearance of a return to the old days of secular statism. With one swing of the electoral pendulum, the gains of the settler movement seemed to have stopped for the first time since the early 1980s. The return to a secular agenda, the shifting of the focus from the territories—the West Bank and Gaza Strip—to Israel proper, and the resumption of a civic program influenced the place and role of religion in state culture.[22] With that shift came also a reevaluation of ethnic tensions of the Bourekas kind, so that the cultural gains of Mizrahim as bona fide Jews, coupled with their political gains since 1977, made their association with religion less useful or relevant in the new era. Several films throughout the 1990s tried to come to terms with these changes. Some of them, like director Savi Gabizon's 1990 *Shuroo* and his 1995 *Lovesick on Nana Street* (Chole ahava Beshikun gimel), as well as Doron Tsabari's 1997 *Shuli's Guy* (Habachur shel Shuli), took pains to disassociate Mizrahim from religion. Others, like the 1993 *Sh'chur* (Black magic; dir. Shmuel Hasfari), acknowledged the old-fashioned associations and stereotypes but confined them to the older generation.

Shuroo is the story of a quasi-Mizrahi guru, Asher Yeshurun (Moshe Ivgy), who becomes the spiritual guide of a group of Tel Aviv Ashkenazi and Mizrahi bohemian socialites. Asher is a charismatic loafer who lives in Tel Aviv with his wife, Shimrit (Keren Mor), a university student and a poet. His latest project is a self-help book on how to lead a happy life by teaching readers to be idiots. Surprisingly, Asher's new "religion" attracts a small group of acolytes who hope to escape their numbing bourgeois life to find love, hope, meaning, and redemption through him.

Although *Shuroo* does not take direct note of its characters' ethnicity, the trained Israeli eye and ear can nevertheless pick up on it. In addition to obvious Mizrahi accents and appearances, like those of the taxi driver, Zhaki (Albert Iluz), or the vegetable grocer, Mordecai (Yigal Adika), there are other hints. Asher's ethnic background is never discussed, but his nonnative Israeli accent, with its rolling *r*, his probable Mizrahi name, and the way his aging father looks (he wears pajamas, a French beret, and stubbly facial hair) identify him almost certainly as Mizrahi. None of these matter. Unlike the obvious signs of difference in *Sallah Shabati*, which drive the film's drama, the distinctions between Mizrahim and Ashkenazim in *Shuroo* are blurred and unimportant from a dramatic standpoint.

Because Asher Yeshurun is Mizrahi, his status as guru, a "secular religious leader," is significant. His disciples are a motley bunch that includes academics, businesspeople, wealthy socialites, and miscellaneous others, Ashkenazim and Mizrahim. The group's diverse makeup illustrates the film's tendency to obscure or in fact flatten ethnic distinctions in order to talk about a general "Israeli condition." Aside from the group's significance as a symbol of the Israeli collective, all its members seem to suffer from acute ennui. Some of them, like Shimrit, write ludicrous poetry, while her mentor, Professor Konar (Ezra Kafri), cultivates sadomasochistic tendencies. Others, like the greengrocer Mordecai and the pub owner Eli (Moshe Ferster), explore their sexuality together, while others, like the television producer, Tal (Sharon Hacohen), try to express themselves by "flying" out of the window and end up crashing on the sidewalk beneath. All of these function more as eccentricities rather than as the real problems of a privileged bourgeoisie who have nothing more serious to worry about.

Asher's newfangled secular religion fills the vacuum in these people's lives. Nevertheless, his cultivation of idiocy as a way to happiness goes beyond the obvious satire of the self-help industry, with its faddish dogmas and gurus. In a way, the inanity and nonsense Asher promotes are a negative mirror image of the high idealism of previous Israeli generations. To counter, resist, and protest the fervent ideals of the forefathers—ideals that have become not only irrelevant but also harmful—Asher, the grandson, chooses no ideology at all in an attempt to vacate from the mind any thought whatever. "Didn't you notice how idiots always smile?" he asks his interviewer on TV. "It's because they're happy." His goal is to make people happy by encouraging them to act like idiots. "Start by doing one inane thing a day," he says to viewers. "You'll immediately feel better."

Although the film never says it quite so directly, Asher is an exorcist of sorts. He tries to cleanse people of an excess of lofty deeds or ideals, which at the historical moment he occupies in Israeli history have become far more damaging than inspiring or constructive. He voices an inchoate protest against an Israeli nationalism gone awry—a national ideology that has changed from redemptive to oppressive, from redeeming Jews to oppressing Palestinians. The ennui that afflicts the sated burghers in *Shuroo* is shockingly irresponsible in light of the problems that Israel faced at the time and especially in light of the plight of the Palestinians, their very close neighbors. Asher's pursuit of idiocy, his encouragement to be "about nothing," as the contemporaneous American TV star Seinfeld put it, is a biting satire. His failure at the end to help his followers reach a state of blissful emptiness is actually the only constructive outcome of his life.

Asher's new idealism is to have no idealism at all. To that end his relationship with his mute and crippled father is telling. Asher's wheelchair-bound father highlights the shift between the first generation of Mizrahi immigrants and their Israeli children. The father's immobility and silence stand for his generation's inability or reluctance to participate in Israeli politics and culture. The father is literally crippled and dumb—a handicap for which the son compensates with his dynamism and his impressive communication skills. If the Mizrahi father has been silenced and disenfranchised, Asher, his Mizrahi son, is now completely in control, a guru of a new Israeli generation.

Asher's ambiguous Mizrahi identity is also a function of his mixed masculine identity, which is part Mizrahi, part Ashkenazi. Although he is slightly dark, has a slight accent, and an obviously Mizrahi father, Asher is an integral part of a Tel Aviv bohemia. He sports fashionable sunglasses, has a fashionable hairdo, wears smart clothes, has a poet for a wife, and consorts with wealthy, sophisticated friends. These trappings were not usually associated with Mizrahim in films. In *Salomonico*, for instance, these are precisely the marks that separate and alienate the protagonist's Mizrahi family from their wealthier, more educated neighbors. Asher is also the author of a book that helps people get in touch with their emotions. From a macho perspective, nothing can be more geeky than this expression of mind over body. "Real" men do not do such things. However, Asher is not a geek at all. He is confident and self-possessed; he is clearly a leader who commands respect from people and he is very attractive to women. He ably combines both masculinities, the Mizrahi and the Ashkenazi. That is part of the reason why his ethnic background is ambiguous. It is also part of the film's message, which is predicated on a fruitful mixture of opposites: men and women, Mizrahi and Ashkenazi.

Shuroo clearly brings an end to decades of cinematic separation between Mizrahim and Ashkenazim and presents a much more integrated society. In some respects, it can even be argued that the film presents Mizrahim in positions of control or at least authority. The film charges Asher with the responsibility to question the past, fill the void created by the dawn of a new era, and perhaps even articulate a new vision for the future. By integrating the Mizrahi Asher completely into Israeli society, *Shuroo* ends the identity politics of the Bourekas film genre—the attempts to legitimize Mizrahim as Jews and incorporate them into the Israeli body culture. His advancement to the center or even the forefront of Israeli society, the solid footing on which he stands in *Shuroo*, opens up Israeli cinema to a new kind of Mizrahi identity exploration. This is no longer the apologia of the Bourekas, with its sociocultural agenda, but a more genuine attempt to come to grips with Mizrahism.

Shuroo thus changed the dynamics of the old Bourekas identity politics; but it did not eliminate them. A new kind of Mizrahi identity politics developed during the 1990s as part of the general privatization of Israeli society and the shift from a melting-pot ideology to a postmodern sensibility that emphasized difference.[23] The new statism of Israel's so-called Third Republic encouraged economic opportunity over social cohesion. The long-awaited peace was seen as a chance to move Israel closer to a Western capitalistic model of the American kind and away from the old socialism of the Eastern European kind. For more than forty years, Israelis were asked to stick together and find common ground in order to cohere and stand strong against their Arab enemies. With the signing of the Oslo Accords, it was time to relax and let go, and especially, to try to enjoy some of the many luxuries that had been withheld by the long state of emergency.[24]

The capitalist statism of the 1990s emphasized and thrived on secularity. But it was a very different kind of secularity from the anticlericalism of pioneering Zionism. The latter was deeply connected to the traditional, Ashkenazi Judaism it rebelled against but whose laws, rituals, and institutions it transmuted into its own new Hebraism.[25] Initially, early statism tried to subject Mizrahim to the same transformative process it demanded of itself and of all other citizens. It was only after the failure to do so that official state culture suffered a modified version of Mizrahi religiosity. But by the 1990s, even this modified religiosity seemed backward, out of step with the exciting new rush to join Europe and America. The challenge faced by Mizrahim, then, was twofold: how to preserve their group identity while simultaneously finding a way to shed their cumbersome religious associations.

The 1993 film *Sh'chur* tried to negotiate these tensions in its story about a successful psychologist and television host, Rachel (Hana Azoulay-Hasfari), whose journey back home to take part in her father's funeral becomes a journey back in time to her small parochial town, her turbulent family life there, and the painful memories they evoke in her. As Rachel travels down to the small, dusty town of her childhood, accompanied by her autistic ten-year-old daughter and her mentally disabled big sister, Pnina (Ronit Elkabetz), a series of flashbacks unravel her life's story as a gifted child who resented her big, dysfunctional Moroccan family and felt stifled in the backward town she grew up in. It was only after she received a scholarship to a prestigious boarding school in Jerusalem that she succeeded in escaping her miserable life and eventually climbing the socioeconomic ladder. By and large, *Sh'chur* manages to deal with both of its challenges successfully: the alienated and agitated Rachel finds peace only after she has learned to acknowledge and accept her past.[26]

At first, the film sets a very sharp distinction between the adult Rachel, now an urbane television host of a highbrow talk show, and the Rachel of her backward and impoverished past. Religion is one of the first images the cold and aloof Rachel associates with a past she remembers as too warm and sticky, a religion that is epitomized for her by her blind father, Eliyahu (Amos Lavie). Although not a bad looking man, the father is tellingly blind, has a gold tooth, a very thick Moroccan accent, and an obsession with the national Bible proficiency competition.[27] Rachel's memories of him are as a nagging old-timer who keeps demanding that she help him practice for the competition by going over the materials with him. When he first asks her to read the questions to him, bent over his work in his home carpentry shop, engaged in making what we later find out is a Torah ark, she tricks him. Wishing to go play with her friends and not be stuck in the dusty shed with a tedious father, she makes up an impossible question that requires him to count the number of times the ubiquitous phrase "and he spoke" (וידבר) appears in the Book of Genesis. Thinking that this is an actual question, the simple father starts counting laboriously. In the meantime, Rachel sneaks out quietly and leaves him there to stand and count like the idiot she thinks he is.

The father's image is naturally informed by previous Bourekas images like Sallah, Salomonico, and Azulai. But whereas these men were respected by their families, even if and especially when the Israeli culture at large rejected them, Eliyahu is ridiculed by his own family and most of all by his daughter, Rachel. His obsession with the Bible competition signifies the reason for it. Unlike previous images of the Mizrahi man as paterfamilias, Eliyahu's religiosity does not serve to bind his family together as a vestige, a remnant of an alleged blissful past in their country of origin. It is a disruptive irritation—nagging, annoying, irrelevant. He is not Sallah, whose recitation of a religious blessing unites his family upon arriving in Israel for the first time. He is not Salomonico, who presides over his family during the Sabbath for a few comforting moments of peace and harmony. Nor is he Azulai, who uses his Jewish erudition constructively in the service of the state. The father's interest in the Bible competition has nothing to do with the prestige the competition enjoyed during the first decades of statehood. In fact, he is not even that proficient, asking Rachel to help him again and again, and repeatedly failing the same questions. His references to the book of books, then, are an empty gesture that stands for nothing. They are as blind as he is and as alien and un-Israeli as his thick Moroccan accent.

The same holds true for the holiday meal, which is also featured here in an homage to its various Bourekas versions. Yet in *Sh'chur*, as in several other films, it is no longer a unifying moment, a chance for family mem-

FIGURE 2.3
The holiday meal in ***Sh'chur*** *(1993).*

bers to come together briefly and celebrate their tradition. The scene opens at the end of the holiday meal—it is the Feast of Weeks (Pentecost)—when everyone has already finished eating and the table looks messy, littered with dishes and remnants of food. There is not much festivity in the proceedings, either, save perhaps for the fact that the family is sitting together, dressed in white, around a big table. When the father attempts to discuss the significance of the holiday, he is mocked by his children: even his one daughter, who apparently attends a girls' seminary, answers him with pronounced sarcasm and derision. Neither the father nor the holiday is a symbol of unity and pride anymore. They are but sad shadows of their former selves, tattered remains.

The most significant moment of change comes one day when Rachel blatantly refuses to cooperate with her father and help him practice for his "silly" Bible competition again. The father tries to grab her and force her to stay, but she resists. The very fact that the two scuffle is shocking. Here is a young teenage daughter of a Moroccan family who physically opposes her father—over the Hebrew Bible. Even Sallah's children, who would have been justified to deride and abuse their lazy, drunk father, almost stand at attention when he speaks. Rachel, on the other hand, refuses. The symbolic moment comes when she accidentally knocks over the Torah ark her father has been lovingly working on up to that point. To the horror of both father and daughter, the ark falls down and crashes. With that decisive gesture the younger Mizrahi generation is tearing the tenuous bonds that tied them to their parents' religious heritage and discarding them altogether.

Worse still is the portrayal of the mother's "religiosity," which is presented here as pure witchcraft, the *sh'chur* of the film's title, meaning "black magic" in Jewish Moroccan Arabic. Looking traditional and matronly in her kerchief, housedress, and slippers, the mother (Gila Almagor) is nevertheless a witch. The only rituals she engages in are voodoo-like ceremonies she performs to get one of her sons to stop peeing in bed, to ensure her daughter' success on an important test, to set aright the romantic relationship of another son, and so forth. Everything she does is informed by elaborate superstitions to which she subjects her household. And although her children dismiss her magic, they seem more tolerant of her sorcery than of their father's religious observance, perhaps because some of her spells seem to work and perhaps, too, because they are part of the film's other agenda: to present Mizrahi heritage as real and authentic, not a cinematic concoction made for cheap laughs. Unlike the image of Sallah, there is no mistaking the ethnic origin of the Ben-Shushan family, who look, speak, and behave Moroccan. But because by the 1990s the adjective "Moroccan" had come to epitomize Mizrahiyut, the effect is similar. Even though the family is specifically and convincingly Moroccan, it also functions as an Every Mizrahi family.[28]

This is precisely how the film handles the twofold agenda referred to above. It rejects Jewish religiosity but at the same time promotes ethnic signs of authenticity, like language, accent, dress, and customs, even if they are problematic, like the mother's black magic. These external signs confer a unique identity on the group—Moroccan in this instance—as part of a new, postmodern Israeli society in which signification comes from representation and not from more tangible values that can perhaps be more helpful in bringing about social change. Image and perception, which are the currency of postmodernism, take the place of old, conventional politics. Change occurs not through social, educational, and political work, but by engaging in the politics of representation. This is also how the adult Rachel comes to terms with her rejected past—by acknowledging her difference and embracing it.[29]

At the end, after having aired the skeletons in her Moroccan (read: Mizrahi) closet, Rachel finds a measure of peace that had eluded her until then. In a symbolic gesture, her autistic, uncommunicative daughter finds a new friend in her "crazy" aunt, with whom no one has communicated since she was put in a mental institution. Rachel's sins of omission have been visited upon her daughter, who literally lost the ability to connect with the world. But when she meets Pnina, the aunt, the two immediately bond in a way that signifies Rachel's return to the family's fold. It is true that what unites the aunt and niece are the unspoken, special powers both possess. But the fact that the little language Pnina has is often Moroccan signifies the peace Rachel has made with the person she was and still is. The special powers the daughter and the aunt share also signify the power of self-knowledge. So while the film minimizes the Jewish traditional religiosity of its Mizrahi characters, it boosts their ethnic signs of identification.

Two other such identity films from that decade are Savi Gabizon's 1995 *Lovesick on Nana Street* and Doron Tabari's 1997 *Shuli's Guy*. Both films repeat the dynamic in which religious associations of Mizrahim are discarded in favor of richer portrayals of their ethnic heritage. *Lovesick on Nana Street* is a story about a mentally unstable young man who is obsessed with the idea of love. Victor (Moshe Ivgy) runs a pirate cable television station in his poor neighborhood, which he uses to broadcast cheap melodramas (Turkish and Arab films mostly) to his customers, with occasional commentary. When a young blond student moves into the neighborhood, the delusional Victor starts stalking her, becomes mentally unhinged when she rejects him, and is put in a mental institution. At the asylum, Victor meets Levana (Hana Azoulay-Hasfari), an Orthodox woman whose post-divorce distress is manifested in obsessive sexual delusions, and eventually falls in love with her.

Religion, which is almost absent from the film, nevertheless makes two telling appearances in the images of the old rabbi and Levana. Rabbi Shmuel, whose religious authority is not clear in the film, is a minor character who helps Victor's mother hospitalize her son. Like Sallah, he is still wearing the perpetual jacket, which early in socialist Israel came to epitomize diasporism.[30] But this figure has significantly changed since the 1960s. The new "Sallah" has grown a beard and is wearing a fedora as well, all signs that have come to be associated with the Mizrahi religious party SHAS, which adopted them from Ashkenazi orthodoxy.[31] The rabbi is insignificant not only because he is a minor character and because his rabbinic authority is unclear but also because his irrelevancy comes especially from the rude, dismissive way Victor talks to him, telling him at one point to do him a favor and "get the hell out of here, Rabbi Shmuel, you and your hat." Another time Victor tells him about one of his imaginary sexual escapades, specifying that the sexy woman he fucked "had a clit as big as your head." Even for a mentally ill person, this is an extremely disrespectful way to speak to anyone, but most certainly to a rabbi. Levana's image as a sexually voracious Orthodox woman is too obvious a joke and requires little explanation beyond the correlation it makes between religion and mental illness.[32]

FIGURE 2.4
Israeli-Arab actress Marlene Bajali as a Mizrahi matriarch in ***Shuli's Guy*** *(1997).*

Shuli's Guy yields more interesting insights, since the fifty-minute film correlates the ascendancy of Mizrahiyut with the election of Likud in 1977 and serves it up as an allegorical Cinderella story. The film takes place on election day, which is a national holiday in Israel. Shuli's family is gathered to wait for her fiancé, Avner, to come and ask her hand in marriage. But when another young man, Ezra, shows up to ask her sister, Mazal, to go out, everyone mistakes him for Avner. Mazal is Shuli's unlucky sister, a divorcée who has moved back home with her young child after her separation. Her decision at the end of the film to follow Ezra, her prince, to his "palace" is associated with the victory of Likud, which like the down-and-out Mazal has finally been rewarded and acknowledged. As Mazal and Ezra drive away in Ezra's ice cream truck, they pass by a local café where a crowd of people are intently watching the election results on TV and then erupt with excitement as the announcer declares victory for Likud, the political champion of Mizrahim.[33]

Significantly, this story about Mizrahi empowerment also makes a passing reference to religion in the image of uncle Lilo (Arieh Elias). Looking like the rabbi in *Nana Street* in his jacket, fedora, and short beard, uncle Lilo enters the film dragging a bleating lamb behind him. The uncle, who is addressed as "rabbi" by everyone but who is probably only a ritual slaughterer, a *shochet*, later slaughters the frightened creature. Unlike Rabbi Shmuel in *Nana Street*, uncle Lilo is a benign elder, respected and liked by all. The party does not begin before he arrives. But he is still a very marginal figure in a film that celebrates Mizrahi agency. None of the other family members seem concerned with religion. The film pays careful attention to dress, body language, hairstyles, speech, home decor, and music as a way to emphasize the Mizrahi identity of its characters. The matriarch of the family, in fact, is played by Israeli-Arab actress Marlene Bajali. Both the story and the casting in *Shuli's Guy* seem less anxious than in the past about associating Mizrahim with Arabs.

By the end of the 1990s, then, although *masortiyut* continued to be associated with Mizrahim, it became a much less pronounced part of their identity. Instead, more "anthropological" details that distinguished them as a unique Jewish-Israeli community gradually replaced religion, which was spread more thinly onto, or mixed more thoroughly into, their overall Israeli identity. In fact, what is meant by "anthropology" here is not so much specific customs of various communities that marked them as Moroccan, Iraqi, Yemeni, and so forth. Few Israeli films engaged in that sort of classification, and *Sh'chur* is perhaps unusual in this respect. The ethnographic details were used to deepen an already existing, all encompassing Mizrahi identity that classified them as non-Ashkenazi Israeli.[34]

At the same time, religion remained an important element of Mizrahi identification, even if it was less pronounced and more stylized, as in the 2008 film *Shiva* (Seven days; dir. Ronit Elkabetz and Shlomi Elkabetz). The film explores the fraught relations between members of an extended Israeli-Moroccan family during the ritual of Shiva, the seven days of mourning for a dead family member. In some ways, there is nothing particularly religious about the film. In other ways, it is hard to see it out of its religious context. This ambiguous quality, an existence informed by religion, or rather Jewish law, a law that at the same time is interpreted freely, remains one of the strongest identifying markers of Mizrahiyut. *Shiva* demonstrates it so well because of the visually powerful way it frames the mourning family, confining it in time to the religious, seven-day ritual, and confining it in space to the house of the deceased. As a result, the extended family as an institution, the Moroccan [read: Mizrahi] particularity of that family, and the religiously traditional context of their existence become intertwined to create a vivid picture of Mizrahiyut.

Shiva is an impressive film first and foremost about family, the Mizrahi family. In the film, that family has come a long way since the poverty of, say, Sallah Shabati, who languishes unkempt in the squalor of a transit camp before receiving a new apartment that twenty years hence would probably turn into a slum. Now, in 1991, when the film takes place, we see a self-possessed and quite well-to-do Moroccan family. Dressed elegantly in black, they occupy the spacious and well-appointed house of the deceased, striking poses that evoke Renaissance paintings with their display of the new wealth of Europe's rising bourgeoisie.[35]

Striking poses, or posturing, rather, is an important element in *Shiva*, a film that undermines the venerable institution of the traditional Mizrahi family and questions it as a cultural trope. On the most obviously symbolic level, the family has acquired its wealth with the help of one of the brothers' Ashkenazi wife, whose own family accumulated it through German reparations. That is, the bold display of Mizrahiyut in the film is seen as propped up or at least financed with Ashkenazi money. But wealth is not the only facade the family maintains. Closeness, warmth, and unity, some of the most popularly recognizable traits of Mizrahiyut, are also undermined in the film. Acute tensions, deep rifts, and explosive feuds, which are echoed by the incoming SCUD missiles of the Gulf War, threaten to tear this Mizrahi family apart.

The most obvious example is the dramatic scene during which Simona (Hana Azoulay-Hasfari), one of the sisters, lashes out at her family and reveals the grievances she has long held against them. As everyone settles down to sleep on mattresses that are laid out on the floor in the main room, reminiscent of the closeness and intimacy of yore, Simona and her other sister, Vivian (Ronit Elkabetz), begin a spat that soon encompasses the entire room. Shouts, physical violence, and finally tears roil the crowded room, which looks like a visual representation of unleashed emotions. This is no longer a picture of a happy Mizrahi family, which we saw on the previous night and in the very same room, when the siblings and their partners huddled cozily on the floor, laughing and being playful as if they were children again.

The ritual meal, which is featured here again in an ironic homage to its prominence in many Israeli ethnic films, shows family discord. Because of the mourning, the family members all squat on the floor, gathered around a rectangular space that denotes a table. The ritual meal around the "table" no longer functions as an island of calm that alleviates the rough Israeli routine with nostalgia. It is now another space and another occasion for the family's unity to be undone. Seething old hatreds reach a visual and aural climax here as they spill out and tear apart the gathered family. The most jarring moment in this scene comes when the oldest son, Meir (Albert Ilouz), pleads for his mother's forgiveness for his sins of omission. The profoundly grieving mother, without uttering a word of rebuke, suddenly slaps her son across the face as he bends on his knees before her. The

FIGURE 2.5
The ritual meal in ***Shiva*** *(2008).*

shocking gesture fells perhaps the last and deepest symbol of that family, the bonds between the Mizrahi materfamilias and her children.

One of the basic elements that keeps the family together is religion, which is both visually and spatially pronounced in the film. Save for the ultra-Orthodox, it is hard to imagine an Ashkenazi Israeli family gathered together thus for seven straight days for the purpose of mourning its dead.[36] The very premise of the film, then, depends on the religious affiliation of Mizrahim, their so-called *masortiyut*. By dressing everyone in black, by crowding everyone into one place, by making everyone perform similar rituals, the film conflates Mizrahi with religion. And while the Mizrahi family on display implodes, it is still held together, at least superficially, by some of the religious rituals that bond it for the time being.

We see this most arrestingly, even hauntingly, in the final scene of the film, when the family is back in the cemetery. Gathered tightly and almost uncomfortably together, we see the black-clad members of the family advance toward us, walking through the cemetery. Headed by the mournful matriarch, whose silent, grim face has been a constant rebuke to her feuding children throughout the film, the family walks slowly and stiffly forward, moving from a long to a medium shot and finally to a close-up, gradually filling the screen until they go down a flight of stairs and disappear at the bottom of the frame. Here it is, says the film, the essence of Mizrahiyut, an Israeli Jewish family that is symbolized and embodied by the religious rituals that keep it together. While language and territory mark it—Hebrew, Moroccan, and French are used interchangeably by the family members—and incoming SCUD missiles draw it together, blood and religion are the bonds that tie the members of the family together and define it.[37]

Finally, one of the most interesting developments of religiosity in Israel with respect to Mizrahim has been its association with masculinity. The connections between Judaism, or rather, Jewishness, and masculinity are not new, of course. The issue was extensively studied in the last few decades of the twentieth century, and this work has yielded some of the richest insights into the development of Zionism. Earlier in the chapter, this phenomenon was mentioned briefly in connection with the film *Shuroo*, whose main character, Asher, is allowed to become a Tel Aviv bohemian only by shedding all connections to Jewish religiosity and even *masortiyut*, despite his vague Mizrahi identity. In order to become a leader, a guru, he also has to shed strong ethnic (read: non-Ashkenazi) markers, especially ones connected with criminality. In other words, as the new Mizrahi man, Asher gets "whitewashed" and becomes as Ashkenazi as possible.[38] In the new, capitalist statism of the Oslo years, Asher's "metrosexuality" guarantees his cultural relevance and even grants him a leadership role, provided that he leave at home his Mizrahi religiosity and other ethnic traits.[39]

But the pax Israeliana after Oslo was a chimera, as has been discussed widely.[40] Eventually, and especially after the outbreak of the Second Intifada in 2000, Israel reverted to a tribalism that was in some ways worse than its earlier, more innocent, versions.[41] First, the renewed war with the Palestinians was bloodier than previous wars because suicide bombings drove it closer to home. Second, the return to a state of emergency after the disappointment of Oslo embittered the country's mood and made it more extreme. Third, the postmodern era had deepened the fault lines of Israeli society. While the Ashkenazi-Mizrahi divide began to blur, the ultra-Orthodox and settler communities became larger and stronger and began to push their agendas in ever more demanding ways.[42] This also meant that for the first time in Israeli history, the country's secular heritage was seriously threatened.

A riveting picture of these changes unfolds in the 2012 film *God's Neighbors* (Ha'mashgichim; dir. Meny Yaesh), which concludes this chapter and presents the most recent iteration of Mizrahi religiosity as well as a metamorphosis of Israeli masculinity. In its blending of neo-Hasidism and Mizrahi criminal masculinity, the film suggests a new Israeli religious moral code that challenges the old secular statism. *God's Neighbors* paints a picture of an Israel that is no longer guided by a coherent national narrative. Instead, its society is ruled by violent men whose so-called religion has replaced the redemptive secularism of the past.

FIGURE 2.6
*Ro'ee Asaf in **God's Neighbors** (2012).*

The film opens on a peaceful Friday eve with Avi (Ro'ee Asaf), a rough-looking but attractive young man who performs the ritual of Kiddush, or sanctification of the wine, that ushers in the Jewish Sabbath. When he is done eating alone with his father, Avi retires to his room to study scripture, basking in the sweetness of the Torah and relishing the peace and quiet of the holy day after a long week of hard work. But his blessed reverie is soon interrupted by loud music that comes from the street below. Looking down, he sees a group of young Russians drinking and loudly making merry in the yard to the sound of booming music. Faint cries by neighbors in surrounding flats to keep the music down in honor of the Sabbath are rebuffed vulgarly and dismissively by the carousing Russians. This incenses God's first neighbor, Avi, who calls on God's two other neighbors, his friends Koby (Gal Friedman) and Yaniv (Itzik Golan), to help him drive the Russians out. What follows is probably one of the most articulated action scenes in Israeli cinema to date—a rapid action sequence in the course of which the Russians are violently beaten and forced to leave, bleeding and humiliated, to the sound of cheering neighbors.

Piety and violence distinguish God's three neighbors—Avi, Koby, and Yaniv—who, since their return to the faith, have become religious vigilantes in their working-class urban neighborhood of Bat Yam. Avi is the leader of the gang. During the day he helps his father in their produce store. In his free time, he mixes religious trance music. Having recently joined the Breslov Hasidic sect, the three friends practice their newfound faith in some of their former gang ways, imposing God's laws on their neighbors by force: they beat up drunks, impose the Sabbath on local businesses, force neighborhood women to dress more modestly, and fight a rival Arab gang. Their lives are a strange mixture of a lackadaisical drug culture, religious faith, and tough street action.[43] But Avi's life changes when a pretty young woman, Miri (Rotem Zisman Cohen), moves into the neighborhood. At first Avi tries to impose a stricter dress code on her, but eventually he falls in love with her and is transformed by his love into a kinder and less vengeful religious person.

Thus, *God's Neighbors* marks a significant cultural moment in the legitimation of Jewish religiosity in Israel and records an important milestone in the country's metamorphosis in recent years from a secular, liberal society to a more fundamentalist, religious one. The film demonstrates this change in three interrelated ways. First, by combining Jewish religiosity with a powerful and aggressive Israeli Mizrahi masculine identity, the film relegitimizes Jewish religiosity, presents it as attractive and sexy, and declares it as the new Israeli hegemony. Second, by not killing off the members of a rival Arab gang, the film symbolically minimizes the conflict between Jews and Arabs and advances the importance of mythical Jewish time over Zionist historical time. Finally, by ending happily with a union between Avi and his girl, Miri, the film provides a neat closure that offers an alluringly simple, Hasidic-like tale of Jewish life in Israel today, promising rewards to the righteous who believe in Hashem, the Lord.

The first way *God's Neighbors* advances a religious agenda is by changing or reversing the association between religious Judaism and weakness and femininity. While the film is not the first to do this, the "un-Zionist" alliance it creates between Jewish religiosity, power, and violence is one of the most poignant articulations of an evolution that has long been under way in Israel. By making the main characters strong, masculine, attractive, and religious, *God's Neighbors* breaks the old Israeli associations between Jewish religiosity, weakness, and un-sexiness to present a new kind of Jewish-Israeli hero for the twenty-first century. The Mizrahi heroes' identity is an important aspect of their character as well.

Generally speaking, Israeli religiosity and Israeli masculinity were separated as cultural idioms. This is certainly true of films that cultivated the image of the New Hebrew, as noted before. But it also obtains for Bourekas films, which do not emphasize the connection. When these idioms were brought together for the first time after the rise of the settler movement on the West Bank following the 1967 war, the combination proved highly problematic. A poignant illustration of this is found, for example, in Joseph Cedar's 2000 *Time of Favor* and his 2004 *Campfire*, which are discussed in the next chapter.

In contrast to Cedar's films, the innovation of *God's Neighbors* is to bind masculinity and Jewishness in another, more positive way that leaves out militarism.[44] Cedar's main critique is animated by the settlers' abuse of everything around them, including the Jewish religion; their attitude toward the state; and most of all, their attitude toward the Palestinians. And although few of these excesses actually appear in his films, the consequences of these abuses for the settlers' own community are translated into the Ashkenazi religious-military freaks that populate them. Yaesh replaces this kind of problematic Ashkenazi masculinity in his film with a more benign and "genuine" Mizrahi masculinity that lacks overt nationalistic characteristics. Avi, the intense hero of *God's Neighbors*, is a simple guy, an unsophisticated street thug who relates to the god he recently found as a kind of gang leader, whose command(ment)s must be loyally obeyed. At the same time, his religious beliefs do not seem to inform his political opinions or stand in the way of his natural physical urges.

This seemingly superficial analogy, which continues in the next chapter, nevertheless exemplifies the differences between the two masculinities and their relationship to Zionism. Compared with the fraught Israeli Ashkenazi masculinity forged in the crucible of European anti-Semitism and changed by the country's prolonged state of emergency into overt military machismo and finally mutated into the settlers' evil super-Jew, the Mizrahi masculinities in Yaesh's film seem uncomplicated and benign. As former street gang members, with their menacing looks, masculine bravado, and adolescent group behavior, Avi and his friends may pay homage to the Bourekas stereotypes of Mizrahi men as criminals, but they are tamed by their religious affiliation. However, this is no longer the Mizrahi traditionalism of previous decades, as displayed in Bourekas and other films. In order to break out of this mold, Avi and his friends adopt a form of ostensibly Ashkenazi religiosity—Hasidism.

In some ways, the three former gang members have simply changed one gang for another. Instead of a group of thugs who deal drugs and collect protection money, they attend Torah study and then go out and impose on their neighbors the Jewish laws they learn. The film's opening scene is a chilling demonstration of their ruthless vigilantism, an example of their personal interpretation of God's laws. This jihadist mode repeats itself several times in the film, as they break the bones of a porn CD seller, shut down a local hairdresser who stays open after sundown on the Sabbath, and coerce a young woman into dressing more modestly. But their religious affiliation also holds the promise of amelioration, and eventually the laws they purport to uphold indeed tame them. Whereas their Bourekas predecessors always seemed lost—drifting victims of an absorption process that ignored them and against which they rebelled through crime—Avi and his friends are essentially in religious group therapy. They are pretty wild at the beginning of the film, but by the end of it, Avi has improved and mended his ways. He avoids killing a rival Arab gang member during a vendetta, and he gets together with his girl at the end, disbanding in effect the piety patrol he ran throughout the film.

Religion, which appears to contain and tame the aggression inherent in the stereotypical Mizrahi "criminal" masculinity, becomes the most signifying characteristic of these three young men, which defines them as Israelis. This is not an identity created as a reaction to a negative impetus in the way the Zionist New Hebraism was a reaction to anti-Semitism. Rather, it is an identity that combines a subjective or personal particularity (Mizrahi) with a bigger communal identity (Jewish and national). That it is Hasidism, a specific Ashkenazi kind of Judaism, that forms the basis for this identity is all the more important, for it may suggest a genuine hybrid form of Israeli Judaism, one that is no longer divided by ethnic or sectarian differences.[45] By joining a Hasidic sect, Avi and his Mizrahi mates transcend the narrower definitions that have always stood in the way of true integration. Their success may perhaps also mark the final death of statism and its discourse of ethnicity, which religion seems to have usurped in this film as a national organizing principle.

Avi is an Israeli Everyman and so are his "gang" members. His neighborhood looks like similar neighborhoods throughout Israel. There is nothing remarkable about it, which is precisely the point. Even his membership in the Breslov Hasidic sect does not diminish his all-Israeli image, and perhaps even enhances it. This claim is powerfully made in the opening scene of the film, as mentioned earlier. The fight with the Russians stages an Israeli show of force during which the invading and polluting outsiders are repelled from the midst of the "holy" community. The Russians exhibit aggressive un-Israeli behavior, as Friday evenings are among the most peaceful times on the Israeli calendar, when many Israeli Jews get together with their families and eat a festive meal. Public drinking of alcohol is also a rarity in Israel, or at least it was so until fairly recently. Speaking Russian loudly, drinking alcohol in public, and especially disrespecting the eve of Sabbath all paint the Russians as foreign and alien to the Israeli space. Avi's fight against them and their defeat are readily perceived, therefore, as a triumph not necessarily of a religious agenda but of a civic Israeli one.

Consequently, Avi's first commanding appearance in the film is not that of a jihadist or crusader. Like the neighbors who cheer him on, viewers initially see him as a vigilante for a common Israeli civic agenda. It is only subsequently that we understand the degree of his religious involvement. But by that time, he has already found a warm place in our hearts as a defender of the civic status quo. We may disapprove of his violence, but we applaud its results.[46]

Another factor that diminishes the alienation his religious affiliation might raise in viewers is the fact that Avi is fully integrated into the community. Unlike Moshe Bellanga's religiosity in *Ushpizin*—he was once a hardened criminal who turned his life around at the price of cutting himself off from society by joining a seclusive religious sect—Avi's religiosity is not regarded as an obstacle or as isolating him from the greater community. If anything, and especially after the terrific violence he displays in the opening scene, it is seen as calming and therapeutic. His religious schooling provides a positive framework that curbs his violent tendencies and harnesses his negative energy. Better a Hasid, as it were, than a gangster. Moreover, Avi's Hasidic affiliation also gives him a leadership role. Since the working-class Mizrahi community he lives in is already traditional, studying Torah elevates him and adds a value to him that he formerly lacked. Toughened and sexualized by a Mizrahi masculinity, and ennobled by the study of Torah, Avi is not simply a leader but specifically a Jewish leader.

This is another reason why it is not just his love for Miri that tames the violent Avi; religion civilizes him as well. The local neighborhood beauty would probably not have considered the menacing gangster as a lover had his religious observance not evoked in her a gentle nostalgia for her own traditional upbringing, as she confesses to him one night. So in spite of her unpleasant encounter with him at the beginning of the film, when he exhorts her to dress more modestly, religion is also what brings them together. At the end Miri, too, becomes enthralled by religion, and she finds a respite from her troubled life in its comforting bosom. However, this is not the sectarian Judaism of *Ushpizin*, but rather a Judaism that is much more Israeli and encompassing.

Finally, then, the "Hasidic" or naive narrative elements in *God's Neighbors* become a story for and of the nation at large, not just a simple tale about the faith of one righteous couple in a small and exotic religious community. The trials Avi is put to, his clash with the Arabs, and his happy union with Miri at the end make up the simple elements of the tale as well as the modern love story. Generally speaking, such narrative features are unusual for Israeli cinema, where most ethno-national clashes end badly, and where happy endings are an even greater rarity. *God's Neighbors* flouts this pattern, and in so doing proposes a different national pattern, one in which Jewish religious time and Jewish religious practices figure more prominently as determining factors.

These new parameters are elegantly suggested in the film, whose closure neatly complements its opening. Whereas the film opens with the ritual of Kiddush, the sanctification of the wine that ushers in the Sabbath, it ends with the ritual of Havdala, which announces the end of the Sabbath and the beginning of the new work week. The opening scene "sanctifies" Avi and anoints him as a kind of local Jeanne d'Arc who goes out to fight for God and country. The concluding scene shows that he has matured and learned to differentiate—to literally make a *havdala*, which means "separation" in Hebrew. Both scenes take place around the Sabbath table. In the opening scene, Avi and his father dine alone. In the concluding scene, Miri has joined them as Avi's bride-to-be. This neat and happy ending is a reward for Avi's good behavior and a fulfillment of his quest for meaning and purpose. That it is the Jewish religion and not the Israeli state that provides both is certainly ironic. And whether it is a wish or a warning remains an open question until the very end of the film.

CHAPTER 3

JEWISH *and* FANATIC: IMAGES *of* RELIGIOUS ZIONISTS

Perhaps the least expected changes in the place of religion in Israeli culture have been those brought about by the rise of the settler, or national religious, movement since the 1967 war. As the historian Tom Segev demonstrated so evocatively, the 1967 war had a tremendous effect on the path Israel took in the second half of the twentieth century.[1] According to Segev, Israel's spectacular military victory was ultimately the country's undoing and the cause of most of its political problems later on. The country was catapulted into the heights of euphoria, which followed on the heels of a debilitating period of national existential anxiety, but the triumph quickly turned into hubris that grew with every passing decade. Feeling invincible, Israeli governments refused to discuss possible settlements with the Palestinians, writes Segev, and preferred the status quo, which almost doubled the country's size and added a large and cheap labor force from the captured territories. Moreover, the de facto annexation of the territories, especially the West Bank, was important, because of the religious significance that Judea and Samaria, as they came to be called, had for religious Zionists, who have become a formidable political force in the decades since that war.[2]

It was perhaps inevitable that this should happen. Zionism was a paradoxical national movement from its inception. Unlike the national movements that inspired it, Zionism had as its foundation the Jewish historical connections to the land of Israel as these were preserved and enshrined in the Jewish religion. The central pillars of modern nationalism—territory, history, language, ethnicity—were all based on notions of indigenousness. But Zionism, even if parts of it were invented, was a secular national movement whose ideological justifications rested primarily on a religious belief. It is true that long before the rise of modern nationalism Jews embodied many of the principles of the modern nation. Jews shared religion, language, historical consciousness, and in the various areas of their habitation around the world, ethnicity. Jews shared a territory, too—except, of course, that for nearly two thousand years that territory was a spiritual religious concept much more than a real place.[3]

The secular nature of Zionism, especially its forceful anti-diasporism, was a reaction precisely to its religious origins. Zionists could not deny the religious basis that gave them claim to the land of Israel, or Palestine, nor did they try to do so. But in order to define themselves as a new, secular Jewish national movement, they took great pains to emphasize their difference from older, post-biblical forms of Jewishness. This was one of the main reasons for the antagonism of the Jewish religious establishment toward Zionism, which it considered sacrilegious. Although the proto-Zionist movement of Hibbat Tziyon, the Love of Zion, late in the nineteenth century, was supported and in some instances initiated by rabbis, once Theodore Herzl's vision for a secular Jewish nationalism caught on, the Jewish religious establishment opposed it with few exceptions.[4] One of these exceptions was the minority of religious Zionists who banded together in 1902 to form what came to be known as Hamizrahi, a Zionist religious movement that worked closely together with the secular Zionist establishment.[5]

From the outset, leaders of Hamizrahi wished to influence the nature and direction of Zionism. Like other Zionists, they saw great value in the opportunity that the movement gave Jews to shape their own lives. Unlike the general Zionists, however, Hamizrahi based their Jewish nationalism on the tripartite bonds between the land of Israel, the people of Israel, and the Torah of Israel. But it was not until the work of one of their most influential leaders, Rabbi Abraham Yitzhak Hacohen Kook, that this belief was invested with an eschatological meaning, whereby Zionism, the establishment of Jewish sovereignty in the land of Israel, was seen as the first sign of the Messiah's approach (אתחלתא הלואגד).

In many respects, then, religious Zionism made much more sense than the more prevalent and secular variety of it. The heart of the Zionist paradox was the elimination of religion, or *halakha*, from the new Jewish life in Palestine. Herein lay one of its most revolutionary aspects. In the historical context of its development in Europe, the nature of Zionism as a secular national movement made good sense, and the practical solutions the movement offered Jews in Eastern Europe were valuable as well. The biggest problem, of course, was the lack of a common territory in which to express the Jewish national aspirations. The land of Israel was an obvious choice, but only from a religious perspective. This was one of the main reasons why the thoroughly assimilated Theodore Herzl, the founder of political Zionism, was happy to consider a territorial alternative to it—Uganda. So when religious Zionists added Torah to the more general Zionist tropes of land and people, they were being closer to Jewish traditions and far less revolutionary than their secular Zionist co-idealists.

Still, religious Zionists made up a small proportion of the movement. In this respect, the real revolutionaries were the other kind of Zionists, the secular Zionists, who made up the majority of the movement. Their call to sever Jews from Judaism and replace religion, or Jewish law, with the land of Israel, was a radical break with the nature of the Jewish religion, Jewish practice, and Jewish history. Since they were the majority, and since their efforts succeeded in establishing the Yishuv and eventually the state, it was their vision that initially shaped it. The Jewish state that was founded in 1948 was a thoroughly secular political entity. Some of its trappings were based on Jewish traditions (Sabbath, holidays), but in terms of Jewish law, *halakha*, it was a secular entity. And it was precisely this secular nature, as expressed by Ben-Gurion's statism, which the eventual rise of the settler movement influenced so greatly.

The fact that it was not the territory of historical Israel, which Zionists first settled in Palestine, made little difference to them. Biblical Israel lay to the east of the coastal plain, which the Zionist pioneers first cultivated and on which they established their state in 1948. The biblical hill country between the coastal plain and the Jordan River (West Bank) was more densely populated with indigenous Arabs, and so initially it was not included in the territories of the Yishuv nor in those of the UN partition plan and the State of Israel until they were captured in 1967. Again, this was not a problem for the majority of Zionists, who were not religious. And most religious Zionists accepted it as well and accommodated themselves to the situation. It was only the seizure of the old biblical territories in the 1967 war that changed the situation radically for them.

In his book about the Six-Day War, Tom Segev vividly conveys the psychological effect that war had on Israelis, who rose in its wake from the depths of despair and gloom to euphoric heights. Other historians also dwell on the messianic nature of that euphoria, which is perhaps hard to understand today. For religious Zionists, it was an event of momentous import, which catapulted them in a completely new direction, a direction that would change the nature of the Israeli state and the course of its history. The spectacular military victory in that war was seen by almost all Israelis, not just religious people, as almost miraculous, and the conquest of the West Bank was immediately referred to as a "return" to ancestral lands.[6] For religious Zionists it was considered nothing short of divine intervention, and it stirred them into a great settlement thrust the likes of which surpassed in some respects even that of the early Zionist pioneers.

The relationship between these two waves of settlement is extremely important, of course, and is at the heart of this chapter.

Although much has been written on the Zionist pioneering project, both old as well as newer histories, cinematic records of the period are scant. There is some historical footage of early settlement efforts by Jews in Palestine, but fiction films are not numerous. Nevertheless, and as a prelude to discussing the continuation of the early Zionist settlers by their self-appointed inheritors, modern-day settlers, it would perhaps be good to look at a few visualizations of the creation of New Hebraism at the beginning of the twentieth century. Of those, the most striking is no doubt Helmar Lerski's celebrated 1935 film *Avodah* (Labor), a cinematic ode to the pioneering men and woman of Palestine and their efforts of settling it and building a new Jewish society there. The film is neither a documentary nor a fictional account. Although it looks like propaganda for the dissemination of the Zionist idea, it was actually a personal project of the avant-garde Lerski, whose celluloid panegyric on Zionism is a captivating work of modern art.[7]

Lerski, whose work is often associated with that of the futuristic movement, conceived and directed an unusual film that manages to translate the core revolutionary ideas of Zionism into powerful visual images. Chief among them is the materialization or embodiment of Zionism's idea of a new Jewishness. That is, the film de-spiritualizes Judaism and expresses adherence to it through a physical connection with the Eretz-Yisraeli soil rather than by rituals and commandments that commemorate and worship it from afar. The value of *Avodah* as a work of art resides in its wondrous conflation of Zionist ideology and Lerski's artistic genius.

Modeled after the nationalist movements that inspired it, Zionism has also placed the human body at the center of its national "revival."[8] Indeed, the creation of New Hebraism found its most succinct expression in the young men and women who literally carved the ideals of the Zionist revolution onto their own bodies. Upon arrival in Palestine they threw away their study books, shed their heavy European clothing, exposed their bodies to the bright Mediterranean sun, tanned their skin, and strengthened their muscles with hard manual labor. Helmar Lerski succeeded in recording that metamorphosis so well because, as a photographer, he was fascinated by the abilities of the new medium of photography to capture the human form. Even before he trained his eye and bent his talent to the Zionist revolution, he explored the beauty of working men and women in his striking photographs of them. In his arresting portraits of the German proletariat from the 1920s, for instance, Lerski turned working people into godlike creatures. Angled yet smooth, their skin appears taut and dramatic in his pictures, evoking the white Greek marbles that inspired it, yet looking like well-wrought iron statues in modernistic shades of gray.[9]

In *Avodah*, Lerski extended this treatment to the moving image to create a modernist installation in which man and land blend into a unified whole. In the dramatic opening sequence of the film, Lerski demonstrates his fascination with body and form, to which he joins the particular articulation of the filmic medium. Framed tightly in a close-up around the legs and dusty, beaten shoes of a walker—wanderer? pilgrim?—the camera follows his marching legs as they make their way arduously but determinedly over difficult terrain. To a low beat, monotonous and ominous, the feet go on and on across sands, rocky soil, streams of water. When they finally arrive at their destination, the camera slowly pans up to reveal their owner, a weather-beaten pilgrim, a pioneer. Trumpets blow, the music crests. We see a sign that reads, "Palestine." The joy of our pilgrim-pioneer is unbounded and he is smiling broadly at the sights and sounds of the long lost homeland he has finally reached.

Most fascinating in *Avodah*, which proceeds to show the Zionist settlement and development of Palestine through a string of sequences, is the transformation of men like the pioneer we met at the opening of the film. One of the most captivating chapters of the film, in which Lerski's genius finds an especially articulate expression, is the part dedicated to finding water in the dry land. After hauling water from afar in small portable tanks drawn by mules, the pioneers decide to drill for a permanent source of water closer to their settlement. Pipes are gathered, drills are piled, a drilling tower is erected, an engine is brought over to power the drilling, and eventually, after a lot of hard work, water is found and revives the pioneering settlement and ensures its continued existence.

While the fabula of the drilling is fairly simple, the *syuzhet* is remarkable: a bold and powerful expressionist montage in which the group of pioneers, the engine operator in particular, becomes one with the machine in order to husband the land. The monotonous, backbreaking work on a dusty plain under a blazing sun is transformed in the sequence into a visual ode to labor, a cinematic symphony of human body and machine parts. The working men are rarely shown in full. Mostly it is their limbs, hands, arms, legs, and heads that are blended together with pipes, drills, cogs, turning wheels, and gears to the tune of Paul Dessau's early twentieth-century modernist score. They make love to the land and worship it. Intent, determined, with great purpose, they try again and again to penetrate it, thrusting the drill deeper and deeper into it. They make love to the land and penetrate it in a Freudian sense. But there is also a spiritual aspect to their labor: bent over and holding a long lever, with only their hands and feet showing in the frame, they hum deeply to a repeated beat as they pull on the lever like priests in a temple.[10]

If the walking pair of feet that opened the film tells us that the Jew can become whole only in the Land of Israel, the drilling section breaks his body again into parts. But now it is not just one body part, feet, whose only purpose is to carry their owner to the land of Israel. The drilling montage breaks the pioneers' body into different parts again in order to reassemble them in the minds of viewers. As man and machine work intensively together, the engine operator is no longer the bedraggled, emaciated fellow who arrived in Palestine at the beginning of the film. He is strong now, muscular, tanned. He is a new Hebrew man who gives a new life to an old land. The water that orgasmically bursts out of the drilled well gushes and flows and floods the land. To the sound of a heavenly choir it becomes a land of plenty, thick with vegetation, crowded with women and children who carry its fruits, grapes, and wine as they frolic and dance upon it.

If there is anything religious about these images, it is the new Zionist pioneering faith in what came to be known as New Hebraism. Stripped of any external signs of traditional Jewishness, the men and women in *Avodah* are nevertheless worshippers in a new Jewish community, the Jewish national community that was established in Palestine at the beginning of the twentieth century. Men may have shaved their faces and exposed their bodies "immodestly" by dressing skimpily—the women all the more so. Jewish law is discarded and the people of the new Jewish Yishuv live on the land like so-called goyim, non-Jews. But as *Avodah* expresses so well, Zionist pioneers can be said to have been deeply religious in other ways. Their attachment to the land was quasi-religious, and in many ways they worshipped it, turning its settlement and cultivation into their new religion, for which they wrote a new Zionist-socialist *halakha*.[11]

Zionists were as zealous as other revolutionaries. But since they came from a long and well-recorded religious tradition, and in the name of it, too, they could not ignore it. Their revolution was informed by their Jewish legacy, even if they rebelled against it. If rabbinic Judaism replaced the once central temple in Jerusalem with *halakha* after the loss of Jewish sovereignty, Zionist pioneers replaced *halakha* with the land of Israel when they came to restore that sovereignty. Since they were secular and nationalist, they did not wish to rebuild a temple.[12] Instead, they worshipped the land both as a figurative, symbolic entity and as a real object of desire, which they mapped, settled, tilled, and hiked across.[13]

Since the Zionist revolution has been examined thoroughly, there is little point in repeating those studies, except, of course, to note the fact. What has not been emphasized as much, however, is the "religiosity" of

Zionism as an ideology, the religious-like zeal with which it was pursued, preached, and practiced by its adherents (or disciples).[14] Lerski's *Avodah* is so successful because it shows the devotion to Zionism not only in the actions of its subjects, the pioneers featured in it, but also in the unusual construction of the film itself. By creating such a distinctive work of art, the filmmaker himself becomes a worshiper at the altar of the new Hebrew "religion."

One is reminded here of Freud's *Moses and Monotheism* and his idea about the Egyptian origins of Western monotheism—and perhaps even more so of Jan Assmann's *Moses the Egyptian*, which elaborates on Freud's ideas.[15] Following Freud, Assmann makes the intriguing hypothesis that Jewish monotheism as described in Exodus and beyond was formulated as an inversion of Egyptian theology and religious practices. Might a similar dynamic have taken place under Zionism as well? Did the Zionists, like the Israelites fleeing Egypt, create their nationalist ideology as a negative of the rabbinic Judaism they despised and ran away from? Although this may be an overstatement, in some ways Zionism was anti-Jewish as well as very Jewish, throwing away *halakha* while making its own alternative version of it. And while Zionists may not have literally inverted *Jewish law*, as, according to Assmann, the fleeing Israelites inverted Egyptian religion, they certainly changed it by replacing its religious values with secular ones that were closer to their nationalist ideas: in their reinstatement of biblical holiday traditions, in their secular-nationalist interpretation of the Passover Haggadah, and most conspicuously by the resurrection of biblical Hebrew as the people's vernacular.[16] And while Assmann's hypothesis can never be proven, given the scant archeological evidence, the inverted connections between *halakha* and Zionist ideology and practice are well recorded. This would become important later on, in the 1980s, when the New Hebraism of the Zionist pioneers was changed into another kind of Zionism by the settlers in the West Bank.

Another, much later example of pioneering imagery can be seen in the 1960 film *They Were Ten* (Hem hayu asarah; dir. Baruch Dienar). The film is a little confusing historically, as it blends the story of the first wave of proto-Zionist immigrants to Palestine, known as the First Aliya, or the Biluyim, with the Zionist pioneers who came to Palestine three decades later in what is known as the Second Aliya. The Jews who came to Palestine in the 1880s came to settle the land before the articulation of modern Zionism a decade or so later.[17] They were far more conservative religiously, economically, and even politically than the young revolutionary pioneers who arrived in Palestine in the first decade of the twentieth century, ready to establish a new Jewish society and eventually a new Jewish state. Although

They Were Ten takes place in the 1880s, the story it tells is that of the Second Aliya, a few decades later.

The film follows nine men and one woman who attempt to settle the wilds of Palestine. Equipped with nothing but their idealism, the young and inexperienced Russian students arrive at a remote tract of hilly land and spend the rest of the film trying to husband it. The difficulties they face are enormous. They have no agricultural experience, they have inadequate farming equipment, their dwelling is cramped and in ruins, they sometimes do not have enough food, and their Arab neighbors are hostile. They also suffer from various social ills brought on by their isolation and by the gender imbalance.

Naturally, however, the greater their difficulties, the greater the meaning and magnitude of their sacrifice. This is precisely what the film aims at: to elevate the pioneers and make them into the stuff of legends. While there is nothing particularly religious about the lives of the pioneers themselves, the film can be seen as a work of hagiography the likes of which were prevalent in Israel until the early 1980s. The opening sequence of the film is particularly illustrative of this hero worship. First we see a close-up of a wagon's wheel making its way up a rocky hill with great difficulty. A choir of men hums a low and somber tune and, as the wagon continues its slow climb, its advance is intermittently cut to reveal, one by one, the nine men and one woman who accompany it on its ascent. Each of these cuts is a medium to a long shot of one of the pioneers, who stops in his or her turn to rest and look around at the expansive view of the barren hills in the offing. The sequence is arranged to personally acquaint viewers with each of the pioneers and set them against the enormity of their undertaking, which is emphasized by the repeated close-ups of the arduously climbing wagon. As a result, the way up the hill is symbolically decorated, so to speak, with pedestals on which the busts of the pioneers are put for display and veneration.

As Ella Shohat has shown, *They Were Ten* shares various sensibilities with Hollywood Westerns.[18] Indeed, the opening sequence borrows elements from various Westerns to set up the Zionist pioneers as mythological founders of a new Jewish society. The empty land, its dangers, the natives who resist civilized settlement, and the eventual overcoming of these challenges are at the heart of the Western genre. The film sets up these Zionist pioneers just as cowboys were set up by American cinema as the founders of the North American civilization and the embodiment of its spirit.[19]

Moreover, if the cowboy's triumph is often a result of his technological as well as his moral superiority as a white man and a Christian, the Zionist pioneers in *They Were Ten* succeed because they are Jews. The commandments they keep are not the halakhic minutiae of the rabbinic Judaism they left behind in Europe. Theirs is a higher commandment, or *mitzvah*, of settling the land of Israel. The film makes repeated allusions to the kind of biblical associations that figured prominently in modern Jewish culture, even before Zionism.[20] It does so with respect to the "biblical" plow they find in the field, repair, and use to till their land. It does so especially during the harvest, which paints a veritable orientalist picture, a reenactment of the Book of Ruth, featuring scythe-wielding harvesters, a biblical threshing ground, donkeys laden with sheaves of wheat, women bearing earthenware jugs of water for the harvesters, dancing Arabs, and a score of Arabized flute trills.

In the most traditionally religious scene in the film, the pioneers celebrate the good harvest with a big loaf of challa they prepared from wheat they grew and harvested themselves. Seated around a long table and dressed in white, they raise the challa up and say the traditional blessing over it, proceeding to break it into pieces and pass it around as Jews do on the Sabbath. But as this is not the Sabbath—it is broad daylight—the pioneers take the Jewish ritual out of its traditional context, applying it to their new, secular way of life, as they have with many traditional customs. However, they are not blessed by heaven until one of them is sacrificed on the altar of the new homeland. Only after Manya, the only woman, dies from complications after childbirth do the heavens release the water they have held up for so long. As Manya passes away, the cries of her baby reach up to heaven, which finally opens and quenches the parched earth with good rain.

Both *Avodah* and *They Were Ten* exemplify the quasi-religious zeal of the Zionist pioneers and the reverence with which these efforts were regarded by early Israeli culture. In *Avodah*, Helmar Lerski invents a new kind of art to express a new kind of ideology. His experimental film creates a unique artistic language with which to describe the great creational mythology of Zionism. Although the film includes some documentary parts, it still offers an original cinematic poetics to describe an original ideological poetics, a revolutionary Jewish poetics that rises in the film to lofty heights. Baruch Dienar's cinematic approach in *They Were Ten* is more conservative. The so-called religious elements of his film reside in its hagiographic nature.

The value of these two early films comes from the example they set and the point of departure they establish for the evolvement of the settler movement later on. By the time Gush Emunim, the Block of the Faithful, as the early settlers called themselves, began to grow in the 1980s, Zionist pioneering had long been relegated to the past. When, following the 1967 war, and especially after the rise of Likud to power in 1977, the West Bank began to be settled, the fortunes of the Labor movement waned considerably. The pioneering ethos that nourished the Labor movement and kept it in power for almost thirty years had dissipated by that time, replaced by growing bourgeois sensibilities. This was only logical. Every revolution eventually runs its course. The greatest revolutionary will always be slowed down by middle age and become less zealous and more moderate with time—all the more so if the revolution is successful, as Zionism most certainly was.

The Block of the Faithful wished to reverse this natural progress and bring back the pioneering ethos of yore. Claiming the heritage of the Zionist pioneers, and in the name of their legacy, they began to agitate for the Jewish settlement of the captured territories, which, soon after the war ended, began to be called "freed territories," and not only by the settlers.[21] The invocation of the old Zionist settlement ethos proved to be one of the most successful political maneuvers the settlers ever devised. It was so successful, in fact, that not only the more naturally sympathetic Likud-led government coalitions supported them, but also leaders of the Labor Party, like Shimon Peres and Yitzhak Rabin, who were the first to do so.[22] Indeed, the early Zionist settlement ethos was so powerful and so ingrained in Israeli culture that when the settlers invoked it in support of their very different kind of project, the country at large accepted it almost immediately.[23]

It is at this point that the religious instability of Zionism, the creational or existential paradox that has always been at its core, began to show. The possession of the actual lands of the Bible, the truly ancestral Jewish lands, proved a powerful potion. It is true that even before the capture of the territories in 1967 the religious faction of Zionism reached a crisis of faith, which the war and especially the access to the territories helped alleviate.[24] It is also true that, long before the war, ideological foundations were laid for the kind of religious settlement activity that began after it. But neither the Bnei Akiva religious Zionist movement, out of which the first settlers came, nor Rabbi Zvi Yehuda Kook, who was the real ideologue of the settlement movement, foresaw the great changes that the seizure of Judea and Samaria would bring about and the way it would change the course of Israeli history.

Zvi Yehuda Kook was the son of Rabbi Abraham Yitzhak Hacohen Kook, who was instrumental in "koshering" early Zionism and making it palatable to religious Jews. Suspicious of the secular nature of Jewish nationalism, most rabbinic authorities in Eastern Europe were reluctant to acknowledge Zionism as a viable Jewish way of life. Most rabbis considered the movement heretical. The call for establishing Jewish sovereignty in the land of Israel was especially problematic as it undermined the millennial belief in messianic redemption. Founding a Jewish state independently, without the Messiah's assistance, was considered sinful among many Orthodox Jews. But the support that the well-respected Palestinian rabbi Abraham Yitzhak Hacohen Kook gave Zionism early in the twentieth century helped legitimize Zionism for some religious Jews. The argument, which Kook Sr., who in 1921 became the chief Ashkenazi rabbi of the Yishuv, offered in support of Zionism was that Jewish settlement of the land of Israel—anywhere on it—is not problematic or heretical at all. On the contrary, it paves the way for the Messiah—and even hastens his coming. It was Kook Sr. who coined the phrase אתחלתא דגאולה, the "beginning of redemption," which became a catchphrase later on in the century, especially for settlers.[25]

What the senior Kook did not manage in his life, his son, the junior Kook, completed in his. The elder Kook died in 1935. His son, who died in 1982, developed and expanded his father's legacy concerning the redemptive value of the land in ways that were greatly aided by history.[26] Among the biggest challenges that stood before religious Jews who advocated the return to Israel and its settlement before the coming of the Messiah were the many laws Judaism set concerning the land of Israel. As mentioned before, since the second century CE, rabbis spent a lot of creative energy on turning these laws into useful commandments that would fit life outside of Israel, in the Diaspora. The two Kooks dedicated their lives to reversing that trend—to adjusting an essentially diasporic Jewish law to life in a Jewish land again. Special creativity was called for here, too, since the Israeli state was not a religious state.

True to halakhic tradition, elaborate argumentation was used by the Kooks to present existing customs or ways of life as evidence of preordained divine meaning. "Jewish sovereignty in the Holy Land," Kook Jr. said in his famous homily given on Israel's nineteenth independence day on the eve of the 1967 war, "that is, the State of Israel and its army, in addition to being the revealed end, is forsooth a clear and important commandment for all Jews."[27] "What we learn from this," he continued, "is that we must perform this commandment which is incumbent upon us—to conquer the land. . . . We are, all of us, commanded to do it, and therefore, all that pertains to it, all the various weapons made by us or by non-Jews, everything that makes possible this day of celebrating the establishment of the Jewish kingdom (*Malkhut Yisrael*), is completely holy."

Prophetically, Kook Jr. opened his homily with this political statement:

> The resolution by the nations of the world to establish the State of Israel called for its partition as well. Nineteen years ago, on that famous night, when the decision of the leaders of the world to establish the State reached Israel, when the people poured into the streets to celebrate their joy together, I could not come out to join them. I sat alone, enraged, greatly disturbed. During those first hours I could not accept the decision, the terrible realization that the words of the prophets did come true: "they have divided my land" (Joel 4:2). Where is our Hebron—are we forgetting it?! And where is our Shechem [Nablus]—are we forgetting it?! And where is our Jericho—are we forgetting it?! And where are our lands on the other side of the Jordan [*Ever Hayarden*]?! Where is every single clump of soil?! Each and every part of God's land?! Who are we to give up even a millimeter of it? God forbid.

Less than a month later, the very lands whose loss the rabbi lamented were under Israeli control. These hysterical words give a good impression of the kind of effect the conclusion of the war had on Kook's disciples. But it was not only his students who were affected thus. As Tom Segev describes so well, the entire country was seized by a quasi-messianic fervor. Newspapers were filled with biblical references, and popular culture, especially music, reflected a new kind of religious sensibility that had been absent from Israeli public life before.[28] The rabbi's students rode that wave and very quickly began to utilize it politically as well.

Gideon Aran described this process particularly well in *Kookism*, which examines the early years of Gush Emunim. The value of Aran's study resides in its articulation of what I referred to earlier on as the crisis of faith among religious Zionists. Faced with the spectacular success of the secular Israeli state—and the marginalization and even derision of Jewish religiosity within it during its first decades—religious Zionists were at a loss for action, for direction. The religious seminary Yeshivat Harav, which was founded by the elder Kook and headed by his son, and which hatched many of Gush Emunim's first leaders, was a small and insignificant institution until 1967.

Before 1967, then, the future of religiosity as part of Israeli culture was not brilliant. It is, of course, useless to second-guess history, but the early success of the state privileged its secular elements, which threatened to prevail and perhaps even eliminate the existential paradox that lay at the basis of Zionism.[29] But then came the 1967 war, which changed the course of Israeli history, stirred the dormant religious elements within Zionism, and brought them to the fore, where they have remained ever since, gaining increasing power with the passage of time.

Yet even if the ideological pendulum of Zionism has shifted from the 1970s on toward the more religious elements that were inherent in it, Israeli culture at large failed to internalize it significantly for decades afterward. The success of the settlement project was apparent already toward the end of the 1980s. So was the increasing danger of its permanency. It was not as if people were not aware of it, but as with any other phenomenon, especially a social trend, it takes time to perceive it and even longer to understand it. Amos Oz's prophetic 1983 *In the Land of Israel*, which appeared just a few years after the beginning of the settlement project, identified some of its most alarming dangers—the souring relations with Palestinians, the undermining of a future peace treaty, the religification of Israeli society, and the dangers it would pose to democratic principles. Few people heeded his words at the time.[30]

It is hard to understand the reason for this blindness, certainly after the First Intifada in 1987, which made the high cost of Israel's continued occupation of the territories very clear. If before the Palestinian popular uprising the occupation benefited Israel in many ways and helped the country ignore or forget the injustices that inhered in it, the Intifada made this impossible. On a conscious level, the Intifada made it difficult to continue ignoring the very existence of Palestinian peoplehood. On a diplomatic level, it made the occupation less acceptable internationally. On a practical level, the cost of policing the territories became burdensome. The settlers were an objective obstacle to any concessions regarding these categories by their very presence; moreover, in the wake of the First Intifada, they actively resisted such concessions by increasing hostility toward their Palestinian neighbors. Yet the usually politically motivated Israeli culture paid little attention to them.

Perhaps the culture's inability to perceive the dangers inherent in the settler movement had to do with its deep sense of persecution and siege and the military ethos it developed as a corollary. In the face of a perceived external threat, the culture closed ranks, as it were. It may also be that despite the robust growth of the settlements, the West Bank and Gaza Strip were still far away for most Israelis, somewhere in a mentally remote periphery. And perhaps the signing of the Oslo Accords in 1993, which were eagerly seized by the leftist, creative establishment as the longed-for peace with the Arabs that had been fantasized since 1948, assuaged its potential critique.[31]

Prior to the establishment of the state, in the 1940s and the decades after independence, Israeli literature, especially poetry, engaged closely with the country's life and times, or its "politics." These issues were forcefully described and fiercely debated in the works of all the major poets and writers, including Nathan Alterman, Haim Guri, Leah Goldberg, Yehuda Amichai, Nathan Zach, Dahlia Ravikovitch, Moshe Shamir, S. Yizhar, Amos Oz, A. B. Yehoshua, Aharon Appelfeld, and others. But as I showed in my previous book about Israeli culture between the two intifadas, artistic culture in Israel, especially new literature, changed significantly in the 1990s. It not only expanded and diversified but also in some ways disengaged from politics. And then, after the Second Intifada, it reengaged with culture and politics in different ways.[32] However, by the beginning of the twenty-first century, the written word no longer enjoyed the centrality it once had in Israeli culture—or culture at large, for that matter. Visual art has replaced it and was now the arena in which the culture's most vibrant creative energies flowed. In short, films and television series replaced books in the 2000s as the country's most dynamic artistic medium and filmmakers replaced authors and poets as the culture's seers.[33]

And yet, even the establishment of the Ma'aleh School in 1989, a communications school founded by the national religious community, did not help to increase the visibility of religious Israelis in the creative media for years to come. The school was founded with two expressed intentions. The first was to combine the world of Torah with the visual arts. The second was to educate filmmakers who would combat the negative images settlers had in the so-called leftist media. Despite these intentions, works produced by graduates of the school failed for many years to achieve the kinds of changes envisioned by its founders; it wasn't until the end of the 2000s, twenty years later, that such change began to be felt. The reasons for this are not clear, although the fact that the school was established in the first place is significant. It pointed both to the expansion of the Zionist religious community and to its growing understanding that it needed to become culturally relevant in order to thrive. One explanation for the school's inability to resonate culturally might have been the deep animosity toward religiosity in Israeli culture—an animosity that persisted into the 2000s, certainly on the part of the intelligentsia. Another reason might have been the popular resentment against settlers among Israelis—especially more radical settlers, whose anti-Arab violence is frowned upon even by those who identify with the right.[34]

Be that as it may, the first serious artistic engagement with religious Zionists occurred in the beginning of the 2000s with filmmaker Joseph Cedar's *Time of Favor* (Ha-hesder, 2000) and *Campfire* (Medurat hashevet, 2004). By that time, the religious faction within Israel's body politic was formidable. As noted before, the political fortunes of religious Zionism as they were expressed in the settler movement have been on the upswing since the early 1980s. And while the 1993 Oslo Accords slowed that swing, and at some point even threatened to reverse it, the assassination of Premier Rabin in 1995 revived it again. Fearful that the assassination would inspire greater violence, the center-left in Israel, led by Shimon Peres, sought a compromise with the settlers, which radicalized them even further. Thus, with the Second Intifada in 2000, the ideological pendulum of Zionism moved discernibly to the right, where it has stayed ever since. It was only then that the culture began to seriously engage with the influence of messianic Zionism and its meaning for the country's politics and culture.

The first two films of Joseph Cedar exemplify these changes—both the culture's re-engagement with politics and with the medium through which this was done, cinema. What makes these films so compelling is their clear focus on the ways settlers usurped and "religified" the tenets of Zionist pioneering. Both *Time of Favor* and *Campfire* look at the changes that religion brought to the old pioneering ethos and to the old concept of New Hebraism. The first notable change is the films' very engagement with these old cultural idioms, which seemed to have run their course by that time, made extinct by a naturally evolving culture. But the settlers revived them and by doing so created two problems. The first problem was that they resurrected a dead body, a corpse. The second was that they gave the secular corpse a new religious brain. The result, according to both films, was Frankensteinian indeed.

In its portrayal of the making of *yeshivot hahesder*, the Jewish seminaries that combine Torah study with military service, *Time of Favor* examines the literally explosive combination of religion and politics.[35] The young men in the film, yeshiva students who train to become soldiers in designated religious units, are torn between their allegiance to their charismatic rabbi and their loyalty to the state. The rabbi's surreptitious political agenda—to infiltrate the Israeli military and political power structure in order to usurp it—is carried to extremes by his students when one of them plots to blow up the Dome of the Rock mosque on Temple Mount in Jerusalem, hoping to hasten preparations for building the third Jewish temple.

Time of Favor examines old labor Zionist paradigms through their distorted modern interpretation. Whereas Labor Zionism extolled military duty as the ultimate service to the state, the religious soldiers in *Time of Favor* pervert that secular dogma by putting God before the state. The film takes the image of the fighting Sabra to an extreme, exaggerating it and creating a monster that rises against its master. Cedar seems fascinated by this kind of bastardization, especially the mixture of masculine and religious ideals as part of the settlers' claim that their settlement efforts and their resistance to Arab violence make them the true inheritors of the early Zionist pioneers.

Unlike the rest of the country, which betrayed Zionism in its search for middle-class comforts and its increasing criticism of Israel Defense Forces policies, the settlers offered an old-new alternative.[36] Their willingness to establish new communities in the "wilderness," their determination to defend that territory against hostile Palestinians, and their high rate of participation in army combat units were cited as proof of their patriotism. For the settlers, these were modern iterations of the settlement and defense ethos that distinguished the early Zionists. But to Cedar, the analogy rings false, and he presents the settlers as living comfortable lives in villages built for them by the government, working in cushy government jobs, and being conveniently protected by the IDF. One of the most intriguing ways Cedar criticizes the discrepancy between the image of settlers as pioneers and their image as members of the bourgeoisie is by examining the new connections the settlers' society creates between Jewishness and masculinity.

As mentioned before, the early Zionist pioneers were famously secular. Against their diasporic Jewish parents—cautious, compliant, and meek—they cultivated a more defiant persona that was daring, independent, and bold. These traits were most sharply displayed by their very physical appearance. As seen in *Avodah*, for instance, the shaved and tanned faces of pioneering men, their scanty clothes and their sandals, were a reaction against the beards and heavy clothes of their tefillin-bound fathers.[37] Many posters from the beginning of the twentieth century clearly display this new aesthetic by setting up strapping young men who are usually poised in the middle of a field, holding a plow in one hand and a gun in the other. These images are not different from the kind of symbolism that was used at the same time in other European countries to represent "the nation." In other words, there was nothing particularly Jewish about them, which was precisely the point.

From the 1970s on, under the influence of the settlement movement and its new ethos, these early Zionist images slowly began to undergo an aesthetic metamorphosis that incorporated more distinguishing Jewish signs. Modeling themselves after the early pioneers, the religious settlers in the West Bank cultivated many of the same traits, but they modified them to accommodate their religious beliefs. For reasons of modesty, the pioneers' shorts were replaced with long trousers, the tanned faces were covered with beards, and the famous *blorit*, the prodigious forelock of the early sabra, the native Israeli, was topped by a yarmulke. A gun was also added sometimes, especially as Palestinians in the territories became increasingly resentful of the settlers and resisted their presence.

Both *Time of Favor* and *Campfire* present this image as Frankensteinian: a golem that has risen against its master, as the Hebrew saying goes. In *Time of Favor*, the wholesome yeshiva students—cleanly turned out in their pressed white shirts, neat haircuts, and skullcaps, with their fresh faces bedewed with Hebrew youth, in the words of poet Nathan Alterman—turn out to be evil terrorists. The film provides chilling glimpses of these distortions. After receiving operating directives from his rabbi, thinly veiled as a blessing to go forth and multiply the religious soldiers in his unit, Lieutenant Menachem (Aki Avni) is celebrated as a new prince in his synagogue. As he stands quietly smiling, Menachem is surrounded by dancing circles of young yeshiva students who solicit heaven's good will for his new military appointment. The young men are dressed in their Sabbath best, but they are also his soldiers, including his second-in-command, Itamar (Micha Celektar), who will later help steal explosives from the army base to use in a Jewish terrorist plot.

Indeed, the problem with these zealous New [religious] Jews is foreshadowed by their alter ego, Pini (Idan Alterman), a gifted yeshiva student whom the rabbi designates as groom for his pretty but rebellious daughter, Michal (Tinkerbell). Unlike Menachem and the others, Pini is not a quintessential model of the new Jewish manhood, cultivated in the seminary hothouses of Judea and Samaria. Both as a Torah prodigy and as someone who is disqualified from military service for health reasons, he echoes the old, diasporic Jew. When Michal refuses to marry him, this darker side of the more proper and clean-cut *hesderniks* goes berserk and nearly succeeds in blowing up the mosque on Temple Mount. The dichotomy represented by the differences between the wholesome and manly Menachem and the diasporic Pini might be a holdover from a previous era. Inasmuch as Menachem is the only one genuinely troubled by the religious-political tensions of his role, his image harks back to the veteran, ethical sabra. But Menachem is both alone in this fight and not very determined. The future, warns the film, lies with the malevolent spirit that Pini represents.[38]

The sense of Jewish power the rabbi and his disciples have is no longer a constructive compensation for persecution in the Diaspora, as was the case for the Zionist pioneers. Instead it is viewed as extremist. Cedar's critique resides precisely in the fanatical image that emerges from the combination of Jewish religiosity and aggressive masculinity. His men look clean-cut on the outside but turn out to be morally soiled on the inside. In one of the most poignantly subversive moments in the film, Lieutenant Menachem is taken into custody for being an accessory to the terrorist plot and brutalized violently by Israeli secret police agents. The humiliation of an IDF officer, the apple of Israeli consensual culture and a representative

FIGURE 3.1
Aki Avni as Menachem, the religious officer in ***Time of Favor*** *(2000).*

of its re-created Hebrew masculinity, who falls on his knees and begs for mercy in his prison cell, becomes a punishment for his confusion of roles, for mixing Zionist (military) politics with Jewish religion.

A similar analogy, perhaps even more symbolic, is created in *Campfire*, Cedar's other film about the national religious community. The film takes place in the early 1980s and is the story of a family of three, a widow and her two teenage daughters, who struggle for recognition and respect as independent women in an oppressive, masculine world. The mother, Rachel (Michaela Eshet), tries to qualify as a member of a group of settlers who plan a new community in the West Bank by trying to conform to their righteous requirements. In the meantime, both she and her daughters are subjected to the demeaning, pious, patronizing, and sexually predatory practices of the men in their religious community.

At one point in the film, a religious youth group watches for the umpteenth time the 1977 action film *Entebbe: Operation Thunderbolt* (dir. Menahem Golan), about the daring IDF commando operation to release hostages from a hijacked airliner in Entebbe, Uganda. The young religious boys and girls are shown watching one of the most patriotic highlights of the film, during which the operation's commander, Yoni (Yehoram Ga'on), gives his men a pep talk before they go into action about their duty as soldiers and as citizens of the Jewish state. The scene ends symbolically enough with an excerpt from *Entebbe* that announces, "Yoni is dead." This statement suggests an intriguing proposition: the death of the kind of exemplary manhood of earlier times, the demise of the mythological citizen-soldiers of the past. The proposition is exemplified later in the film when the younger daughter, Tammy (Hani Furstenberg), is sexually molested by a blondish (= Ashkenazi?) religious soldier on leave, as well as by another boy from the youth group, the son of the leader of the religious community. What Cedar may be suggesting here is that when the defiant masculinity inherited from pioneering Zionism is combined with religiosity, the concoction is lethal and explosive.

The identification of Tammy's two sexual molesters as Ashkenazi is important because it highlights the connection to the Zionist legacy and especially to its problematic relationship with religion. Indeed, Tammy's attraction to Rafi (Oshri Cohen), a Mizrahi-looking classmate she fancies, can be understood as a critique of the Zionism-religion relationship. Although Rafi is also a member of the religious youth movement, he is gentler and less religiously fanatical than his friends, suggesting perhaps the sort of more commonsensical religiosity usually associated with Mizrahim. A similar dynamic is played out in the relations between Rachel (Tammy's mother) and her suitor, Yossi (Moshe Ivgy). After a year of widowhood and a number of failed dates, Rachel finally settles on an old bachelor. A virgin at forty-something, the Mizrahi-looking Yossi is accommodating to a fault, a refreshing change from the string of menacingly aggressive Ashkenazi men Rachel and her daughters have to contend with in the film.

A counter-image to Cedar's Frankensteinian masculinity can be seen in two other contemporary films worth mentioning here, the 2007 *Beau-*

FIGURE 3.2
Danny Zahavi as the molesting soldier in ***Campfire*** *(2004).*

fort (dir. Joseph Cedar) and the 2008 *Waltz with Bashir* (dir. Ari Folman). Although neither film deals directly with religiosity, some of the ways they handle the metamorphosis of Israeli manhood have a bearing on the religious masculine imagery just discussed. Both *Beaufort* and *Waltz with Bashir* engage in what I would term the return of the repressed, that is, the return of the repressed image of diasporic Jewish masculinity. And since that repressed image was often connected in early Zionist rhetoric to traditional (read: religious) Jewish stereotypes, its resurrection in those two films serves to illuminate its opposite—the settlers' religious masculinity—from another perspective.

Beaufort is the story of a group of young soldiers who man an IDF redoubt close to the ruins of the eponymous Crusader fortress in the south of Lebanon on the eve of Israel's withdrawal from that country after eighteen years of occupation.[39] The film dramatizes the soldiers' great enthusiasm to serve their country, especially the soldiers under the fort's commander, Liraz (Oshri Cohen), and the futility of their naive zeal in the face of the greater forces of history: the public fatigue in Israel and the unwillingness to continue supporting the occupation in Lebanon. Unable to reconcile their self-perception as brave and patriotic and their image as an obstacle to settlement by a public resentful of the protracted war, the soldiers experience a deterioration of morale and eventually blow up the bunker and withdraw.

The film introduces an important twist to the history of Israeli masculinity by severely criticizing it. Throughout the film, even though the fortress is constantly under attack, the soldiers never shoot back or take any action against the enemy. Forced by an adamant high command that expects a withdrawal any day, they are not allowed to retaliate—not even when Ziv (Ohad Knoller), the commander of a special army engineers corps squad, is killed in an attempt to clear an approach road to the fortress. Ziv's death enrages Liraz, who is eager to avenge it, but to no avail. He is strictly forbidden to do so.

A few days later, despondent and deeply frustrated, Liraz is surprised to see the father of his dead friend Ziv interviewed on the television evening news, speaking about his son's death. In this arresting scene, Ziv's father calmly confesses to the interviewer—on national TV—that he is personally to blame for his son's death. "Are you angry, are you blaming anyone for your son's death?" he is asked. "No," he says, "I am only blaming myself." The interviewer is puzzled. The father then explains that the army doesn't know his son, nor is it really responsible for him. "I am responsible for him," he says, "he is my son. I educated him, and apparently, I didn't bring him up properly." Now the interviewer is really confused. Aren't you proud of him, he asks, for volunteering to serve in an elite unit and for serving his country? Isn't that what Israeli society considers the highest duty, the highest calling? In response, the father talks about his own upbringing and how his parents instilled in him the sense that he is the most precious thing on earth. He confesses sadly that he failed to do so himself, to teach his children to be afraid for their lives. This is precisely how he puts it: "to be afraid" (לפחד).

Liraz, who watches the broadcast alone and in silence, is resentful of the father's words, yet at the same time he is also increasingly receptive to their subversive message. The meaning of the father's words clashes with everything Liraz believes in, with his entire military career, built on a passionate desire to serve his country and a willingness to die for it if called to do so.

But the words of the bereaved father go deeper and farther than that. In some ways they amount to nothing less than a revolutionary negation of Zionism. To eliminate Jewish fear was one of Zionism's most vigorous calls; fear of violence to one's person as well as violence to Jews as a group. The elimination of Jewish fear was also one of Zionism's most spectacular successes—so much so, in fact, that its opposite, military bravado, became one of Israel's most distinguishing characteristics after 1948 and especially after 1967. It also became one of the country's most dangerous excesses, as the film makes very clear. The clarity and self-possession of the bereaved father set him against the uncertainty and doubt that pervade the film. His solution to both, to an IDF bloated from pride and drunk with power, and to its blunder in Lebanon as an expression of a hubris that leads to the anxiety and confusion of the soldiers in the film, is a call to bring back a measure of the old Jewish fear. This is not a post-Zionist call for a return to the Diaspora by any means. Ziv's father is neither a deconstructionist nor a defeatist. His is the voice of sanity, of common sense, long lost, it seems, in the tribal wars of the Middle East.[40]

The 2008 film *Waltz with Bashir* engages in a similar reversal of Zionist masculine tropes, which have been bastardized by the settlers. The film is an animated documentary in which the protagonist, the director himself as a young man, processes his participation in the 1982 Lebanon War, twenty-something years earlier. Haunted by his persistent inability to recall anything clearly from that war, the main character begins a therapeutic journey. Visiting former army buddies who served with him, he interviews them about their war experiences. Going further and further back in time, his memory is gradually jogged until he finally understands the reason for his mental block: he was indirectly involved in the infamous Sabra and Shatila massacre, during which Lebanese Christian forces, assisted by the IDF, entered Palestinian refugee camps and massacred thousands of men. At that point, the film suddenly switches from animation to live documentary footage from the massacre's aftermath. These were the horrors that the protagonist witnessed and then repressed.

Waltz with Bashir is an impressive film for many reasons. Aside from its distinct animation the film is noteworthy also because of the unusual way it uses the symbolism and fantasy inherent in drawing to articulate very real psychological and emotional affects. It is also one of the latest and most elaborate iterations of an Israeli cultural phenomenon called יורים ובוכים. Literally meaning "shooting and crying," the term refers to a certain tendency, in literature and other arts, including journalism, to acknowledge Israeli wrongs against Arabs without actually taking responsibility for those wrongs. At best, such public hand-wringings are indeed tragic, as in S. Yizhar's famous 1949 novella *Hirbet Hizah*, which describes the suffering of the women, children, and old people who are expelled from a recently captured Arab village during the War of Independence, as well as the compunction felt by the Israeli soldiers who drive them away. Struck by the tragic irony of one diasporic experience that leads to another, the Jewish soldier-narrator is racked by guilt for sending the Palestinians into a new exile in the name of his own old exile.[41] At worst, such sentiments are disingenuous and even specious, as in Golda Meir's famous declaration that she will never forgive the Arabs for making Israelis kill them.[42]

There can be little doubt that the soldiers who took part in the 1982 Lebanon War were traumatized by it. Some of them have gone to great lengths to distance themselves from Israel, and some have suppressed the painful memories along with big chunks of their lives. Yet the revelation at the end of the film serves little purpose other than to make the protagonist feel better somehow for identifying the cause of his trauma and acknowledging his guilt. It is not only the pilgrim's progress, as it were, that elicits our sympathy for his psychological journey of pain and suffering. What raises the film's quotient of "victimhood" are the stories of his friends, who clearly have been leading an anxious life since that war, haunted by memories of it and to some extent deeply scarred by it emotionally. So traumatic was the war for one of them, called Carmi Kna'an in the film, that he fled all the way to Holland, refused to even be drawn for the film, and asked that his name and image be completely altered.[43]

However, the tragedy of the real victims, the Palestinians, and the injustice they suffer remain jarringly absent from the film. In compensation, the film seems to punish the soldiers who took part in that war by portraying them as antiheroes, or more precisely, anti-Zionist heroes. In one of the most visually arresting scenes in the film, Carmi Kna'an tells Folman of a recurring dream he has about the war: while the soldiers in his

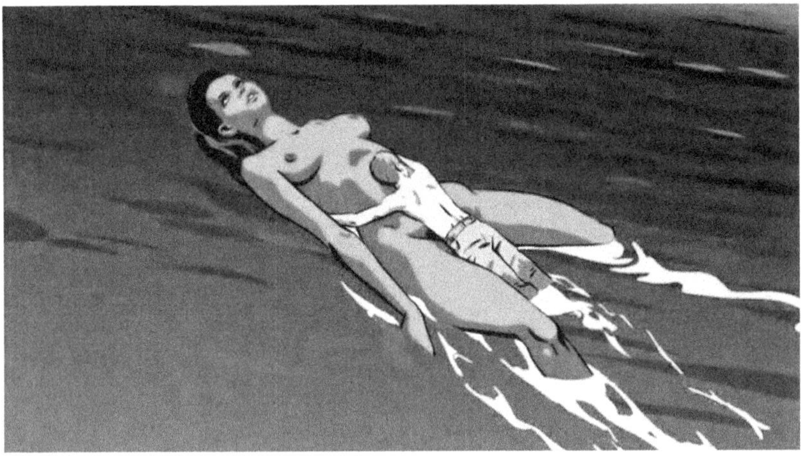

FIGURE 3.3
The emasculation of Israeli manhood in ***Waltz with Bashir*** *(2008).*

unit dance without much care on a boat that brings them to the shores of Lebanon to fight, Carmi, who is deathly afraid of the approaching battle, gets sick and goes off to the side and begins to hallucinate. In his dream, a giant attractive naked woman comes out of the sea, climbs onboard the ship, picks him up in her arms, and clasps him into her enormous bosom and then goes back into the sea with him. The listless body of the man-boy, the soldier who represents the nation as the epitome of virility, is now drooped over the gigantic vagina of his savior, a symbolic mother/wife/nation/giver of life/temptress and emasculator all at once. As the big woman slowly swims away, the boat gets hit by a missile and explodes, killing everyone on board.

The visual eloquence of this scene is stunning, especially in the context of Zionist history and the construction of the New Hebrew man, which is taken apart here almost literally. Yet the film fails to raise any kind of protest against those who sent these Israeli soldiers into a battle they care little for: Israeli society? Israeli government? And because Carmi and his comrades are presented as the victims of a cynical but amorphous system, the revenge they take is a passive-aggressive one, directed primarily at themselves. Carmi's story is one of the most visually expressive stories of trauma. The complement to his vision is the story of another of Folman's friends, Rony Dayag, who, following an attack by armed Palestinians on his tank, and after fleeing the tank and losing contact with his unit, cowers behind a rock in great fright, hoping not to be spotted and killed by the Palestinian fighters, who are close at hand. When night falls, he goes back into the sea and swims south in search of friendly Israeli forces, where he can take refuge. At no point does he even consider getting up behind the rock and attacking the Palestinians, who do not suspect his presence.

These stories, like the film itself, paint a picture that is very different from the more prevalent associations of Israeli manhood as heroic. *Waltz with Bashir*, as well as *Beaufort* to some extent, emphasizes what might be termed as "cowardice" in macho or jingoistic jargon, behavior that stands in sharp contrast to the standards of heroic masculinity, which were cultivated by early Zionism and which subsequently were enshrined by the image of the Israeli fighter. Thus we can see two kinds of masculinities developing in Israel in the beginning of the twenty-first century, both of them different iterations of the Zionist Ur-masculinity of the New Hebrew. On the one hand we have the jihadist masculinity of the settlers, soldiers in a so-called god's army (צבא השם). On the other hand, we have a less macho masculinity that tries to shed some of its former muscular-heroic associations and adopt more "diasporic" Jewish traits.

CHAPTER 4

JEWISH *and* POPULAR: IMAGES *of* RELIGION *on* TV

This chapter examines several contemporary television shows that summarize or exemplify the metamorphosis that religious images have undergone in Israeli culture in the last half-century or so. Television provides a different kind of cultural commentary than film. The differences between them can be illustrated by noting the affinity between films and novels. Even though the production of films, unlike the writing of novels, is an artistic group effort that involves a greater number of people, the finished work is associated with the creative genius of one person—the director. Both types of works also go through a similar process of reception. Since films and novels are completed before they are released to the public, the resonance of their artistic vision is unpredictable. The success of a film, like the success of a novel, is arbitrary and depends on the ability of the work of art to provide a screen, as it were, for viewers' innermost desires and anxieties—that is, to reflect their psyche and give it a cathartic expression.

To some extent, television dramas function similarly. But because television shows are less associated with the creative genius of one person and because they are more strictly beholden to commercial considerations, their creation is more susceptible to interference, both during the planning process and after a show is released. In a commercial market, television shows are pitched to networks, which tend to support projects that promise to be profitable or popular. As a result, television programming includes many derivative shows that are made according to specific formulas. Although these formulas can never guarantee popularity, they can reduce the risk of failure by repeating specific features that were received well in the past, changing them only slightly. But interference can also occur after a show is released. The public reception of a television series can determine not only its continuation but also its future episodes. This is not to say that films are free of commercial considerations. There are many derivative films that follow successful formulas, as well as films that did not succeed and have been forgotten.[1]

These differences between television shows and films also determine their documentary value. Because commercial television has to be more attuned to the public's taste, it is arguably more reflective of viewers' values and the zeitgeist in general. If the greater sophistication of films can sometimes obscure their "message," even as they make it more valuable, television expresses these values in a clearer and more direct fashion. In other words, while the value of films resides more in their artistic interpretation of a specific reality, the value of television programs resides in a more direct reflection of that reality. These considerations may be more significant in Israel than they are in older commercial television markets, such as those in the United States or Great Britain, because its commercial television channels are relatively new. It was only in 1992 that television in Israel was deregulated, ending a twenty-four-year monopoly of the country's single, government-controlled TV channel, which began broadcasting in 1968. Shows that were deemed to have educational values by a patronizing television administration were replaced by a plethora of commercial shows that were more attuned to public tastes, more eager to satisfy them, and less artistically adept at concealing that eagerness.[2]

It may be argued that the close proximity in time to the shows that are discussed in this chapter—the earliest is from 2007—affords little perspective. But precisely because contemporary TV shows have clear documentary values, they can be good indicators of social change. If one of the first shows that focused on religious society, like the 2007 show *A Touch Away* (Merchak negi'a, 2007), legitimized religious images, subsequent shows like *Srugim* (Knitted, 2008–2012) and *Shtisel* (2013) popularized those images. More interesting still is the cultural exchange that occurs in those shows with respect to the secular-religious divide in Israel. In a "made-to-order" show like *A Touch Away*, the exchange is more programmatic or artificial, as discussed below. But in subsequent shows, like *Srugim*, *Urim Vetumim* (Guiding lights, 2011), and *Shtisel*, as well as shows without a clear religious focus, like *Hasamba 3rd Generation* (Hasamba dor shalosh, 2011), all of which are reviewed in this chapter, the exchange is already much more nuanced or complex and involves a genuine incorporation of religious sensibilities by the secular culture in addition to an internalization of secular values by the religious society represented.

It is worth noting that the creation of the first properly "religious" TV show, *A Touch Away*, was partly contrived. The show was funded in part by the Avi Chai Foundation, an American Jewish charity set up after Rabin's assassination in 1995 to encourage rapprochement between different fac-

FIGURE 4.1
*Henry David and Gaya Traub in **A Touch Away** (2007).*

tions of Israeli society, primarily between secular and religious factions and primarily through the arts.[3] But while the series may have circulated under Avi Chai's "make peace" imprimatur (צו פיוס), its immense popularity was something its creators could have neither predicted nor entirely controlled. The series ran for only a single season, but it broke all TV viewing records in Israel and generated a lot of public interest and debate.[4]

A modern-day Romeo and Juliet story about a love affair between two good-looking young people, a secular Russian immigrant and his religious neighbor, *A Touch Away* tells the stories of two families: Russian Jewish immigrants who move into an apartment in Bnei Brak, an Orthodox city adjacent to Tel Aviv, and their religious neighbors. True to its mission, the series examines the relationship between the fiercely secular Russians and their religiously devout neighbors, a relationship that is exemplified by the romance that buds between their children, the Russian Zorik (Henry David) and the Orthodox Rachel (Gaya Traub). In the first episode, for instance, as Zorik cleans an apartment he has just rented in preparation for his family's arrival from Russia—Zorik immigrated earlier and has already served in the army—he is locked out of it. Sweating and shirtless, Zorik knocks on the neighbor's door across the hall to ask for help. When the door opens, a fetching young Orthodox woman, Rachel, stands in the doorway. Although she is confused and embarrassed by the shirtless young man before her, and although she hastens to shut the door, murmuring something about the prohibition to see him thus and talk to him, she furtively casts appreciating looks at his strapping torso and handsome face. Zorik, too, is taken aback by the striking beauty of the modest girl, and the two go on to have a torrid romance in the next episodes, which explore the possibility, meaning, and consequences of such a relationship.

It is pretty easy to understand, even from this short description, why the show became a hit. But while it is well known that sex sells, this was one of the first times that a television drama actually used it in a religious context constructively, so to speak, and not critically. The show presented Orthodox society not as sexually abusive, as *Kadosh* did, for instance, but as attractive, in the manner most Hollywood films "sell" ideas. In other words, by using aestheticism and sex, the show subjected religious society to the cultural codes of the majority secular culture. Whether this was intended or not, it became part of the Avi Chai's rapprochement agenda. Here was a pretty member of a secluded religious sect paraded before the viewing audience, who were encouraged to gaze precisely at those physical attributes that are usually covered up and hidden from view in Orthodox society.

At the same time—and despite the fact that the Russian immigrant family, which moves into Bnei Brak, is new to Israel—the series was aimed at conciliation, not divisiveness. It took viewers for the first time into the homes of Orthodox people and made them familiar, as television programs are wont to do. Through continuous exposure, viewers became intimate with the series' characters, who no longer belonged to an adversarial and faceless crowd. Sex and intimacy, then, normalized Orthodox society in the show. And while these may have been secular categories, which may have been manipulated, such is the nature of the visual medium.

A Touch Away was only the first sparrow, as the saying goes, that heralded a veritable flock of programs that continue well into the 2010s. But it was also an old-fashioned program in a way, especially in the neat, sitcom-ish symmetry it created between its various parts. It is true that it did not artificially solve problematic situations at the end of each episode, as sitcoms do. In fact, the show did not even solve the difficult predicament the lovers gradually found themselves in, torn between the calls of their heart and those of their respective societies. That was partly why the show did so well. Were it to elide the deep rifts that inhere in Israeli society, it would have rung false with viewers. But the show's very premise was programmatic: to bring together disparate social factions and make them get along, as it were. As such, it was a holdover from an older era and sacrificed its mission on the altar of the genre.[5]

FIGURE 4.2
A Sabbath meal of eligible religious singles in the first season of **Srugim**.

Another popular show, the television series *Srugim*, which began broadcasting a year or so later, was a different creature altogether.[6] Unlike *A Touch Away*, it left behind blatant references to politics, hiding its agenda in more sophisticated, updated ways. Conceived as a *Sex and the [Holy] City* kind of program, the show explored the dating travails of a group of several almost thirty-somethings, two single men and three women from the national religious community.[7] Although they live in Jerusalem, not the territories, they belong to the same religio-political milieu. If the dating woes of the four main characters in the American television show *Sex and the City* (1998–2005), which inspired *Srugim*, stemmed from their agency as self-aware, independent women who battle conservative perceptions of and expectations for women, the romantic worries of the characters in *Srugim* stem from their agency as self-aware modern members of an otherwise antiquated religion.

One striking aspect that lent *Srugim* such freshness was the very contemporary context that was given to a community that hitherto had been perceived as outdated and culturally irrelevant. *Srugim* served this exotic tribe, as it were, in weekly installments to a public curious to go on safaris into the depths of that territory and observe their mating rituals. The national religious was, after all, a growing sector of the Israeli public. Yet it was virtually unknown, culturally marginalized by an increasingly capitalistic Israel that frowned at its enthusiastic involvement in a "boring," intractable, tribal-political conflict while the rest of the country tried to have fun.[8] Yet here they were, these curious religious "creatures," interested in the same mundane but oh-so-human concerns we all share. It was new and surprising—and titillating, too.

Moreover, the show was served up as a kind of soap opera, which is not only one of television's most commercial formats but also a format predicated on an open-ended story line. The combination was striking: the seriousness and morality of religion presented in television's most frivolous format, originally designed to sell products, and an open-ended story line about a society whose members' lives are restricted and fixed. In a market saturated with derivative products, the show made a splash.

But *Srugim* was even more sophisticated, if not outright subversive. In episode 5 of season 1, for instance, two of the male leads, Nati and Amir, fill out an online dating questionnaire for Amir, who is recently divorced and is looking to date again. Asked about his political affiliation, left or right, Amir is not sure what to put in. "What's better?" he asks Nati, who gets annoyed, assuming Amir, like everyone else in their group—nay, in their sector—is right-wing. Reluctantly, Amir agrees to the designated affiliation. "What's the problem?" Nati asks him, noticing his unease. "I don't know," Amir replies. "Maybe it doesn't suit everyone. I don't want to exclude anyone."

Ignoring the political aspects of the national religious and presenting them as simply "human," without the baggage that is usually associated with that sector in Israeli public discourse, virtually de-politicizes religion. This is also where the soap-operatic genre becomes so important. The characters in *Srugim*, like the characters of all soaps, are disconnected in many ways from a spatial-temporal context, isolated in interior spaces and "trapped" in the maze of their own intricate relationships, which go on and on forever. Interior close-ups and medium ensemble shots characterize the show stylistically, as in all soaps. In a telling production coincidence, the interior scenes of *Srugim* were shot in Tel Aviv; establishing, documentary-like scenes were shot in Jerusalem and later spliced in for authentication.[9] While the reason for this was primarily financial, to cut production costs, it can nevertheless be used to illustrate the kind of disconnect that the show presented—its subversive elision of politics. Jerusalem of both heaven and earth, as the Hebrew saying goes, the holy city with its burdensome religious connotations, as well as the seat of the country's government, with its own set of divisive associations, becomes merely decorative. The real action, the real meaning, moves inside and is almost cleansed of any political referents.

In other words, by disconnecting the "religious" from the automatic political connections they usually have in Israel, the creators of *Srugim* insured the popularity of the show at the expense of politics. Given that the creators of *Srugim*, Hava Divon and Laizy Shapiro, were graduates of the Ma'aleh School, one wonders if this was what the founders of the school had in mind when they established it. While the show generated a lot of controversy in the national religious community, most of it was about its alleged raciness. Very little debate, if any, dealt with the careful political cleansing it underwent.[10]

Was this the only way to have made the religious visible again? Were they legitimized artistically at the cost of a more serious engagement with the political consequences of their beliefs and actions? Joseph Cedar's films show us that art does not necessarily have to come at the expense of politics. Yet, by their very nature as independent works of art, films can be more poignant than television programs, which require more of a consensus to produce and in a capitalist market are subjected to commercial concerns.[11] Television is much closer in Israel to its commercial cable models in the US. Ratings are therefore important for the success of a program and determine its viability and longevity. *Srugim* was an extremely popular show. It did not scale the viewership heights of *A Touch Away*, but it had a robust following, which it sustained and increased from season to season.

The proliferation of television shows toward the end of the 2000s and beyond focusing on religious characters and themes or including them as subplots certainly indicates that the exposure and perception of religious people and religiosity in Israel have changed tremendously over time. Both *A Touch Away* and *Srugim* opened the way to a number of religion-themed shows, which have since become common on Israeli TV. Most if not all of them adopted *Srugim*'s innovation and keep religion separated from the controversial political connotations it has in Israel. Commercially, this makes sense, of course, especially for those shows that are still partly funded by the Avi Chai Foundation, whose chief mission is to create bridges between the secular and the religious in Israel. And while this might make many such shows less relevant politically, the loss is compensated for by a politics of representation instead.[12]

The rest of the chapter examines three of these shows: *Shtisel*, *Urim Vetumim*, and *Hasamba 3rd Generation*. These shows exemplify the changing attitudes of contemporary Israeli culture toward Jewish religiosity. *Shtisel* is a good point of departure because the Israeli community it depicts is so visually different. Focused on the personal lives of members of an ultra-Orthodox family in the religious neighborhood of Me'ah She'arim in Jerusalem, the show is a fairly straightforward television drama series. Like many recent Israeli TV shows, *Shtisel* is a sleek, commercial product.[13] That alone, though, cannot explain its relative popularity, which derives from its innovation: a regular show about a very irregular group of people, Orthodox Jews. Like many of the shows supported by Avi Chai, *Shtisel* takes religious—in this case, Orthodox—characters, strips them of their problematic political associations, and serves them up as "ordinary" people.[14]

Moreover, the show revolves primarily around the love lives of its characters, Sholem Shtisel (Dov Glickman), the patriarch of the family and a widower who is courting several women; Akiva Shtisel (Michael Aloni), his young, handsome son, who is in love with the twice-widowed and good-looking Elisheva Rotstein (Ayelet Zorer); Giti Weiss (Neta Riskin), his married daughter, whose husband abandoned her and who is struggling to care for her family on her own; and, as a sweet touch, Sholem Shtisel's old mother, Bube Malke (Hana Riever), who is enamored of the TV soap opera *The Young and the Restless*. As such, the show is obviously directed at secular audiences, and the preoccupation with love as life's most meaningful aspect is not the only device that gives it away. Most of the characters on the show seem unhappy with the religious strictures that limit them, something which would appeal to secular viewers but would not necessarily reflect genuine Orthodox sensibilities.

Although the show is named after the widowed patriarch and follows his relationships with members of his family, the main focus of the show is the youngest son, Akiva, and his tortuous love life. Akiva falls in love with a twice-widowed older woman, Elisheva, whom he pursues despite pressures from his family and his community to marry a virgin his age, and even despite being rebuffed by Elisheva herself. Having been married twice before and with a son by one of her previous husbands, Elisheva is reluctant to get involved again. Although the show is not focused exclusively on their relationship, its ups and downs comprise the series' dramatic core.

It is here, at this romantic juncture, that the show engages in the kind of cultural exchange mentioned above. Matrimony in the Orthodox world is a practical arrangement that has little to do with romance. It is preferred, of course, that the intendeds like each other, but it is by no means a requirement. Eligible young singles are expected to make their decision after meeting once or twice, which allows them little time to develop any meaningful feelings. Akiva goes on such a date in the show's first episode. The meeting starts to go wrong when he realizes the woman is humorless. But the date fails completely and abruptly when he realizes that she is also unfeeling and lacks imagination. In his free time, Akiva draws and paints. Although an artistic career is not a real option in his Orthodox world, he is still proud of his talent, which allows him to express his individuality and

FIGURE 4.3
Akiva (Michael Aloni) about to meet Elisheva (Ayelet Zorer) for the first time and fall in love with her in **Shtisel** *(2013).*

escape the strictures of his confining world. So when his date asks to see a notebook of his sketches and then dismisses it as "nonsense," the sensitive Akiva is disappointed and loses interest in the practical young woman. After his awkward and unromantic date is over, and in order to recover from it, Akiva goes off to the zoo to draw animals and practice his art. It is there, inspired by the muse, as it were, that he meets his other muse, the beautiful Elisheva, and becomes infatuated with her.

The contrast between the two dates and the connection to art is significant here. It is perfectly acceptable, even in the Orthodox dating context, not to like someone for any reason whatever. But what Akiva hopes for is that his future wife will appreciate his art and be sensitive to it. This is not a simple request, as anything not connected to the study of scripture in the Orthodox world is considered frivolous—unworthy of time and attention. Akiva's expectation, then, that he would have an intellectual and emotional connection with his future bride and that she would appreciate his art, is uncommon. But it is unusual only in an Orthodox context—even in the Israeli Orthodox milieu, which has internalized many values of the Israeli majority culture.[15] For Western, secular culture such concerns—true love, professional fulfilment, and especially artistic fulfillment—are of utmost importance and are the ultimate goals in life. That these are also Akiva's concerns and that they occupy center stage in a show about the Orthodox reveals the kind of cultural exchange this and other "religious" shows exhibit.[16]

Admittedly, the story line is not very original. Love, artistic freedom, the pursuit of individual happiness—all are clichéd tropes that the show treats convincingly, but simplistically, too. What is unusual about them is that they unfold in a society that purportedly does not subscribe to them. The show remains authentic in the accurate ways it portrays the Orthodox—their habitat, their ways of life, their speech. The drab interior spaces, with their sad, cheap, generic furniture, match the exterior shots of the winding, unkempt streets of their poor Jerusalem neighborhood, cluttered with tattered ads, dotted with laundry hanging out to dry, teaming with poor folk running about with hardly a car in sight. Even the Orthodox language, a Yiddishized form of Hebrew, is impressively and convincingly reproduced by the cast. Yet in the middle of this sad modern *shtetl* love shines as a redeeming virtue.

Episode 3 in the series establishes Akiva's romantic woes and provides a good example of the power of love and its centrality in the show. Still hesitant to express his feelings for Elisheva, Akiva is pressured by his father to go on a second date with a young woman he met a week before. The reluctant son confesses to his father that he is not sure he will be able to tell the woman that he loves her. "Do you think that in all of our thirty-eight years together I ever told your mother, 'I love you'?" Sholem quips. Using the English expression derisively in the midst of his Hebrew speech, the father imparts to his son that marriage is an important duty that should not be confused with some sentimental American movie nonsense. Yet even after Akiva meets the girl and agrees to marry her, he is unsure of himself. His doubts continue to grow the next day during an outing in the woods with his bachelor friends.

In a fascinating scene that evokes nineteenth-century Jewish Enlightenment literature about the *shtetl*, Akiva and a few young male friends go out for a stroll in the woods outside Jerusalem. While many of his friends walk about among the pines, steeped in thought, Akiva and his friend Levy Yitzhak (Mottie Brecher, also called "the koirech," or bookbinder) sit under a tree and discuss philosophy and love. Koirech is reading the writings of the Danish philosopher Søren Kierkegaard and tells Akiva of the Dane's unfulfilled love for his fiancée, Regine, whom, Koirech says, he never married, fearing that his happiness would eventually make him smug. This is a personal interpretation of a question that has never been resolved concerning Kierkegaard's life. But it does set the tone for the show, in which Akiva's love for Elisheva remains unfulfilled as well, and for unclear motives. Thus, the show places love at its center, making both Akiva and Elisheva into quintessential lovers in the great nineteenth-century romantic tradition.

The archaic sensibilities that proscribed the relationship between two unmarried young people two centuries ago obtain here, and they are played out in the traditional Orthodox society in similar ways. Lovers are not allowed to be alone together, nor can they have any physical contact before they marry, no matter how passionate they feel about each other. After Akiva gets engaged, Elisheva calls him one night simply in order to hear his voice, to connect with him, and be close to him without violating her society's rules about such contacts. Elisheva uses the excuse that her son studies in Akiva's class to call him and ask about his schedule. In one of the most endearingly romantic scenes in the show Akiva then recites to her, quietly and longingly, the various school subjects, making love to her over the phone by almost whispering the words—Pentateuch, Laws, Prophets—as he slowly goes over them. Under the infatuated gaze all things become special and unusual; ordinary becomes extraordinary in the bright eye of love, which sees everything through its subjective prism and shines a magical light even on a mundane list of school subjects. This tender moment exemplifies the successful way *Shtisel* negotiates tradition and modernity, convincingly incorporating both.

It might be argued that these cultural references, that is, the incorporation of love and the pursuit of personal happiness, are artificial add-ons designed to make the show more palatable to potential non-Orthodox viewers. While there may certainly be some truth to this argument—television more than film scripts needs to make such concessions—for all the reasons mentioned above, the show still creates a certain "reality" or image that stays with viewers. It definitely succeeds in making the Orthodox community culturally visual and perhaps even relevant. And even if members of that community do not watch television, the cultural resonance and residual effects of a show like *Shtisel* eventually reach them, too. If attention is complimentary and if compliments are seductive and make one compliant, the contrived portrayal of the Orthodox community as more all-Israeli than it really is will perhaps also lead, eventually, to its greater participation in the state's culture at large. At any rate, this is the logic behind the support the Avi Chai Foundation provides to shows of this kind.

Such relevance is also evident in the masculine imagery the drama presents. On the one hand, most of the young men in the show are contemporary iterations of Boyarin's "feminine Jew," his well-known and much debated image of an alternative, softer masculinity that Jewish orthodoxy set against "manlier" nationalist models in the nineteenth century.[17] Boyarin's more domesticated, compliant, unaggressive Jewish man, who is more confined to the home, is displayed almost farcically in the outing to the woods mentioned above. While Akiva and Koirech sit and discuss romantic love, their friends walk about among the trees crying loudly to God.

"Father," some shout in Hebrew, while others prefer the Yiddish "Tatteh," lathering themselves up into spiritual excitement in a Hasidic manner as they walk about, trying to unite with God. This ludicrous scene of whiny masculinity ends poignantly with the injury of one of the men, who apparently stumbled and fell during his rounds. At first, Akiva and Koirech cannot distinguish his cries of real anguish and pain from the loud supplications of his fellows. But when he adds "Help!" in Hebrew (הצילו) and then "Gevald" in Yiddish, they rush to his side to discover him lying on the ground over a pile of rocks. Although he is only slightly bruised, he whimpers like a small child and complains that he might have broken his leg.

The word "broken" is crucial here because the men in Akiva's small group also refer to themselves as "the broken," probably referring to their fragile mental state as problematic seminary students and young men who do not fit well into their rigid Orthodox society. But "broken" can also describe them as incomplete men who cut a sorry figure in their hesitant, anxious, fretful state. Akiva may not be as badly broken as his friends are, but he is definitely a nebbish of sorts, perhaps even a schlimazel. Both of these Yiddish words describe precisely the kind of unflattering, Old World Jewish masculinity that is often associated with the image of the American film director and actor Woody Allen. The question that arises, then, is whether the men in *Shtisel* are portrayed that way because they are Orthodox Jews. Does the show engage in the same kind of demeaning stereotyping that was common in an earlier era, around the time of the state's establishment?

The answer to this question is probably negative. A century after the beginning of the new Jewish society in Eretz Yisrael and more than half a century after the establishment of the state, Israeli society no longer subscribes to these cultural imperatives. As has been demonstrated in previous chapters, especially the chapters about orthodoxy and Mizrahi religiosity, the Zionist anxiety over Jewish masculinity has subsided with the passage of time. Israeli standards of masculinity have become much closer to those in the West, where a host of factors have tamed the hypermasculinity that developed with the rise of the nation-state.[18] The Orthodox men in *Shtisel*, especially Akiva, subscribe to those models much more than to Boyarin's models, which in the post-postmodern age are beginning to lose their relevance as well.[19]

Even though he is Orthodox, then, Akiva subscribes to those milder masculine models, which is also why he is more relatable to the show's general viewership. But it is not just Akiva's updated masculinity that makes the show relatable. The different models of masculinity it contains also lend it authenticity. The scene in the forest certainly refers to older forms of Jewish masculinity from the nineteenth century. It would be almost impossible to ignore this given the setting, the characters involved, and their actions. But while the show makes perhaps an unintended historical gender reference here, it also presents a host of other masculinities and in doing so marks the Orthodox community as just another multifaceted, ordinary community.

As the main lead, Akiva is closer to Hollywood's image of the postmodern romantic hero. The romantic Hollywood hero in the last twenty years is shy and awkward around women in general and around his object of desire in particular; his manliness resides in his defiance of the odds against him and the obstacles he overcomes on his way to win his beloved's heart. Although he often appears to be "feminine" in that he is hesitant, eager to please, and apt to avoid confrontation, his "masculine" bravery is manifested in his determination to pursue his love and his faithfulness to her as an ideal.[20] Postmodern chivalry has modified the older demonstrative feats of valor with a quieter determination. Akiva is a romantic hero of this sort.[21]

Urim Vetumim, though produced two years prior to *Shtisel*, demonstrates yet a further stage in the evolution of religious imagery in Israeli culture, that is, the near disappearance of religiosity as an "issue." This statement may seem a bit quizzical, as *Urim Vetumim*, which can be translated as "Guiding Lights," is a drama that unfolds in a boarding school seminary, a fictional yeshiva for high school boys.[22] Politically speaking, members of the seminary staff as well as the students are immediately identified as belonging to the national religious movement. Yet the show is about much more than that and in fact uses the boarding school as a conceit to examine Israeli religiosity per se.

The drama of the show is composed of two complementary stories, the mysterious death of one of the seminary boys and the various tensions and conflicts between the staff, the students, and the parents that unfold as a consequence. The attempts to solve the mystery around the boy's death rock the seminary, which is experiencing leadership and financial difficulties that threaten not only its educational reputation but also its very financial viability and existence. The story is built around four main characters, two good-guy/bad-guy pairs. The first adversarial pair is that of the students, Yaacov Mazuz (Tom Hagai) and Bini Meltzer (Tom Avni). The second adversarial pair is that of the present head of the seminary, Rabbi Chaim (Danny Geva), and the former head of the seminary, his father-in-law, Rabbi Grant (Yehoram Ga'on). As Yaacov tries to solve the inexplicable death of a former student whose body he finds one night as he sneaks back to the seminary after a forbidden trip to the nearby city to watch a film, Bini tries to stop him. And as Rabbi Chaim tries to introduce institutional and educational reforms, Rabbi Grant constantly undermines him.

At first, the show appears to be dealing with many issues that pertain directly and exclusively to the national religious community, which runs these kinds of educational institutions in Israel. Early on in the show, it becomes evident that the seminary has been very badly run, and that Rabbi Grant, its former head, was a corrupt administrator and a manipulative educator. He dipped into the school's funds and ran down the institution. His pedagogy was equally problematic, based mainly on threats and power games he played among the students and staff. So the overall picture that emerges early on in the show, and quite explicitly, is the corruption of a religious institution that, if it were run according to the religious principles it purports to uphold, would have been an exemplary place.

As such, the show fits into a long critical tradition in modern Hebrew culture, beginning in the Jewish Enlightenment in the eighteenth century. The literature of the Haskala is full of scathing critiques of the contemporaneous rabbinic administration, which is lambasted as backward, ignorant, corrupt, and reactionary. Educational institutions in the various Jewish towns, the *shtetls* of Eastern Europe, mostly the *cheyder* and the *melamed*, were especially targeted by *maskilim*.[23] In the nineteenth century, as part of the reforms that the Jewish communities in Eastern Europe underwent, the *cheyder* was the primary target of critique for perpetuating ignorance and standing in the way of reforms and progress. In addition to the limited curriculum and backward pedagogy, which consisted mainly of rote learning, the *melamdim* came under severe critique for being cruel and greedy—much more interested in the tuition they could get for their young charges, whom they were frequently accused of physically abusing, than they were in education. The pages of many maskilic works are full of their foul ways and evil deeds. *Urim Vetumim* can readily be seen as part of this critical tradition, then. Moreover, the creators of the show come from within the religious establishment, just like the *maskilim* who criticized the *cheyder* before them. Having grown up in the bosom of the national religious community, Shuki ben Na'im and Ohad Zackbach, two of the show's creators, who wrote this and other shows dealing with various religious aspects of life in Israel, are intimately familiar with its workings and educational institutions. This is also the source of the show's veracity and power.[24]

At the same time, when the *maskilim* were writing their poignant critiques of traditional society more than a hundred years ago, it was practically the only kind of Jewish society that existed at the time in Eastern Europe. They were, therefore, writing as insiders for readers who were in the know. The institutions they described were familiar to the majority of their readers, who were educated in them and who later sent their own boys to study there. That is one reason why those critiques were so hard-hitting and why they resonated so much with their readers and with the religious establishment of that time. In contrast, the national religious are not a majority in Israel today, and so the creators of *Urim Vetumim* could not expect many of their viewers to be familiar with the religious world the show describes.

But if only a relative minority of Israeli television viewers today would be familiar with the inner workings of religious seminaries, the tradition of criticizing the Jewish religious establishment remains very much alive in contemporary Israeli society. So even if the religious details the show presents are not generally known, the critical sentiments that animate it would be not only familiar but also welcomed. As shown in the previous chapters, the secular Israeli state had a long anticlerical tradition that routinely rejoiced in exposing the inequities of the so-called religious. For secular Israelis, differences between various religious sects or affiliations were of little interest. The key factor that secular society repeatedly focused on was the difference between the moral rectitude of the professed religion and the moral frailty of its practitioners, especially its leaders. *Urim Vetumim* fit into that paradigm as well, even if the majority of viewers were not religious cognoscenti.

And yet, as this book argues, this dynamic began to change after the 1980s. By the time *Urim Vetumim* was broadcast, the culture was much more familiar and comfortable with religious imagery and references, which had become progressively more nuanced and complex. This was a dialectical process to which *Urim Vetumim* surely contributed. It was also one of the changes that turned the series into a metaphor and not just a sectarian show or a religious safari, as the slightly earlier *Srugim* might have been. For after all the obvious critique of the fictional seminary of Har Tzur is said and done, the show also functioned as a microcosm of Israeli society that transcended its ostensible parochial purview. As such, it introduced two innovations. The first was the matter-of-fact way in which it presented religious content. The second was the way it used that religious content to go beyond the narrow confines of the sector portrayed to say something about Israeli society at large.

The latter point bears some elaboration. In some important ways, *Urim Vetumim* can be compared to the so-called school novels that proliferated especially in English literature in the eighteenth and nineteenth centuries and beyond.[25] Novels such as *Tom Brown's School Days* (Thomas Hughes, 1857), for instance, took place in exclusive educational institutions that only a very small part of the population attended. The schools for boys and girls, where most of these novels take place, were private institutions for a select few, children of the aristocracy and the wealthy. Yet they were tremendously popular works that circulated widely and constituted a veritable literary genre. Among the many reasons for their success was the important socializing factor they played in the formation of the middle classes in Europe during that time. The small community of fledgling adults in those schools functioned as a symbolic microcosm of the nation, where relationships between individual and community, negotiations of control, and important values such as honor, loyalty, and camaraderie could be articulated. *Bildung* could be emphasized quite openly precisely because the subjects of these stories were young people who needed to be educated, just as the nation needed formulation. The fact that these institutions were exclusive was not really paradoxical, since they were deemed to represent the country's heritage and legacy, which were quite literally concentrated in them both in their impressive architecture as well as by the fact that they educated an elite that would continue to lead society in the name of those values.[26]

The analogy to *Urim Vetumim* is suggestive. The show might be making two related points. First, religious Zionism, as represented by the seminary, has come to replace the kibbutz as the ideological cradle and vanguard of the state. Second, religious Zionism has become the ethical source of the national community and the inspiration for it. The fact that both are found wanting in the show is irrelevant for determining its centrality and may in fact be further proof of it. One does not expend great efforts to expose and critique a thing of no importance. The 1960s works of Amos Oz and A. B. Yehoshua, which harshly criticize the labor-Zionist establishment and especially the kibbutz, are an obvious case in point.[27]

What is interesting to note in *Urim Vetumim* are the ways some of the culture's old tropes get reworked against the new background of religious Zionism, which has replaced labor Zionism by this time. The most immediate of those is, again, the preoccupation with masculinity, which continues to reverberate in the show. This is despite the alleged adherence to *halakha*, which has greatly changed by this time, and in some cases has usurped statism as a leading ideology. This issue was explored at length in the previous chapter, but it is articulated differently in this show.

The rivalry between the Mizrahi Mazuz and the Ashkenazi Meltzer certainly rehashes an old and somewhat hackneyed dynamic—all the more so when we consider the very obvious physical "ugliness" of the darker Yaacov Mazuz, whose face is scarred by a cleft lip, and Bini Meltzer's generic European good looks. These clichéd differences are further highlighted by Bini's social and institutional popularity, his academic excellence, and finally by his dream of joining the air force and his passage of its rigorous entrance exams (albeit by cheating). Even within religious Zionist culture this image has become trite. As the previous chapter makes clear, toward the end of the twentieth century religious Zionism completely internalized and domesticated these masculine-military values.

The difference here is that the show does not promote or proliferate these differences and images as much as critiques them. Fairly quickly we find out that Bini Meltzer, the seminary's star student, the apple of everyone's eye, is in fact a nefarious character. At first, his wholesome good looks and seeming kindness fool viewers, as it does Yaacov, who, as an unsure newcomer, confides in him. In fact, when Yaacov finds the drowned body of one of the seminary students cast on the shores of the pond outside the school, he goes directly to Bini for guidance and help instead of to his teachers. Bini's response is remarkable. He not only soothes the shocked and frightened Yaacov and tells him not to worry, but also promises to take the blame on himself and tell everyone that it was he, Bini, who found the drowned boy. Yaacov will not have to come forward and confess to it, exposing the fact that he snuck out at night and risking suspicion that he was somehow involved in the boy's death.

Bini's altruism is commendable, almost too good to be true. Can anyone be so selfless, so considerate as to risk their own reputation? We soon learn, however, that it is not empathy or the desire to help Yaacov that motivated Bini to act so. As the story unfolds, Bini is discovered to be a sinister manipulator whose wholesome exterior hides the fact that he is deviant and possibly a murderer. His mask peels off gradually the deeper Yaacov digs into the death of Yaniv, the drowned student. At first Bini cooperates and helps Yaacov, who tries to understand the reasons for Yaniv's so-called suicide. But the closer Yaacov comes to unraveling the mystery, the nastier Bini becomes and the more malicious his attempts to thwart Yaacov. In an escalating process of resistance to Yaacov's honest efforts to uncover the truth that culminates in a full-scale attempt to sabotage and even murder Yaacov, the truth about Bini is revealed. It turns out that the poster child of religious Zionism is cowardly and cruel, a liar and a cheat, a latent homosexual who probably drowned Yaniv in order to hush the affair he had with him and who would have murdered Yaacov, too, had he not been stopped at the last moment. Bini organizes a nightly beating of Yaacov, subjects his entire class to a humiliating and terrorizing hazing ceremony, and finally tries to burn Yaacov alive in what would look like an accident.

In trying to understand the show's agenda it may be useful to consider again the critical spirit that animated the early works of Oz and Yehoshua. As Gershon Shaked has shown, Yehoshua and Oz railed against the corruption of the labor-Zionist administration and lamented the gap between the high ideals of Yishuv Zionism and their disappointing realization after independence. Their critique was impressive because it was leveled at a very powerful and triumphant establishment that was celebrating independence and bullishly exercising its newly gained authority. It was also prescient and courageous, because the state's power structure had just been created, and instead of extolling its achievements, Oz, Yehoshua, and other contemporaries chose to warn against early abuses of state power.[28]

With obvious differences, this is also the critical agenda of *Urim Vetumim*. Herein lies the innovation of the show and its significance. Instead of celebrating the triumph of religious Zionism—that it has inherited and acculturated the legacy of labor Zionism, seized control of the country's politics, and led it according to its sectarian agenda—the show alerts viewers to its corruption and abuse of power. The show thus levels its critique at a movement that has a lot to celebrate. Religious Zionism has come a long way since the early days of the Yishuv and later the state, when it was an insignificant and often derided part of the political and cultural establishment. Even in terms of the categories that are examined and discussed in this book, that is, the visibility and viability of religious representation and expression in Israeli public life, it has made great strides. And yet the creators of *Urim Vetumim* critique their own culture, like the earlier so-called prophets of the (modern) house of Israel, Oz and Yehoshua.

Actually, the show's critique is much harsher, more acerbic, than the New Wave's reproach of labor Zionism in the 1960s. Consider, for example, A. B. Yehoshua's 1977 novel *The Lover* (Hame'ahev), in which the decline of the old Ashkenazi labor-Zionist hegemony is represented by the listless Adam and his disconnected wife, Assia. The worst that can be said about both is that they are emotionally detached, dried up, and dysfunctional, as opposed to the vibrant, dynamic, sexually charged forces that undermine them: the Mizrahi Arditi, as Assia's lover, and the Arab Na'im, who loves Dafi, the Ashkenazi couple's daughter. This is a simplistic analysis, perhaps, but one that illustrates the kind of critique writers of the New Wave staged at the time in order to protest and alert readers to changes that had actually transpired twenty years earlier.

Urim Vetumim creates similar dynamics and uses many of the same images, including Mizrahi and Arab characters. Here too, the Mizrahi Yaacov Mazuz is less attractive, poorer, academically mediocre, and less socially connected. Yet he is clearly the show's "good guy," its sung hero, a champion of truth, integrity, honesty, and kindness. So is Fadi, the Arab cook and kitchen manager, who is a literal stand-in for the Palestinians in the real-life conflict between Arabs and Jews. An illegal immigrant from the territories who somehow managed to fake working papers and get employment at the seminary, he is a well-meaning and conciliatory man. Nevertheless, he is shockingly abused by some of the nastier boys in the seminary, who literally try to kill him. In an ironic reversal of a dynamic that is often cited by the right in Israel, and with which many religious Zionists identify, the Palestinian Fadi is presented as peace loving and willing to compromise. Conversely, the Jewish seminary boys who try to hurt him are shown as quarrelsome and vicious. In popular Israeli culture, Arabs are almost always blamed for their domestic misfortunes as well as for the continuation of the war with Israel. *Urim Vetumim* disrupts this pattern and blames Israelis as well. That the boys who are charged with it are also religious is all the more significant, as it is not a critique that is often heard.

But this is not all. To some extent, beastliness is a common feature of the school novel genre. And while the attempt of two of the boys to kill Fadi is extreme, it is not outside the genre's conventions, something that cannot be said about Bini's character. Unlike the other "bad guys" in the show, who hide their true nature from their teachers but openly menace their peers, Bini tries to uphold his saintly facade as long as he can and with as many people as possible. The depth of his depravity and wickedness is inversely proportional to his exemplary image as a scion of the religious Zionist establishment. Borrowing from another genre, the "who-done-it" detective story, the show keeps up Bini's good character for a very long time. But when we finally learn of his true nature, his fall from grace is swift and precipitous.

Urim Vetumim paradoxically identifies religious Zionism as a leading contemporary ideology but also exposes its hubris, corruption, and evil. It is worth pointing out again the irony in the full circle that is created here, or the dysfunctional repetition, rather, of a Zionist historical imperative. The invention of New Hebraism, which began as a genuine reaction to adversity in early Zionist culture, was usurped by religious Zionism later on and modified for its own use. Initially, the adaptations of labor-Zionist tropes by religious Zionists may have been genuine, too, an honest attempt by a disadvantaged political movement to compensate for its underdog status by borrowing elements from its rival movement. Eventually, though, as *Urim Vetumim* and the films of Joseph Cedar demonstrate, that adaptation or acculturation has mutated into something sick and deformed. And while the show is ostensibly apolitical, the message it sends is most decidedly political, directed both internally and externally. It censures religious

Zionism for its excesses and loss of way as well as for its shortsighted and cruel way of dealing with Arabs. The important thing, however, is that it does so from a position of power, from the privileged position of a well-connected insider, who comes from the heart of the establishment. This is the real revolutionary meaning of the analogy to Oz and Yehoshua.[29]

The third and last show I want to discuss is *Hasamba, 3rd Generation* (Hasamba dor shalosh). This show is unusual because in many ways it cannot be considered a religious show, as the other shows discussed here are. Before it became a cable TV show, *Hasamba* began in 1949 as a series of action-adventure-detective books for teenagers by playwright and author Yigal Mossensohn (HASAMBA is a Hebrew acronym for Havurat Sod Muchlat Behechlet, loosely translated as the Absolutely Secret Society, or the Secret Bunch). Initially published as a newspaper serial, it soon grew to be a phenomenally successful book series that spanned decades and numbered forty-four volumes. Probably modeled after Enid Blyton's famous children detective series *The Famous Five*, *Hasamba* has the same premise: a group of young teenagers are engaged in various hair-raising adventures that have an underlying educational value.[30] In the case of *Hasamba*, that value is Zionist patriotism, which stands to good reason given that the stories began appearing less than a year after the state's establishment.

The book series had two print cycles before it became a cable television series in the 2010s. The first cycle spanned ten years, from 1949 to 1959. The second appeared from 1966 to 1994. Although the second cycle of the series was successful, it was the first that left the biggest imprint on Israeli culture, for two major reasons, both of which had to do with the series' patriotic premise. First is the proximity of the series' launch to the state's foundation. Second, a high level of nationalist sentiment animated the small and young Jewish state after independence, which was augmented by its perceived state of emergency. The adventures of the young Israeli detectives in *Hasamba* dealt directly with dangers to the young state, mostly, though not always, Arab elements that threatened to infiltrate it, compromising the safety of its citizens and undermining its precarious hegemony. Thus, the Secret Bunch comprised symbolic representatives of the young nation, including the gang's commander, Yaron Zehavi, and his beautiful deputy, Tamar, both Ashkenazi and connected to the labor-Zionist establishment; the Yemenite Menashe as the so-called Mizrahi representative; and various other characters, presumably Ashkenazi, including two comically useful characters known as Thin Uzi and Fat Ehud, as well as various others with decreasing degrees of symbolic significance.[31]

In the years leading up to the establishment of Israel, and afterward as well, the local Jewish community was consumed with the momentous business of state building. The fact that Yaron Zehavi and his teenage mates were allowed to participate in these efforts felt very rewarding to young Sabras, even if it was only a fantasy. To fight the British, as the youths did in first books, to help Jewish immigrants get to Palestine, to guard the country's borders and capture spies who threatened to undermine the new state—these acts were the stuff of the Hasamba books. Riding in jeeps, wielding guns, and capturing dangerous villains were suddenly the purview of young teenagers as well, who were finally permitted to contribute to the welfare of the fighting nation just like their parents.

The series also evinced the spirit of the Yishuv and the young state, and promulgated the Sabra culture of initiative, improvisation, self-reliance, and native Israeli humor. The books privileged life on the kibbutz or close to the land in dangerous areas near the country's borders. All of these connected the series quite clearly with labor Zionism, whose ethos informed the series. In short, Yaron Zehavi, Tamar, Menashe, Ehud, and the other members of the Secret Bunch were model young Sabras, native Israelis who were cut out and made according to the most hopeful dreams of their (mostly Ashkenazi) Zionist parents. As such, they were secular through and through. And while the books certainly foreshadowed the pervasive influence of the military on Israeli society—the Hasambans were children who played war games—none of them presaged the religious influences to come, which followed in the wake of militarism toward the end of the twentieth century.

The second season of the cable TV series, which is discussed in detail below, is inspired by one of the most memorable books in the written series, the 1951 *Hasamba and King Herod's Gold Treasure* (Hasamba ve'otzar hazahav shel hamelech hordus, 1951). In that book about King Herod's treasure, the Secret Bunch comes to the rescue of Israeli archeologists whose discovery of precious artifacts from the coffers of the famed king is threatened by Arab grave robbers.[32] Thanks to the efforts of our alert bunch, the thieves are captured and the treasure is restored to its rightful owner, the Israeli state, true inheritor of the ancient Jewish king. The whole affair is almost completely devoid of any religious under- or overtones. Rather, it capitalizes on the archeological craze that seized the country in its first decades and ties it to a plot of espionage and sabotage.[33]

The search for archeological evidence of Israel's ancient past was one of the only ways early Zionist culture openly acknowledged its Jewishness. For under the cloak of scientifically researching the great heroes of various Jewish texts, sacred and less so, beginning with the Bible and continuing through the Talmud and Josephus, the young Hebrew nation shaped a half-imagined past, sanctioned by academia.[34] *Hasamba*'s pursuit of the thieves of Herod's treasure thus became a show of ownership as well, a powerful demonstration of the nation's right to its past and heritage. That the thieves were Arabs made the whole affair even more poignant and useful, for it tied together the political and military conflict with the state's enemies and its own internal search for cultural identity, all of which were sublimated through children's games.

The memorable book about Herod's treasure is echoed in the second season of the cable television series when the Secret Bunch chases another treasure. Only this time the treasure they seek has distinctly divine qualities, for the Hasambans pursue artifacts from the ancient Jewish temple, and most significantly the *choshen*, the gold breastplate worn by the high priest, mentioned earlier. The season's premise is given in the opening of the first episode, where we see an Indiana Jones–like character who, while digging somewhere in Palestine in 1880, gets shot and killed just as he unearths a treasure chest of artifacts, among them an ancient scroll identifying the hiding place of the *choshen*, a Jewish holy grail of sorts.[35] The moment the archeologist realizes the importance of his finding, the ancient scroll is snatched from him and is lost until it resurfaces again in the show, in danger of falling into the wrong hands, that is, non-Jewish hands. It is the job of the Secret Bunch to find it, recover the *choshen*, and return it to its rightful owner, the Jewish state.

Yet unlike the book series, those wrong hands do not belong to Arabs anymore, who do not figure prominently in the contemporary cable show. After all, in the 2000s the Arab states that border Israel are no longer a match for it and do not pose an existential danger to it as they did in the past. The enemy now comes from within and takes the form of the Jewish arch-criminal Zerach Zorkin, who wants the *choshen* for his own evil plans of power and control. Zerach is the brother of Elimelech Zorkin, who appeared in several of the original book series as a totemic criminal, a nefarious character who tries to thwart the good guys for his own private profit.

Zorkin's ethnic background is not clearly identified in the book series, but in its first cinematic adaptation, *Hasamba and the Criminal Gang* (Hasamba vena'arey hahefker; dir. Joel Silberg, 1971), Zorkin, played by the Moroccan-born Zeev Revach, has distinct Mizrahi characteristics. The identification of Zorkin as Mizrahi was quirky and accidental, most probably owing to Revach's penchant for overtly ethnic performances, for which he came to be known.[36] By the time Zorkin made it to television, his Mizrahi identity had been fixed. In the 2010 cable show it is greatly exaggerated, and he is cast as a deceitful, heartless, cruel, and power-hungry Mizrahi rabbi who manipulates his followers' belief in his supernatural powers as a so-called kabbalist to extort their money. Played by the popular drag comedian Itzik Cohen, Zorkin's character in the cable series is a biting parody of various kabbalist Mizrahi rabbis—Babahs, as they are called—who began taking a greater part in Israeli politics after the rise of SHAS.[37]

The televised version, then, quite unlike the original book series, is much more concerned with both the Jewish legacy of Zionism and the excesses of [Mizrahi] religiosity within contemporary Israel. Both issues are dealt with quite tellingly in the show, despite its fluffiness as a cheap entertainment product. First, the cable show focuses on the third generation of Hasambans, the grandchildren of the first generation, who appear even more secular than their grandparents. Given their obvious secularism, their zeal in pursuing the *choshen* and their acceptance of its divine power is perplexing. Second, the character of Zerach Zorkin reveals another side of the show's preoccupation with Jewishness, which the original book series lacked. For Zorkin is identified not just as Mizrahi but also as a Jewish clown, a ridiculously religious bogeyman. Both of these elements are in fact complementary. Because while Zorkin stands for religious excess, the Jewish awareness of the young Hasambans is promoted as a moderate antidote to it. The relationship between the two is precisely the reason why the show is so telling about the changes this study examines. The book series and the cable television show are expressions of Israeli patriotism that are separated by several decades, in which religion plays very different roles. While Jewishness is completely absent from the books, it dominates the TV show.

Teenagers Renen and Igi, who have now replaced the original Yaron and Tamar, live affluent Western lives that characterize members of the Israeli Ashkenazi upper middle class.[38] Religion has no part in their lives, as it had no part in the lives of their grandparents and parents. Their involvement in the dangerous pursuit of the *choshen* is therefore quizzical. The dramatic reason for it is simple: Renen's grandmother, Tamar, is kidnapped at the beginning of the show in connection with the *choshen* affair. Renen wants to help her grandfather, Yaron, to find her grandmother. Igi joins the chase because he is Renen's boyfriend. Initially, then, this is a fairly generic opening to what is, in terms of television genre, a derivative, third-rate children detective series.[39]

Patriotism is an underlying element of the show right from the first episode, when the existence of an ancient scroll with information about the temple's treasures is discovered in Jordan. The Israeli Secret Service gets involved and brings Yoav Tzur, the commander of Hasamba's second generation, back from retirement and charges him with finding and retrieving the scroll. Yoav readily enlists in a mission "to retrieve a scroll that belongs to the State of Israel," as he puts it, for he is not ready to "sit back and let the country go up in flames." These statements exemplify the show's mixture of Jewish nationalism and Jewish religion, which has, in fact, characterized Zionism from its inception. In this respect, then, the episode and the cable series in general show the endurance of the national-religious mixture that has always characterized Zionism.[40]

Again, *Hasamba 3rd Generation* makes for such an interesting case because it records the gradual shift in this dynamic and the increasing influence and role the Jewish religion seems to be gaining in the national imagination. Precisely because the show does not focus on any of Israel's religious minorities, like the shows discussed above, but revolves around the lives of the country's secular majority, heirs to its founding pioneers, it becomes a telling gauge of these changes. What epitomizes this shift is how the chase after the ancient treasure develops in the TV show: very differently from the search for Herod's treasure in the 1951 book. Eventually, the object of pursuit in the TV series gains a different status altogether when its divine power becomes acknowledged by all and when the Hasambans, especially the young commander Renen, is identified as a messianic figure.

In the second episode of season 2, following a lead they receive, Renen and Igi visit the Museum of the History of the Holy Temple in order to look there for clues about the *choshen*.[41] Walking around the museum, the two meet an Orthodox-looking man—black suit, hat, full beard—who is standing before a large engraving of the ancient Jerusalem temple. With great intent and reverence the bearded man starts talking about the temple, pointing out to the two teenagers the location of the inner sanctum on the map. Igi is not especially interested, but Renen is, and she asks the old man about the *choshen*, a picture of which also hangs nearby. The man readily tells her about it as well, emphasizing that in olden days the high priest used it to communicate directly with God. "Until it was robbed," Renen adds, "and its whereabouts are unknown, right?" The old man confirms, and, looking intently at Renen as the eerie music swells, adds that the day will come when it shall be found by the Intended, who will also save the people of Israel.

Igi, who has no patience for this kind of nonsense, thanks him curtly, rolls his eyes, and mutters to Renen something about tripping lunatics as he pushes her away. Renen, who is later identified as the Intended by the old man and his kabbalist circle, members of a congregation called Adat Hayachad, is obviously more interested.[42] Later in the show her status as the Intended or Chosen is gradually accepted by everyone and certainly by the viewers. It is never really clear who chose her or why, and it is even less obvious how exactly she will save the people of Israel, and from what. No one seems to need saving in the show, which, given the importance of the *choshen* as a redemptive object, is surprisingly lacking political context and references either to Israel's conflict with the Arabs or to world anti-Semitism, to name two of the most dangerous problems for Jews in the twenty-first century. Is this, then, the moment of change when the televised series becomes a different kind of story, one that converts the role of Hasamba from protectors of the nation to its redeemers?

A brief comparison to the films of Indiana Jones, especially *Indiana Jones and the Raiders of the Lost Ark* (dir. Steven Spielberg, 1981) and *Indiana Jones and the Last Crusade* (dir. Steven Spielberg, 1989) may serve to illustrate this point. Both films involve a search for a holy relic whose alleged divine powers have the potential to cause great harm if they fall into the wrong hands—that is, non-Western, liberal, democratic hands. In his pursuit of the Ark of the Covenant in the first of these two films and the Holy Grail in the second, and in his attempt to prevent them from falling into the hands of the Nazis, the archeologist Indiana Jones is a modern crusader of sorts. As an American professor of archeology he represents enlightened science in the service of humanity. That he does not seek the two holy relics for any kind of personal gain is evident from the end of both films, when he gives up ownership of them. The ark is packed up, sealed, and stored away where it cannot be found or tampered with, while the Holy Grail is left where it was found, in a secret cave in Jordan that collapses at the end of the film, entombing the grail forever.

Like Indiana Jones, the original Hasambans of the book series were representatives of their nation, agents of a communal ethos, who were shaped in its image and meant to protect and preserve it. Their pluck, their initiative, their unique sense of humor, and above all their willingness to sacrifice themselves for the well-being of their compatriots made them an apt reflection of the nation. It was no doubt the reason for their enduring popularity as well. In this respect, not much has changed in the televised series. Renen and her comrades are brave, they show initiative, and they also put their lives at risk. At the same time, they become much more than just protectors of the nation or representatives of its ethos. They are designated as redeemers of their people as well. The language used to describe Renen, and the reason she is the only one who can actually get to the *choshen*—a little like King Arthur's Excalibur sword—has an obvious religious resonance. She is the Intended, the Chosen, the Anointed. Such spiritual associations have been traditionally absent from the Zionist narrative. Instead of a biblical connection that emphasizes national sovereignty, as in the early Zionist case, the focus here is on spiritual morality based on Jewish religious beliefs and practice.

And yet, I would like to suggest that the role of Hasamba in the television series has not changed vis-à-vis the nation. Rather, it is the nation Hasamba represents that has changed. If the book series created Sabra heroes in the image of their Sabra nation, the television series creates "religified" heroes in the image of a nation that has become much more religiously minded than it was in the past. The heroes' role remains essentially the same—to represent the nation and protect it. But now that the nation has changed, the mission to protect it has changed as well in order to match the modified national ethos. It is no wonder, then, that the cable show makes few references to the politics on which the book series was based. The external enemies the original Hasambans fought are now gone, faded into a fuzzy background. What has taken their place is an internal enemy, Zerach Zorkin in particular, a "false Messiah" who poses the greatest threat to the state of Israel.

In the second season of the cable show, Zorkin is an arch-crook who pretends to be a kabbalist rabbi with special powers of healing. Calling himself the Microwave, he charges high fees from his simple believers, who come to him for help with various spiritual and physical ailments. Zorkin is a clear parody of the Babah phenomenon—Mizrahi rabbis, usually Moroccan, who in the 1980s began establishing large bands of followers and became fairly wealthy, powerful, and eventually corrupt, meddling in the economic and political life of the country.[43] Zorkin is indeed extremely wealthy and is interested in the *choshen* in order to harness its power and become still wealthier and more powerful.

Like the villains in another action-adventure subgenre, the James Bond films, Zorkin is a master of evil who is interested in power for its own sake. As the show is an obvious parody, and seems to be deliberately made cheaply, Zorkin's plans for world domination are ridiculously nonsensical yet at the same time also shockingly racist.[44] As a biting satire of the Babah phenomenon in Israel, Zorkin's character is a parody of the excess of the only kind of Jewish religiosity that was sanctioned by official Zionism after statehood—Mizrahi, traditional Judaism. Yet here in the show it has clearly stepped out of bounds and has become a warped kind of Judaism, a mutated and false incarnation of it that threatens to infect and corrupt the state's politics and culture.

Comic relief aside, Zorkin is indeed a false messiah. His placement in the show as the greatest threat to the well-being of Israel is another important aspect of the show, where the changes in the nature of Israeli society are demonstrated by the shift in the place of religion and the attitudes toward it. The danger Zorkin poses and the bias against him are very different from the older Zionist animosity toward religion. Some of the older Zionist antagonism against religious Judaism was a result of the historical moment of separation from it in the name of a competing Jewish renewal movement. This is also the reason for the continued suspicion of Orthodox Judaism in Israel even today. For the black-wearing, state-denying *haredim* in Israel remain a constant reminder of both the cradle of Zionism and the threat to its way of life. Unpredictably though, the Orthodox are not the ones who pose a threat to the state in the show. It is precisely the folksy Mizrahi traditional Judaism that threatens it because it is not Judaism anymore but a strange cultic manifestation of it that is suspiciously Arab-like.

The relationship of the Ashkenazi cultural hegemony with Arab-Jews, or Mizrahim, was never easy. Even today, more than fifty years after Mizrahim first arrived in Israel en masse, the pangs of absorbing them into Israeli culture continue. As mentioned in chapter 2, among the most difficult of those pangs has been the religious character of the Jews who came from Muslim countries, which the secular, Ashkenazi Zionist establishment found difficult to digest. When attempts to eradicate it and turn Mizrahi Jews into secular socialists failed, their unique form of religiosity was eventually accepted and came to be known less threateningly as *masortiyut*, or traditionalism. What recommended it most to secular Zionists was its difference from Eastern European Jewish orthodoxy, which Zionism originally rebelled against and which it feared the most.

But when that traditionalism manifested itself politically in the form of SHAS from the 1980s on, the Ashkenazi hegemony found it increasingly difficult to tolerate.[45] This became harder still after strange-looking rabbis, wearing robes and turbans and mumbling all kinds of incantations, began interfering in the democratic process about a decade later. It was bad enough that SHAS had a spiritual-religious leader, Rabbi Ovadia Yosef, whom the heads of the party regularly consulted, mixing state and religion unabashedly in unprecedented ways.[46] But when religious characters of an even more exotic kind—like the Babah Sali—began to be consulted by other politicians who made embarrassing pilgrimages to their cultic courts, the cup truly ran over, certainly in liberal, democratic, Western eyes.[47]

Zorkin's character is an exaggerated, evil representation of those Babahs who was made in their image. His long robe and turban identify him as a so-called spiritual leader of the Mizrahi kind, with his court of sycophants and their underhanded machinations. He is a "bad guy" because he has crossed the line and cannot be ignored anymore. He must be stopped. His religiosity has become unrecognized as a legitimate form of Jewishness. As a consequence, his Arab characteristics become much more apparent and assume a sinister aspect. As long as the different dress, language, accent, and ethnic customs of Mizrahim were accompanied by bona fide Jewish practices, they were accepted. But Zorkin is no longer "Jewish" in any recognizable way. In fact, he reminds one much more of the image Muslim spiritual leaders have in the media, in Iran, in Lebanon, in Afghanistan. He looks like an Arab, dresses like an Arab, talks like an Arab, and behaves like an Arab.[48]

This may be why the show delineates the possibility of a realignment with Jewish orthodoxy of the Eastern European kind as the only authentic form of Judaism and as a legitimate source of inspiration for a Zionism in search of a spiritual dimension. While a bastardized and Arab-like Mizrahi religiosity is rejected outright in the show, the fact that another prominent kind of Judaism, the messianic Judaism of the settlers, is not mentioned at all can be seen as a rejection of it as well. Both kinds of Judaism pose a threat to Zionism because of their aggressive political agendas, which seek to usurp it. Orthodox Judaism, on the other hand, while it deems the Jewish state a sinful entity, is primarily interested in using its resources for its own sustenance. Unlike SHAS or the religious Zionist parties, it does not desire to take political control of it.[49]

Ultimately, then, *Hasamba 3rd Generation* can be seen as a show about Zionist hegemony and about the new place of Judaism within it. The show is entirely consumed with an internal fight to define the character and future of a Zionist Israel, an Israel that is very different from the one we encounter in the Hasamba book series. If the first and second generation of Hasamba managed to secure the country's borders, the third generation is engaged with determining the kind of Jewish nation that shall dwell within them. That Jewishness is an important consideration becomes clear from the show's preoccupation with internal concerns over external ones, with its rejection of what it considers bastardized forms of Judaism, and finally with its acceptance of the sanction and support of "true" Judaism, that is, orthodoxy.

This does not mean that Renen and her friends are going to return to the faith, become Orthodox, and in doing so change the State of Israel completely, putting an end to historical Zionism as we know it. On the contrary. By accepting the sanction of orthodoxy, the anointment by Adat Hayachad, they celebrate the triumph of Zionism not just as a Jewish national movement but as a movement that redefines Jewishness itself. While Zionism always aspired to do so, its insistence on ignoring the paradox that inhered in it prevented it from becoming relevant for all Jews. Despite its hopeful beginnings, the State of Israel eventually became the true home for very specific kinds of Jews—"Hebrew-speaking goyim," as I once heard a Jewish-American friend refer to Israelis; that is, people whose connection to Jewish spirituality has become ever more tenuous despite their conceit to represent and lead world Jewry.[50]

Hasamba 3rd Generation suggests a change in this course first and foremost by its very engagement with this question, and by none other than its hegemonic elite, the grandchildren of its founding pioneers. Second, it eliminates corrupt strands of Judaism that threaten its existence as a Jewish national renewal movement. Third, it brings an end to the denial of its traditional Jewish roots and its rejection of traditional Jewish elements as parts of it. As Tali Artman put it recently in a review of the television show:

> Renen and her friends are the "Newest Jews." They are the best of what all worlds have to offer: the self-confidence of the New Jew, the pure heart of the Hassid, and the natural charisma of a holy woman or man. They are both Israelis and Jews; Israelis not because of their citizenship, but because of their loyalty to the state, and Jews because they hold to higher values of Judeo-Christian ethics.
>
> The "newer Jew" had learned some Bible in school, but no longer sees the bible as justification for his or her right over some of the land she or he was born in or immigrated to. This Newer Jew also does not turn his or her back on two thousand years of Jewish history. This Jew might be orthodox or secular, a rationalist or a mystic, but always determined to do the right thing for the group, for the country and for the world as well.[51]

It is perhaps worth concluding with a reference to Haim Hazaz's well-known 1942 short story "The Sermon" (Hadrasha), in which the protagonist, Yudka, wonders whether the success of Zionism will also be the end of Judaism as we know it. "The Sermon" is essentially a long speech, spoken by a humble and hardworking pioneer, a man of very few words who is suddenly seized by the urge to unburden himself before a committee of his peers and tell them what he thinks about the paradox of Zionism as a so-called Jewish national revival movement. Written more than half a century ago, Hazaz's critique is quite prophetic, certainly with respect to the place Judaism has in the lives of secular Israelis, the inheritors of Yudka and his ilk, Hasamba included, and their relationship with the Jewish religion.

"Zionism and Judaism are two different things . . . perhaps even two things that stand in contrast to one another," says Yudka in the story, which has been one of the most widely debated literary works in modern Hebrew literature and a work that is still featured prominently in schools' curricula in Israel.[52] "Zionism begins where Judaism is destroyed," Yudka announces, and goes on to quip that "when a person cannot be Jewish, they become Zionist." More presciently still, Yudka believes that "Eretz Yisrael is not Judaism anymore." That is, the modern Jewish presence in the land of Israel and the centrality the land has gained in Zionism is somehow un-Jewish. This was apparently the case during his own time, in the 1940s, and he makes the chilling prediction that un-Jewishness may increase in the future. This double-bind prophecy is neatly borne out in present-day Israel by the schism that separates secular Israelis from religious Zionist Israelis. If the first buy pork on the Sabbath and do not circumcise their newborn boys because they think the ritual primitive and barbaric, the second are idolaters who have replaced God with land. While both are two different kinds of Israelis, their relationship to traditional or historical Judaism is problematic.

Hasamba 3rd Generation offers a compromise to this impasse. It suggests another solution that modifies the fierce secularism of its young protagonists by incorporating the more universal rather than tribal ethics of Judaism. The show promotes a kind of ethical Judaism that is socially minded, morally concerned, charitable, tolerant, and forgiving. A Judeo-Christian ethical Judaism, as Tali Artman writes. It is only in the post-postmodern Israeli world of the show that the Hasamba Bunch can comfortably include a religious member, Chofni, his halakhically half-Jewish girlfriend, the Russian-born Luda, a cross-dressing gay guy, the Jewishly ignorant Igi, and the super-secular Renen, who accepts the sanction of Jewish orthodoxy as the Chosen. "If a Kabbalist, a Hassid of Breslau, a gay man, a woman leader and a half Jewish immigrant can unite," writes Artman, "then maybe a new Zionist utopia might just be born and Israeli society might still become the model society that the Zionists of the late nineteenth and early twentieth century had envisioned."[53] That this new Zionist model incorporates self-consciously significant elements from Jewish religion is the very change this book has tried to trace.

AFTERWORD

In an apt coincidence, the events leading up to Israel's 2014 war against Hamas in the Gaza Strip make for a poignant conclusion to this book. Both the protracted search for three Israeli teenagers who were kidnapped and murdered by Hamas operatives in June of 2014 and the war against Hamas in the Gaza Strip that immediately followed the murders demonstrated the erosion of democratic civic values in Israel and the increasing incorporation of religiosity into the national discourse. The search for the kidnapped boys on June 12, which involved massive police and army forces that swept over the West Bank and combed it for eighteen days, was "religiously" named "Return, Brothers" (שובו אחים).

Invoking a biblical reference from Jeremiah 31:16 about the ingathering of exiles to Jerusalem that reads "and thy children shall return to their own border" (ושבו בנים לגבולם), the military search was accompanied by an unprecedented religious discourse in the public and the media. On June 15, twenty-five thousand people gathered by the Wailing Wall in Jerusalem and prayed for the safety and return of the three boys, led by the Sephardi chief rabbi. In Tel Aviv, 250 people gathered in Rabin Square and were led in prayer by the Ashkenazi chief rabbi.[1]

More unusually, prayers for the kidnapped were also held during various television programs by secular hosts. On June 16, on the morning show of one of Israel's major cable channels, Channel 2, a public prayer was held for the kidnapped youths, with one of the secular hosts wearing a large Breslev yarmulke and another scolding viewers for being cynical about the religious content. "It is at this point," wrote television critic Moran Sharir, when the hosts of the morning show "invite viewers at home to open the Book of Psalms, and Rabbi David Stav [in the studio] chants a prayer, the words of which appear at the bottom of the screen so viewers can join in karaoke style . . . that you realize it makes no difference which side is going to win this round, Israel or Hamas."[2]

The war that followed suit, named "Operation Protective Shield" (Tzook eitan), seemed to many in Israel to be the country's first holy war because of the religious rhetoric that accompanied it, from the public's religious expressions of support—mass prayers and the wearing of phylacteries in public—to the religious expressions of soldiers and officers who took part in the fighting. "This was Israel's first religious war," wrote *Ha'aretz* commentator Uri Misgav:

> Facebook, Twitter and Whatsapp turned into synagogues. The IDF became God's army. God became the Lord of Hosts. The army's HQ became a Yeshiva. This would be the only logical explanation why an IDF spokesman distributed pictures of the Chief of Staff speaking to his generals while behind them a digital screen showed biblical verses that read, "Though war should rise up against me, even then will I be confident" [Psalms 27:3]. . . . We need to ask forgiveness of Colonel Offer Vinter, the commander of the Givati division, who in his letter to his soldiers called for a religious war against the Gazan enemy, which vilifies the name of the God of Israel. Last week he was severely criticized; now he can be quickly promoted in rank. All he did is jump the gun by one week. Suddenly, everyone is praying, reading psalms, quoting Holy Scripture. Hours after the beginning of the operation, the social networks almost crashed, flooded by prayers. In the past, artillery and airstrikes used to prepare a ground offensive. Yesterday, it became evident that Israeli soldiers are sent into the battlefield only after viral airstrikes from heaven.[3]

The religious rhetoric of IDF soldiers and officers may be explained in part by the increasing numbers and greater influence that national religious soldiers and officers have in the military.[4] But what the war in Gaza in the summer of 2014 showed for the first time is the resonance such religious sensibilities have with the public at large. The tribalism that always awakens in Israel during times of emergency bore clear religious signs for the first time during that war. For anyone following the changing place of religion in public life in Israel, the appearance of those religious sensibilities should have come as little surprise.[5]

As this book has tried to show, the writing was on screens for a long time before, especially after the beginning of the 2000s, although the cultivation of "screens" or media had begun in the early 1990s. As mentioned earlier, films and TV shows gradually replaced the hegemony of prose in which most cultural ideas had been publicly aired and debated until then. That initially films eclipsed TV with regard to the authentic representation of religiosity may have to do with the nature of the medium—its auteurial quality and its ability to present and articulate a focused message.[6] Television began to pick up the pace and truly raise the quality of its shows in the early 2000s.[7]

In considering the authenticity of television programs that incorporate Jewish religious issues, the early financial involvement of the Avi Chai Foundation in their production should always be borne in mind. The foundation's support has certainly contributed to the popularity of such shows as *A Touch Away* and *Shtisel* by removing from them many of the controversies surrounding religious issues in Israel. "You can always count on the generous support of the Avi Chai Foundation," wrote critic Arianna Melamed in 2012,

> provided that the script possesses some essential ingredients: a diverse assortment of the religious shown in a completely positive light while blurring the enormous social conflicts between them and secular viewers, or turning such conflicts into a moving human story . . . the possibility of seeing [*haredim*] as belonging to an insular sect with offensive beliefs no longer exists now that the Avi Chai Foundation funds the script and the production. This is . . . disturbing.[8]

The efforts of the Avi Chai Foundation in this regard should also be considered in a globalized context, what Arjun Appadurai calls "globalization from below, institutions, NGOs that mobilize highly specific local, national, regional groups on specific issues."[9] Such trends are more often connected to the distribution and cultivation of Western, liberal ideas, like the recent US involvement in Ugandan politics for advancing gay rights in Africa.[10] Although the cultural politics of the Avi Chai Foundation are much more conservative, the principle of their involvement as foreign agents obtains. In the global era, writes Appadurai, "imagination is globally distributed," and "regions are best viewed as initial contexts for themes that generate variable geographies rather than fixed geographies marked by pre-given themes."[11]

But while the push toward a greater visibility of religion in Israel media, especially television, may have been artificial initially, its remarkable reception and the plethora of more complex religious shows it inspired authenticated the trend. That the Avi Chai's *haredi* TV world is a wishful-thinking world, cleansed of controversy and beautified, cannot escape an Israeli public all too well informed about these issues. And yet the popularity of such shows may well reflect, besides the public hankering after greater national harmony, a wish for a more meaningful Jewish national context.

Given these changes, the question arises whether the greater presence of religion in public discourse in Israel is a passing trend or a more permanent change. Can the higher visibility of religious sensibilities belong to what Andreas Huysson and others call the culture of memory in the postmodern era—a tendency that strongly evinces the proclivity toward permanency, tradition, the old and the safe in an era of fluid reality?[12] This is true even if memory is reproduced and even if it is fantasized, as memories tend to be. "Modernization," writes Huysson, "is inevitably accompanied by the atrophy of valid traditions, the loss of rationality and the entropy of stable and lasting life experiences."[13] Is the Israeli public—like other fundamentalist societies, for that matter—reacting to these changes by seeking solace in religious traditions?[14]

It would seem that the various "religious" shows in Israel today try to do something different. If the more simplistic Avi Chai shows like *Shtisel* "pinkwash" religion and promote a feel-good sense about it by eliminating its problematic aspects, shows like *Srugim* and *Urim Vetumim* examine more complexly the place of a restrictive and antiquated religion in the context of modern national life. As such, these shows question the secular nature of Zionism and express an abiding wish to find a way to incorporate a religious measure into Jewish national life that goes beyond the artificial and coercive attempts to do so from above.[15]

In an important opinion piece in *Ha'aretz*, commentator Carlo Strenger identified three major groups in contemporary Israel, which are currently clashing.[16] The first are the liberal Zionists, who support a modern version of the earlier, secular statism and believe in a democratic and liberal state whose citizens are all equal before the law. The second are the Orthodox, for whom the eternity of the people of Israel is of utmost importance and for whom the State of Israel is not essential for Jewish survival, since only religious observance can guarantee that. The third are what Strenger calls romantic nationalists, those religious Zionists who believe that the State of Israel is an expression of the holy connection between the Jewish people and the greater land of Israel. Liberal democracy comes second for the romantic nationalists, who are willing to sacrifice its principles and curb or eliminate the rights of their detractors if they endanger the holy communion between people and land. "We should not dismiss any of these tendencies," concludes Strenger. "At this point in history, the clash between these hallowed principles poses a greater danger than any of Israel's external enemies."

A much more dire prediction comes from Avraham Burg, an observant man and a past member of Knesset for Labor, who served as the chairman of the Fifteenth Knesset and subsequently also chairman of the Jewish Agency.[17] Discussing the nature of Israel as "Jewish and democratic," Burg has this to say:

> As long as the "Jewish" part was a cultural component that included in it history, culture, legacy, ethics, aesthetics, civil society, and religion, which were either confined to individuals or to certain communities, all was well. But things have not been the same now for a long time. Some time ago the "Jewish" project began and its decisive goal is clear: to take over everything and introduce a completely different source of authority, [divine authority]. . . . The Israeli democratic component deposited (and some—like me—would say abandoned) the responsibility for the content and interpretation of the term "Jewish" into the hands of individuals and institutions whose source of authority is not Man.[18]

An alarming example of such interpretations is provided by a growing group of religious Zionist extremists who have been calling for a Jewish return to Temple Mount and the reestablishment of the Jewish temple there: a chilling fulfillment of a threat that was articulated in Joseph Cedar's 2000 film, *Time of Favor*.[19] While the age-old halakhic warnings against such attempts were conveniently met by political expediency after the capture of Jerusalem in 1967, recently this dynamic has been destabilized. All Israeli governments after the 1967 war were careful to respect Muslim religious authority over the Jerusalem mosques, knowing full well the disastrous consequences that would likely result from violating it. State politics happened to fit very well with religious politics in this matter.[20]

In recent years, however, voices calling for a reversal of these policies have grown bolder and more numerous, supported for the first time by members of Knesset as well. Leading those efforts is a man by the name of Yehuda Glick, who on October 29, 2014, was shot and wounded by a Palestinian for his leadership role in promoting Jewish presence on the holy mountain.[21] Glick, who headed the Temple Institute for several years, founded in 2008 the Fund for the Temple Mount Heritage (Hakeren lemoreshet har habayit) and the Project for Jewish Freedom on Temple Mount (Hameyzam lechofesh yehudi behar habayit), for which he managed to get the backing of members of the Likud Party.

The public resonance of Glick's efforts marks an important stage in the development of messianic Zionism. Warnings about the dangers inherent in imbuing a Jewish state with holiness, even in the form of a secular sanctity, were heard early on in the annals of Zionism. In 1953, five years after the State of Israel was established, the philosophy professor Nathan Rotenstreich warned against Ben-Gurion's secular messianism, as he termed it, which he thought dangerously close to religious messianism.[22] Rotenstreich's words were echoed by another well-known Israeli scholar, Gershom Scholem, who in 1971, following the post-1967 messianic stirrings, wondered whether Jewish culture would be able to handle its entry into history without being annulled or usurped by the messianic longings that lurk deep inside it.[23]

This was not a new question, of course, as the religion scholar Tomer Persiko reminded *Ha'aretz* readers in a series of poignant articles following the assassination attempt on Glick's life.[24] The question accompanied Zionism from its very inception and occupied various Zionist ideologues, including Herzl and Ben-Gurion. Herzl's distaste for Jerusalem was well recorded in his diary—a physical aversion he felt for the dirty and impoverished city he saw on his visit, as well as an ideological aversion to its sanctity as a religious location. As a politician with executive powers, Ben-Gurion went further than that and tried to convince his colleagues to leave Jerusalem out of Israeli jurisdiction, perhaps fearing exactly that which has come to pass.

Initially, writes Persiko, the longing for Temple Mount was not cultivated by religious Zionists, but rather by right-wing Zionists, the Revisionists. Despite their pronounced secularity, the Revisionists spoke openly about the Temple Mount as a unifying axis for the new Israeli nation, a mythology around which they envisioned it united. "In a certain sense," writes Persiko, the Revisionists

> took secular Zionism to its logical end, but in doing so they inverted it. . . . Jewish redemption . . . is based primarily on the establishment of sovereignty in a national home. According to Jewish tradition, sovereignty means the rebuilding of the temple and the reinstatement of the kingly house of David. Although Zionism only sought political independence, it could just as well have called for more than that. The fact that it did not was arbitrary in many ways, based on pragmatism and liberal and humanistic values. For those who do not believe in realpolitik and are not humanists, the eschatological push forward [inherent in Zionism] is completely logical.[25]

When the so-called Jewish underground, a group of radical settlers, plotted to blow up the Temple Mount in the 1980s to make way for a Jewish temple, the leadership of Gush Emunim was stunned by their boldness and especially by their defiance of halakhic tradition. As ardent practitioners of Kookism, they feared and abhorred such direct interference in the messianic process. Zionism, the two Kooks instructed, was only meant to begin a redemptive process, whose completion was up to the messiah, not to man. Kook Jr. was very careful to imbed religious Zionism within the Israeli state in the hopes of changing it gradually from the inside through conviction, not through coercion.

But while the various efforts to change the status quo on Temple Mount did not start inside the religious Zionist movement, recent events, especially the 2005 withdrawal from the Gaza Strip, changed this dynamic, according to Persiko. The voluntary unilateral withdrawal from Gaza shocked the Zionist religious establishment because it reversed for the first time a process it had seen advance continuously since the 1980s—a settlement thrust that even during the Oslo years was perhaps slowed but never stopped. The erasure of Jewish settlements in the Gaza Strip radicalized parts of the religious Zionist membership. "The disappointment and obstacles on the way toward the messianic vision," writes Persiko, "do not lead to the abandonment of that vision, but to a radicalization of faith, which tries to force the redemptive vision on a reluctant reality."

> For many religious Zionists, the turn toward Temple Mount replaces the belief in a gradual redemptive process and the sanctity of the state. Supporters of the mountain declare their final goal and by going up to the mountain and praying there deviate from halakhic practice and defy Israeli law. Statism is abandoned together with the patience required for the gradual process of redemption, substituted by vigilante messianism and bold efforts to hasten the end, to bring about the apocalypse.

The longing for the holy mountain and the temple at its top is therefore the endpoint of Zionism, as Persiko writes in his second article, titled, "Temple Mount as the Starting Point and the Endpoint of Zionism."[26] Zionism, which developed a secular version of Judaism, or Jewishness, always made use of the messianic matrix of Judaism and its prophecy of the ingathering of exiles. Yet that prophecy also calls for the erection of a temple and the anointment of a king. Is it possible, asks Persiko, following Gershom Scholem, to revive an ancient political framework without awaking the mythological kernels dormant within it? Scholem was writing in 1926 about the revival of Hebrew, but his words can be applied even more poignantly to politics:

> Each word that is not newly created but taken from the "good old" treasure is full to bursting with explosiveness. A generation that inherited the most fruitful of all our sacred traditions—our language—cannot, however mightily it wished, live without tradition. . . . God will not stay

> silent in a language in which he is invoked a thousandfold back into our life. . . . The revivers of the [Hebrew] language did not believe in the Day of Judgment, to which they destined us by their acts. May the recklessness which has set us on this apocalyptic path not bring about our perdition.

The capture of Jerusalem in 1967 and the access to the Wailing Wall forced Zionism to face the apogee of its earthly success, the final fulfillment of its political goal, wrote literary critic Baruch Kurzweil.[27] It would be unthinkable for Zionism and the State of Israel to give up these gains, seized by force, without betraying the very historiosophic essence of Judaism. "It is not possible," Kurzweil observed, "to stop the ride of apocalyptic messianism in order to let the passengers out to look at the wonders of the sacred sights." But it is not just secular Zionism that must face its own annulment. Religious Zionism shall find itself in the same predicament, for the building of a temple will make it redundant as well, and make *halakha* irrelevant, notes Persiko. A Jerusalem temple will take Judaism back to pre-mishnaic and pre-talmudic times and resurrect a priestly religion that has little to do with contemporary Judaism.[28] Both secular Judaism and rabbinic Judaism understand this risk and so far have tried to prevent access to the Mount precisely because of it. Yet the waning force of orthodoxy and the ascendancy of ethnic nationalism and templar messianism make it necessary for Israel to suppress them—a very difficult task, writes Persiko, that will require the Jewish state to abandon the messianic path it has been following since its inception.

Suppression will not be enough, of course. If Zionism wants to survive and thrive, it cannot ignore the Jewish heritage inherent within it and cannot abandon it to radical forces that will seize control of the conversation in the existing vacuum. In this respect, the later films discussed in this book, and especially the television programs, indicate a real thirst among Jews in Israel for precisely such an engagement, even if the conversation was begun by outside forces. In fact, outside forces like the Avi Chai Foundation, coming as they do from North America, may yet be able to teach secular Israelis important lessons about cultural innovation and Jewish diasporic sensibilities. For while North American Jews have taken a subordinate role to Israel on the Jewish world stage, they have been busy all the while creating a dynamic Jewish community that rose to the challenges of prosperity, security, and legal equality—unprecedented conditions in diasporic Jewish history.[29]

The vibrancy of the North American Jewish community does not rest only on the existence of a strong Israel. First and foremost it is rooted in Jewish heritage and ethics, which have been interpreted brilliantly and very successfully in the New World. Without ever setting out to do so deliberately, North American Jews have in fact developed the ideas of Ahad Ha'am and Bialik and turned Judaism into a veritable modern civilization, a civilization that is deeply rooted in Jewish religious ethics but is not beholden to them.[30] By contrast, after almost one hundred years of Jewish national life, the Jewish character of the State of Israel seems much closer to extinction. Whether it is hijacked by ethnic nationalists or comes under the sway of secular Zionists, its traditional Jewish character is likely to become ever more obscure.[31]

But since Israel is a sovereign state and not a religious community, it should probably handle its Jewish heritage differently than Jewish communities outside of it. One way of doing it—of incorporating a religious heritage into the culture of a secular state—can be seen in the Danish television program *Borgen*, which ran for three seasons between 2010 and 2014 (DR1 TV). *Borgen* is a revolutionary show about politics not because it paints the portrait of a female prime minister but because it is a show about *ethical* politics. While most television shows about politics—films too, for that matter—focus on the moral turpitude of politicians, *Borgen* examines the compromises politicians make in order to preserve their integrity and uphold their society's morals. In *Borgen* these morals are clearly informed by the Protestant ethics of Danish society.[32] As a Jewish state, Israel does not need to look that far. It would do well to begin with the one book that began it all, the Hebrew Bible, in the name of which it claims the land of Israel. But it should abandon the more belligerent and xenophobic parts of that book, which Zionism always tended to cultivate, and seek inspiration instead in some of the great ideas of social justice which that book gave to the world.

NOTES

INTRODUCTION

1. In 1958, after a series of heated debates in the Israeli parliament, the Knesset, the Israeli government decided that any adults who in good faith declared themselves to be Jewish and who did not practice another religion would be considered Jewish for purposes of national registry, immigration, and naturalization. As part of these debates, Ben-Gurion sent letters to fifty influential Jewish "sages" around the world, soliciting their opinion about the appropriate criteria for considering a person to be legally Jewish. Thirty-seven of those sages supported the orthodox, halakhic definition of Jewish identity. The rest defined it as an ethnic, cultural, or national identity. A copy of Ben-Gurion's letter is widely available on the Internet; see, for example, http://in.bgu.ac.il/Pages/news/berlin_bg.aspx.

2. Literature on Ahad Ha'am is plentiful. For an excellent bibliography, see Steven Zipperstein's entry in the *Oxford Bibliographies*, http://www.oxfordbibliographies.com/view/document/obo-9780199840731/obo-9780199840731-0075.xml?rskey=T9Z88J&result=2.

3. Bialik used "The Bookcase" as part of the title to one of his most famous poems, "Lifne aron hasfarim" [Before the bookcase, 1910]. The fuller term, "the Jewish Bookcase," later came to be used frequently in the so-called Kulturkampf between the religious and the secular in Israel in their argument over ownership of the Jewish traditional corpus. In 1952, during a famous meeting between Premier David Ben-Gurion and the influential rabbinical leader Avraham Yeshayahu Karelitz, aka Hachazon Ish (lit., the Visionary), Ben-Gurion conceded that ownership to the religious sector, a concession that transpired primarily due to inaction. Asked how he envisioned cooperation between the secular and the religious sectors in the Jewish state, Karelitz replied that since the religious carry the burden of *mitzvot*, or commandments, they should be given various dispensations. Ben-Gurion vehemently disagreed with the rabbi, arguing that building the land and defending it are practical commandments of equal if not greater importance. But the image that emerged from this public discourse remained: the religious sector draws a cart heavily loaded with worthy commandments, while the cart of the secular sector is empty and light. In the 1990s the image of a cart changed to that of a bookcase that holds the main works of Jewish traditional (rabbinic) wisdom. Because of various historical trends, as well as government educational policies, access to that rabbinic literature has become progressively more difficult

to obtain for secular Israelis over the years. Several initiatives, both private and public, were instituted to reverse this dynamic. Two of the most recent ones include the establishment, in 2013, of the Administration for Jewish Identity (Haminhelet Lezehut Yehudit), a governmental agency dedicated to promoting Jewish values, and an initiative to encourage Israelis to read one Bible chapter a day. In many ways, of course, these initiatives can also be seen as part of the cultural religification this book describes. See "Missionaries in the Service of the State" [Misyonerim besherut hamdina], *Ha'aretz*, December 30, 2014, http://www.haaretz.co.il/opinions/editorial-articles/1.2524749.

4. Avraham Shapira, *Or hachayim be-or ktanot: Mishnat A. D. Gordon umekoroteha bakabala uvachasidut* [The Jewish sources of A. D. Gordon] (Tel Aviv: Am Oved, 1996); Eliezer Schweid, "Lev'ayat hamkorot bemishnato shel A. D. Gordon" [The problems of the sources of A. D. Gordon's philosophy], *Proceedings of the Fifth World Congress of Jewish Studies* 3 (1969): 345–351.

For information on other ideas that preceded Zionism, see the classic study by Shlomo Avineri, *The Making of Modern Zionism: The Intellectual Origins of the Jewish State* (New York: Basic Books, 1981). See also this useful collection of essays: Avriel Bar-Levav, Ron Margolin, and Schmuel Feiner, eds., *Tahalichey chilun batarbut hayehudit* [Secularization in Jewish culture] (Tel Aviv: Open University Press, 2012).

5. On the nature and importance of statism in early Israeli culture, see Nir Kedar, "Ben-Gurion's Mamlachtiyut: Etymological and Theoretical Roots," *Israel Studies* 7, no. 3 (2003): 117–133.

6. This policy is well known and amply recorded. For a good summary and evaluation, see Tom Segev, "Between the Orthodox and the Secular," in *1949: The First Israelis* (New York: Henry Holt, 1986). For a cultural and philosophical rather than a political consideration, see the proceedings of a conference that dealt with issues relating to what the organizers termed the "Zionist era": Anita Shapira, Yehuda Reinarz, and Yaacov Harris, eds., *Idan hatziyonut* [The Zionist era] (Jerusalem: Zalman Shazar Center for Jewish History, 2000). See especially the final article, by David Vital (337–348), which assesses the revolutionary nature of Zionism. Vital notes the widespread animosity toward Zionism, religious as well as liberal and secular, that was shared by most of the Jewish establishment at the movement's dawn. What contemporary Jewish leaders found most objectionable was Zionism's insistence on questioning the necessity of preserving Jewish tradition. According to Vital, Zionism was anathema to contemporaneous Jewry. The real revolutionary nature of the Zionist ideology, then, was its insistence on advancing the safety and well-being of Jewish individuals over more abstract ideas concerning Jewish religion and tradition.

7. For a representative collection of articles, see Uzi Rebhun and Chaim I. Waxman, eds., *Jews in Israel: Contemporary Social and Cultural Patterns* (Hanover, NH: Brandeis University Press, 2004).

8. For a consideration in English of some of what Leibowitz was warning against, see Charles S. Liebman and Eliezer Don-Yihya, *Civil Religion in Israel: Traditional Judaism and Political Culture in the Jewish State* (Berkeley: University of California Press, 1983). Some of the authors' questions about the inherent tensions between Zionism and Judaism have been resoundingly answered by history in the decades that have elapsed since the book's publication.

9. Yeshayahu Leibowitz frequently appeared in public and on television. Many of these appearances are readily available on YouTube. In 2013 Rinat Klein and Uri Rosenwaks created a short series on Leibowitz entitled "Leibowitz: Faith, Land, Man" [Leibo-

vitz: Emunah, adama, adam] for Israel's documentary channel. A website dedicated to his legacy, including a comprehensive list of his own works as well as reviews of his philosophy by others, can be found at www.leibowitz.co.il.

10. Aviezer Ravitzky, *Messianism, Zionism, and Jewish Religious Radicalism* (Chicago: University of Chicago Press, 1996). The Hebrew version was published three years earlier under the title *Haketz hamguleh umdinat hayhudim* [The revealed end and the Jewish state].

11. Aviezar Ravitzky, *Religious and Secular Jews in Israel: A Kulturkampf?* [Datiyim vechilonim beyisrael: Milchemet tarbut?] (Jerusalem: Israel Democracy Institute, 2000).

12. Aviezar Ravitzky, *Religion and State in Jewish Thought* [Dat umedinah bemachshevet Yisrael] (Jerusalem: Israel Democracy Institute, 1998).

13. Aviezar Ravitzky, *Is a Halakhic State Possible?* [Ha'im titachen medinat halacha? haparadoks shel hate'okratya hayehudit.] (Jerusalem: Israel Democracy Institute, 2004).

14. Maoz Azaryahu, *Tel Aviv: Mythography of a City* (Syracuse, NY: Syracuse University Press, 2007), 79–84.

15. The issue was much discussed in the news in the summer of 2014. For a brief news item, see http://www.globes.co.il/news/article.aspx?did=1000963603.

16. Guy Ben-Porat, *Between State and Synagogue: The Secularization of Contemporary Israel* (Cambridge: Cambridge University Press, 2013).

17. Amos Oz, *In the Land of Israel* (London: Chatto and Windus, 1983).

18. Idith Zertal and Akiva Eldar, *Lords of the Land: The War over Israel's Settlements in the Occupied Territories, 1967–2007* (New York: Nation Books, 2007).

19. Tomer Persiko, "When the Teachings of Rabbi Kook Became Kookism" [Kshetorat harav Kook hafcha lekookism], *Ha'aretz*, March 29, 2013, http://www.haaretz.co.il/literature/study/.premium-1.1973372.

20. For an illuminating historiosophical discussion of the concept of history in Jewish culture, see Yosef Hayim Yerushalmi, *Zakhor: Jewish History and Jewish Memory* (Seattle: University of Washington Press, 1996). In his first chapter, "Biblical and Rabbinic Foundations" (1–26), Yerushalmi notes the conclusion of Jewish historical writing after the Bar-Kochba rebellion in the second century CE and its resumption seventeen hundred years later in the nineteenth century. The settlers, in effect, turn the Jewish clock back almost two thousand years. They re-exit history, as it were, and, if we apply Yerushalmi's argument (24), paradoxically resurrect the postnational spirit of their rabbinic forefathers, whose shock at the failure of the Bar-Kochba rebellion was so great that it made them disavow history and withdraw from it for nearly two thousand years. See also the afterword to this volume.

21. One of the most grating points of friction in the absorption of Mizrahi immigrants was the suppression of their religiosity in favor of a national Israeli socialism under Labor's dominance. In the 1977 election campaign, Menachem Begin, the leader of Likud, appealed to this sense of religious grievance of Mizrahi voters by bolstering his own sympathies toward traditional Judaism. This was one of his chief attractions in the eyes of Mizrahi voters. See Michal Shamir and Asher Arian, "Collective Identity and Electoral Competition in Israel," *American Political Science Review* 93, no. 2 (June 1999): 265–277.

22. Nissim Leon, *Charediyut raka: Hitchadshut datit bayahadut hamizrachit* [Soft orthodoxy: Religious renewal in Mizrahi Judaism] (Jerusalem: Yad Ben-Tzvi, 2010).

23. The most common critique of SHAS is that the party engaged in identity politics at the expense of more meaningful gains for its voters and that it turned Mizrahi traditionalism into a stricter, Ashkenazi form of Jewish orthodoxy, which deepened and perpetuated Mizrahi backwardness. There are numerous studies on the SHAS phenomenon. For a general English introduction see David Lehmann and Batia Siebzehner, *Remaking Israeli Judaism: The Challenge of Shas* (London: Hurst, 2006). See also Moshe Shokeid, "The Religiosity of Middle Eastern Jews," in *Israeli Judaism: The Sociology of Religion in Israel*, ed. Shlomo Deshen, Charles S. Leibman, and Moshe Shokeid, Schnitzer Studies in Israeli Society, vol. 7 (New Brunswick, NJ: Transaction, 1995).

24. The party seems to have disintegrated thirty years after it was established under a bitterly feuding leadership, but more importantly, perhaps, because the national religious agenda has usurped the party's parochial agenda, to some extent making it redundant.

25. Nissim Leon, "Dat vechiloniyut" [Religion and secularity: What shall we call this mysterious phenomenon? Concerning the development of Mizrahi orthodoxy in Israel], *Iyunim bitkumat Yisrael* 16 (2006): 85–107.

26. For a representative sample from 2014 alone, see the following works: (1) "Missionaries in the Service of the State" [Misyonerim besherut hamdina], *Ha'aretz*, December 30, 2014, http://www.haaretz.co.il/opinions/editorial-articles/1.2524749. An editorial about the establishment of the Administration for Jewish Identity as part of the Ministry of Education under the guidance of former chief military rabbi Avichai Ronetzky. The administration develops and promotes school curricula that highlight Jewish religious aspects. Some of its projects include *Project 929*, an online program for reading a Bible chapter a day, as well as "An Israeli Sabbath," which promotes sabbath ceremonies in grammar school classes around the country. (2) Adi Dovrat-Mezerich and Tali Cheruti-Sover, "Conspiring to Stop Commerce on the Sabbath: Businesses, Celebrities, Politicians" [Hahit'argenut hasodit lehafsakat hamischar beshabatot], http://www.themarker.com/news/1.2523928. A report about an initiative to prohibit business people, politicians, and public figures from conducting commercial activity on the weekend. (3) Tomer Rotem, "The National Service Theater Will Produce Shows Based on Jewish Sources" [Bete'atron hasherut hale'umi yu'alu hatzagot hamvusasot al mekorot yehudiyim], *Ha'aretz*, June 5, 2015, http://www.haaretz.co.il/gallery/theater/1.2261634. (4) Or Kashti and Yarden Skop, "An Initiative by the Ministry of Education to Introduce a New Subject of Jewish Studies from Kindergarten to High School" [Misrad hachinuch yozem miktzo'a chadash], *Ha'aretz*, November 12, 2014, http://www.haaretz.co.il/gallery/theater/1.2261634. (5) Yair Etinger, "The National Religious Camp Doubles Its Size: 22% of Israeli Jews Identify with It" [Machane hakipot hasrugot machpil et kolo], *Ha'aretz*, December 27, 2014, http://www.haaretz.co.il/news/education/.premium-1.2522201. (6) Uri Misgav, "Economics for Jews Only" [Kalkala liyhudim bilvad], *Ha'aretz*, April 20, 2014, http://www.haaretz.co.il/opinions/.premium-1.2300297. An op-ed about an economics conference focusing on the nature and implications of economics in a Jewish state. (7) A short report on a funding campaign to raise money for an architectural plan to rebuild the third temple in Jerusalem, www.globes.co.il/news/article.aspx?did=1000959364. For the actual campaign, which met its goal and raised more than the $100,000 target in two months, see www.indiegogo.com/projects/build-the-third-temple—3. (8) And finally, a response to all of the above in the form of a secular contract by the world-renowned sociologist Eva Illouz, who felt compelled to respond to the religious surge: "Here Is Our Torah: The

Six Commandments for the Secular and Proud" [Vehine hatora shelanu: Sheshet hadibrot lachiloni hage'eh], *Ha'aretz*, June 4, 2015, http://www.haaretz.co.il/magazine/the-edge/.premium-1.2340449.

27. See Yaron Peleg, *Israeli Culture between the Two Intifadas: A Brief Romance* (Austin: University of Texas Press, 2008).

28. John H. Weakland, "Feature Films as Cultural Documents," in *Principles of Visual Anthropology*, ed. Paul Hockings (Berlin: Mouton de Gruyter, 1995), 45.

29. Ibid., 50.

30. The loaded Zionist term "negation of exile" is dealt with more extensively in the next chapter.

31. Weakland, "Feature Films," 54.

32. For a concise history of this process and one example of many, see Simon Halkin, *Modern Hebrew Literature* (New York: Schocken Books, 1970).

33. On this cultural change, see the introduction to Peleg, *Israeli Culture between the Two Intifadas*.

34. Gershon Shaked, *Modern Hebrew Fiction* (New Milford, CT: Toby, 2008).

35. Amalia Kahana-Carmon, "The Song of the Bats in Flight," in *Gender and Text in Modern Hebrew and Yiddish Literature*, ed. Naomi B. Sokoloff, Anne Lapidus Lerner, and Anita Norich (New York: Jewish Theological Seminary of America, 1992), 239. Earlier in her evocative article, Kahana-Carmon calls modern Hebrew literature "a kind of national synagogue of the mind" (238).

36. On the influence of postmodernism on Israel and its manifestation as post-Zionism, see Laurence Silberstein, *The Postzionist Debates: Knowledge and Power in Israeli Culture* (New York: Routledge, 1999).

37. See the introduction to an anthology edited by Alan Mintz, *The Boom in Contemporary Israeli Fiction* (Hanover, NH: Brandeis University Press, 1997).

38. This has also partly to do with the development of commercial television in Israel after 1992, which had a big impact on creative energy and consumption in Israel. For a synoptic discussion of this change, see Oz Almog's monumental study, *Preda misrulik, shinuy arachim ba'elita hayisre'elit* [Changing values in the Israeli elite] (Haifa: Haifa University Press/Zmora-Bitan, 2004), 43–240.

39. This dynamic may change with time, especially if Israel's population continues to grow as robustly as it has in the last decade or so. The cinema law, which was passed by the Knesset in 1979 and then amended in 1999 in order to encourage local film production by allocating public funds for it, may become redundant at some point in the future. In 1979 and 1999 Israel's population numbered 3 million and 6 million, respectively. The 2014 census estimated it at over 8 million.

40. Nacim Pak-Shiraz, *Shi'i Islam in Iranian Cinema: Religion and Spirituality in Film* (London: I. B. Tauris, 2011).

41. Dan Chyutin, "'Lifting the Veil': Judaic-Themed Israeli Cinema and Spiritual Aesthetics," *Jewish Film and New Media* 3, no. 1 (Spring 2005): 25–47.

42. This premise is not shared by everyone. See, in particular, Ben-Porat, *Between State and Synagogue*.

43. The word דת (*dat*), which comes to Hebrew from Persian and means "law" as well as "religion," is put here into the causative aspect of the Hifil verb form in the sense of "causing to become religious."

44. Simha Flapan, *The Birth of Israel: Myths and Realities* (New York: Pantheon Books, 1987).

45. Benny Morris, *The Birth of the Palestinian Refugee Problem, 1947–1949* (Cambridge: Cambridge University Press, 1988).

46. Tom Segev, *1949: The First Israelis* (New York: Henry Holt, 1988; Hebrew, 1984); Segev, *One Palestine, Complete: Jews and Arabs under the British Mandate* (New York: Metropolitan Books, 2000; Hebrew, 1999); Segev, *The Seventh Million: Israelis and the Holocaust* (New York: Hill and Wang, 1993; Hebrew, 1991); Segev, *1967: Israel, the War and the Year That Transformed the Middle East* (New York: Henry Holt, 2007; Hebrew, 2005).

47. Baruch Kimmerling, *Palestinians: The Making of a People* (New York: Free Press, 1993).

48. Baruch Kimmerling, *The Invention and Decline of Israeliness: State, Society, and the Military* (Berkeley: University of California Press, 2001).

49. The criticism of Israeli new history continues to this day. For an eloquent and measured example, see Amnon Rubinstein, *From Herzl to Rabin: The Changing Image of Zionism* (New York: Holmes and Meier, 2000), as well as Silberstein, *The Postzionism Debates*. Amnon Rubinstein was a politician, writer, and legal scholar. His book, like those of many of his peers—the new historians would call them the ruling (Ashkenazi) elite—takes issue with the new historians' critiques.

50. For an overview of the new historians in Israel and post-Zionism, see Silberstein, *The Postzionism Debates*.

51. Guy Ben-Porat actually claims the opposite, that Israeli society has become more secular in the last few decades. Ben-Porat shows how large sections of the secular Israeli public are becoming increasingly alienated from a state religion that has grown more beholden to radical Jewish elements. See Ben-Porat, *Between State and Synagogue*. Given the growing influence the Orthodox and the settlers have had on government policies in the last few decades, Ben-Porat's analysis makes a lot of sense. At the same time, some of the resistance to official and more coercive efforts by successive Israeli governments to impose halakhic strictures on the general public, like the most recent debate about opening business in Tel Aviv on the Sabbath in the summer of 2014 (http://www.haaretz.co.il/news/education/1.2361884), is accompanied by a concurrent rise in the engagement with Jewish identity in various popular entertainment venues like music, film, and television. This book focuses on this process.

52. Michael Keren, *The Pen and the Sword: Israeli Intellectuals and the Making of the Nation-State* (Boulder, CO: Westview, 1989).

53. See a seminar paper by Shura Kurtzfeld, "Tmurot beyitzug yehudi dati umimsad dati bekolnoa yisre'eli mehakamat medinat yisrael ve'ad sof shnot hatish'im" [Changes in the representation of Jewish religious people and religious institutions in Israeli cinema, 1948–1990s] (Open University, March 2003).

54. For more on this, see Yaron Peleg, "From Black to White: The Changing Image of Mizrahim in Israeli Cinema, 1960–2000," *Journal of Israel Studies* 13, no. 2 (Summer 2008): 122–145.

55. See Kurtzfeld, "Tmurot beyitzug yehudi dati umimsad dati bekolnoa yisre'eli mehakamat medinat yisrael ve'ad sof shnot hatishim," 11–13.

56. See Roni Parchek, "Haregesh hadati bakolnoa hayisre'eli" [The religious sentiment in Israeli cinema], in *Mabatim fiktiviyim al kolnoa yisre'eli*, ed. Nurit Gertz, Orly Lubin, and Judd Ne'eman (Tel Aviv: Open University Press, 1991).

57. On identity politics in Israeli cinema, see Yosefa Loshitzky, *Identity Politics on the Israeli Screen* (Austin: University of Texas Press, 2001).

58. See Almog Oz, *Preda misrulik.*

59. For more information on this, see Galeet Dardashti, "Televised Agendas: How Global Funders Make Israeli TV More 'Jewish,'" *Jewish Film and New Media* 3, no. 1 (Spring 2015): 77–103.

CHAPTER 1: JEWISH AND HUMAN

1. On some of these developments, see George Mosse, *Confronting the Nation: Jewish and Western Nationalism* (Hanover, NH: Brandeis University Press, 1993; Alain Dieckhoff, *The Invention of a Nation: Zionist Thought and the Invention of Modern Israel*, trans. Jonathan Derrick (New York: Columbia University Press, 2002); Michael Berkowitz, *Zionist Culture and West European Jewry before the First World War* (Cambridge: Cambridge University Press, 1996).

2. Much has been written about the anti-diasporic aspect of Zionism. For a representative article, see Eliezer Schweid, "Rejection of the Diaspora in Zionist Thought," in *Essential Papers on Zionism*, ed. Yehuda Reinhartz and Anita Shapira (London: Cassell, 1996).

3. This has also been amply discussed in academic literature in the last twenty or so years. For two representative examples in English and Hebrew, see Daniel Boyarin, *Unheroic Conduct: The Rise of Heterosexuality and the Invention of the Jewish Man* (Berkeley: University of California Press, 1997), and Michael Gluzman's interpretation of it within the modern Hebrew context, *The Zionist Body: Nationality, Gender and Sexuality in Modern Hebrew Literature* (Tel Aviv: Hakibbutz Hame'uhad, 2007).

4. In literature, early Israeli works inherited the acerbic antitraditionalism of the Haskala—the Jewish Enlightenment—and incorporated it as a critique of Jewish religious culture in general, a sentiment that has percolated into the culture at large. The kind of scathing critiques of traditional Jewish life one finds in the works of Mendaleh Moikher Sforim (S. Ya'acov Abramowitz), for example, have made their way into later works, such as those of Y. H. Brenner and others. See the biting description of traditional Jewish society in Abramowitz's novella *Fishke the Lame* from the 1880s, especially chapter 5, about the town of Kissalon. See also Brenner's similar descriptions in his 1911 story "Nerves" [Atzabim], about some of his travel mates on the sea voyage to Palestine, who are described with almost anti-Semitic language. Such descriptions were part of later stories, like Ya'acov Hurgin's description of the religious community in early Tel Aviv in his short story "Professor Leonardo," and Moshe Shamir's description of the Yemeni characters in his short story "Dr. Schmidt."

For an early example from cinema, see the 1954 film *Hill 24 Doesn't Answer* (dir. Thorold Dickinson), about Israel's war of independence. In one scene, eighty-six minutes into the film, an Israeli soldier captures a former Nazi officer who is now fighting on the Egyptian side against the Jews. During the struggle between the Jewish-Israeli soldier (Arik Lavie) and the wounded Nazi officer (Azarya Rapaport), the Israeli soldier is suddenly transformed into the image of a religious Jewish Holocaust survivor. The image of the persecuted Jew is juxtaposed against that of the Israeli soldier to mark the difference and transformation between them.

The historian Tom Segev summarizes these sentiments comprehensively in "Between the Orthodox and the Secular," in his book *1949: The First Israelis* (New York: Henry Holt, 1988; Hebrew, 1984).

5. These attitudes were not limited to Zionism. They were shared, albeit not as harshly, by liberal American Judaism, which regarded orthodoxy after the Holocaust as a negligible phenomenon whose days were numbered. See, for example, Will Herberg's 1955 comment about it: "The pervasive secularism of American Jewish life has lately been challenged by groups of ultra-Orthodox refugees from eastern Europe" whose "unwillingness or inability to separate their Jewishness from the alien East European culture in which it was embedded has, however, virtually isolated them from the mass of American Jews. . . . there would seem to be little chance that this Orthodoxy will survive the process of acculturation, or succeed in escaping it any better than its predecessors." Will Herberg, *Protestant-Catholic-Jew: An Essay in American Religious Sociology* (Garden City, NY: Doubleday), 1955, 224–225n65. This view was shared by others. Nathan Glazer, for example, wrote in 1957, "The medieval world is gone and Orthodox Judaism is only a survival." Nathan Glazer, *American Judaism*, 2nd ed. (Chicago: University of Chicago Press, 1972), 141.

6. See Segev, *1949, The First Israelis.*

7. Yaniv Goldberg demonstrates this in a telling analysis of the metamorphosis of a skit Ephraim Kishon wrote in the 1950s. The skit was first adapted into Yiddish by the Israeli comedians Dzigan and Schumacher, and then by the writer, singer, and comedian Yossi Banai, who updated it in the 1970s for the comic trio Hagashash Hachiver. Each adaptation emphasizes another element of the original skit that best suits the absorbing culture at a specific point in time. Originally, Kishon's skit dealt with the anxiety many immigrants to Israel—mainly middle class and Ashkenazi—felt about being suckers (*freiers*, in Yiddish), taken advantage of by a system they were unfamiliar with. In their Yiddish version of the skit, Dzigan and Schumacher emphasized the critique of state socialism and its animosity toward bourgeois sensibilities. Yossi Banai emphasized ethnic humor as a way to express the recent rise of the lower, Mizrahi classes and their defiance of Ashkenazi hegemony. See Yaniv Goldberg, "Ephraim Kishon's 'Lefi Ratzon'—'As Much as You Like': The Metamorphosis of a Skit across Languages and Cultures," *Israeli Journal of Humor Research* 1, no. 2 (2012): 52–62. Hagashash Hachiver remains the most expressive manifestation of Israeli ethnic humor to this day.

8. For one of the first serious studies on this topic, see Ella Shohat, *Israeli Cinema: East/West and the Politics of Representation* (Austin: University of Texas Press, 1989). For one of the latest, see Yaron Shemer, *Identity, Place, and Subversion in Contemporary Mizrahi Cinema in Israel* (Ann Arbor: University of Michigan Press, 2013).

9. There were not too many such films. In addition to the Kuni Leml trilogy discussed here, it is worth mentioning the Eskimo Limon "franchise," a series of eight films that were sequels to the 1978 original comedy *Lemon Popsicles*, as it is called in English. Directed by Boaz Davidson, the original film follows the coming-of-age adventures of three high school friends in 1950s Tel Aviv. The first film, especially, qualifies as an Ashkenazi comedy because of its nostalgic focus on a time that preceded the politicization of ethnic tensions between Ashkenazim and Mizrahim that began in the late 1970s. For more on this, see Miri Talmon, *Israeli Graffiti: Nostalgia, Groups, and Collective Identity in Israeli Cinema* (Tel Aviv: Open University Press, 2001).

10. Gefilte fish, or stuffed fish, is the most identifiable dish of Ashkenazi cuisine, served at most Jewish holiday meals. It is used here as a complement to its Mizrahi cinematic counterpart, the Bourekas film genre.

11. Abraham Goldfaden (1840–1908) was a popular Yiddish playwright, many of

whose plays were comedies of errors that promulgated the ideas of the Jewish Enlightenment. The play was written between 1878 and 1880 under the title "Der Fanatic; oder, die Beide Kuni Leml" [The fanatic; or, the two Kuni Lemls]. It has been staged many times since then and continues to be revived. The first translation into Hebrew was by Mordechai Ezrahi-Krishevsky, published in 1900 under the title *Hakanay; o, shney yakatan yakshan* [The fanatic; or, the two yakatan-yakshan]. For one of the latest revivals, see this review: http://www.news1.co.il/Archive/0024-D-87359-00.html. In the original play the two doubles, who vie for the bride's hand, represent two different Jewish societies. The lame Orthodox groom represents the ailing traditional Jewish society, whereas the modern groom, a medical student, represents the enlightened modern world. The distinctions between them were somewhat lost in the cinematic versions of the play, and the Israeli films paint Jewish religiosity as comical in general.

12. The film was not perceived as such when it was first released. In fact, a lot of money was spent on building a *shtetl* set near Tel Aviv that included specially made food for some of the scenes. "A little Jewish town was constructed next to the Geva Film Studios in Givatayim, with 800 extras and 55 actors," writes Nirit Anderman in a retrospective article about the Geva Studios. She goes on to interview the film's star, Mike Burstein, who remembers that "the town . . . looked like a real Jewish *shtetl*, with wooden houses, carriages, horses, cows and chickens. It was as if someone came and transported you to a nineteenth century town in Poland or Russia. I remember that tourists arrived at the set to see the *shtetl*." See Nirit Anderman, "The Last Diary: Geva Studios Last Farewell," *Ha'aretz*, March 3, 2011, http://www.haaretz.co.il/gallery/1.1166245. As in many old films, the set looks decidedly fake now, a problem that was perhaps more exacerbated in Israel, which had a very limited and poorly financed film industry until the 2000s.

13. See Emanuel Levy, "Art Critics and Art Publics: A Study in the Sociology and Politics of Taste," *Empirical Studies of the Arts* 6, no. 2 (1988): 127–148.

14. The film included such local contemporary stage greats as Shmuel Rodensky, Raphael Klatchkin, Elisheva Michaeli, Aharon Meskin, Geta Luca, Shmuel Segal, and Albert Cohen, all of whom were much admired and loved, as well as several young actors who went on to make a name for themselves later on, including Oshik Levi, Mordechai (Pupik) Arnon, Chanan Goldblat, and Shlomo Vishinsky. The film also included several songs that became instant hits and that are still known today, including the title song, "Omrim she'ani eneni ani" (They say I am not who I am), lyrics by Moshe Sahar, music by Sorin Brazovsky.

15. Orthodox society as a society of learners is a post-Holocaust phenomenon enabled by the welfare state in Israel and the United States. Traditional Jewish society in Eastern Europe could not afford to support such a large number of yeshiva students. See Yohai Hakak, *Young Men in Israeli Haredi Yeshiva Education: The Scholar's Enclave in Unrest* (Leiden: Brill, 2012). For a more concise study of this phenomenon, see Menachem Friedman, *The Haredi Ultra-Orthodox Society: Sources, Trends and Processes* (Jerusalem: Jerusalem Institute for Israel Studies, 1991), http://www.jiis.org/.upload/haredcom.pdf.

16. See Gideon Kouts, "The Representation of the Foreigner in Israeli Films (1966–1976)," *European Journal of Hebrew Studies* 2 (1999): 80–108.

17. Although Kuni Leml is purported to be a yeshiva student, this conceit is undermined by his idleness—he does not really do anything in the film—and especially by his obvious idiocy. That he is campily dressed as a modern Haredi man adds to the ab-

surdity of his image and its ready identification with contemporary images of Haredi Jews.

18. In the 1990s, the Orthodox community in Jerusalem began demanding that the Israeli Egged Bus Company not display ads on its buses with images of women in them. The issue has been much commented on in the media over the years. For a recent article, see this 2013 *Ha'aretz* article by Nir Hason: http://www.haaretz.co.il/news/local/.premium-1.2063243.

19. For a cinematic representation of the soldier-citizen, see the 1968 film *Siege* [Matzor] (dir. Gilberto Tofano). Made shortly after the 1967 war, the film both celebrates and critiques the image of the heroic Israeli soldier. For a discussion of the film as well as Israeli cinematic masculinities in general, see Yaron Peleg, "Ecce Homo: The Transfiguration of Manhood in Israeli Cinema," in *Identities in Motion*, ed. Miri Talmon and Yaron Peleg (Austin: University of Texas Press, 2011).

20. For a bilingual version of the poem, see http://zionism-israel.com/hdoc/Silver_Platter.htm.

21. See this YouTube clip at http://youtu.be/WKXwsYqPGCo. The clip is taken from the 1969 docudrama *The War after the War* [Hamilchama acharey hamilchama], written by Moshe Hadar and directed by Micha Shagrir. The film describes Israel after the 1967 war and the incursions by Palestinian fighters (not terrorists, as the film makes clear) through the stories of a wounded Israeli paratrooper and a Palestinian fighter both of whom are treated in the same hospital. The lyrics were written by Rachel Shapira and composed by Yair Rosenblum.

22. For a short history of entertainment in the IDF, see this website, which contains lyrics and vocal performances of the songs and provides a variety of links to further reading: http://www.zemereshet.co.il/article.asp?id=19. For more general reading and musical context, see Motti Regev and Edwin Seroussi, *Popular Music and National Culture in Israel* (Berkeley: University of California Press, 2004). For the YouTube performance of the tank-man song, see http://youtu.be/5zkzS2oGM2w. The lyrics include these lines: "Not for his blue eyes / did I fall in love with him / I am not impressed either / by his height or by his breadth / nor by his impulsive laughter / which captures every woman's heart / the reason must be different / He's just a tank-man / nothing more, nothing less."

23. For more such films, see Peleg, "Ecce Homo."

24. The picture of Mike Burstein as Kuni Leml adorned a 2015 *Ha'aretz* article about the origin of the word "Ashkenazi." In other words, Burstein's goofy face has come to epitomize Eastern European nebbish manhood, that is, Ashkenazim. See Elon Gilad, "How Did Ashkenazis Get Their Name" [Ech kiblu ha'ashkenazim et shmam], *Ha'aretz*, May 27, 2015, http://www.haaretz.co.il/magazine/the-edge/mehasafa/.premium-1.2635118.

25. On the Babah phenomenon see Yoram Bilu and E. Y. A. L. Ben-Ari, "The Making of Modern Saints: Manufactured Charisma and the Abu-Hatzeiras of Israel," *American Ethnologist* 19, no. 4 (1992): 672–687.

26. For one of the most well-known critiques of this dynamic, see Ella Shohat's 1987 lecture, http://www.amalnet.k12.il/sites/commun/library/cinema/comi0378.htm.

27. Orthodox Jews do not view films, as Jewish law generally forbids it. There have been changes in this dynamic in the last few decades, especially with the paradoxical rise of an authentic Haredi cinema. For a study of Haredi men's films, see Yael Friedman and Yuval Hakak, "Jewish Revenge (Yehuda Grovais, 2003–2010): Haredi Action in the Zionist Sphere," *Jewish Film and New Media* 3, no. 1 (2015):48–76. For a study of

Haredi women's films, see Marylin Vinig, *Orthodox Cinema* [Hakolno'a haharedi] (Tel Aviv: Resling, 2011).

28. Studies on these changes abound. For a concise consideration of some of these issues, see Avi Shlaim, "The Likud in Power: The Historiography of Revisionist Zionism," *Israel Studies* 1, no. 2 (Fall 1996): 278–293.

29. Whether the party benefited its voters in concrete ways and improved their standard and quality of living has been widely debated. For an excellent study of Mizrahi religiosity and the SHAS phenomenon, see Nissim Leon, "Dat vechiloniyut" [Religion and secularity: What shall we call this mysterious phenomenon? Concerning the development of Mizrahi orthodoxy in Israel], *Iyunim bitkumat Yisrael* 16 (2006): 85–107.

30. Casting assessments of this nature can be tricky and are useful only up to a point. Having said that: Yossef is played by the Ashkenazi-named Uri Klauzner, who often appears in films in the role of what is known in Israel as an "*ars*," an aggressive, uneducated, and uncultured street youth who is often Mizrahi.

31. Not counting Bourekas films, the romantic comedy genre is conspicuously absent from Israeli cinema, save for a few films that have significant religious elements, like *Ushpizin* and perhaps the recent *God's Neighbors*, as well as *Fill the Void*, which may not correspond very closely to conventions of the genre. There are no studies yet about this curious absence or the correlation between religiosity and romantic happy endings. It may be that since Israeli cinema has not been a profitable enterprise generally, the incentive to produce popular genres like romantic comedies has been absent as well. A reason for the proliferation of romance in religious films may be Judaism's emphasis on coupling and procreation. These propositions are worth further examination.

32. *Ushpizin* means "guests" in Aramaic. One of the most important customs of the holiday of Sukkot is to host guests, with whom one shares roof and food.

33. At one point, they mistake the *etrog*, the hallowed citrus fruit that Moshe bought for 1,000 NIS for his *sukkah*, for an ordinary lemon and use it to make salad. The *etrog* is one of the most visible symbols of the holiday of Sukkot and one that every Jew in Israel learns about in kindergarten, irrespective of his or her family's religious observance. The escaped criminals should also have noticed that the fruit was stored in a special vessel and protected with special padding to prevent damage.

34. Prior to his conversion to Breslov Hasidism, Shuli Rand played various roles on stage and on screen. In most of these roles his accent is free of the guttural speech patterns that are associated with Mizrahim and that his *Ushpizin* character distinctly has. Yaron Shemer also identifies Rand's character in the film as Mizrahi. See Shemer, *Identity*, 222. I should also add that in the early 1980s I served with Shuli Rand in the Israeli Army and can personally attest to the fact that he did not speak that way.

35. See Shmulik Duvdevani, "A Great Miracle" [Nes gadol haya po], *Y-Net*, May 19, 2015, http://www.ynet.co.il/articles/0,7340,L-2958697,00.html.

36. The history of each of these directors is different. Shuli Rand grew up in a religious family in Bnei-Brak, left religion as a young man, and after a brilliant acting career became a disciple of Breslov Hasidism. Rama Burstein became Orthodox as an adult. Meny Yaesh comes from a traditional Mizrahi (Turkish) background and had become more observant before making *God's Neighbors*.

37. For a conversation with the director Rama Burstein about the film and her views as an Orthodox woman filmmaker, see http://www.habama.co.il/Pages/Description.aspx?Subj=4&Area=1&ArticleId=18603.

38. On Orthodox male cinema, see Friedman, *Haredi Ultra-Orthodox Society*. On Orthodox female cinema, see Vinig, *Orthodox Cinema*.

39. Mark Simpson, "Meet the Metrosexual," *Salon*, July 22, 2001, http://www.salon.com/2002/07/22/metrosexual/. For a more recent consideration of metrosexual imagery and its place and influence on contemporary society, see Mathew Hall, "Analysing Discursive Constructions of 'Metrosexual' Masculinity Online: 'What Does It Matter, Anyway?'" *GEXcel Work in Progress Report* 6 (2009): 111–117.

CHAPTER 2: JEWISH AND ISRAELI

1. An excellent early example is the witty 1819 send-up of Hasidism by Joseph Perl, *Revealer of Secrets* [Megaleh tmirin]. For an English-language edition of the Hebrew book, see Dov Taylor, *Joseph Perl's Revealer of Secrets: The First Hebrew Novel* (Boulder, CO: Westview, 1996).

2. היה אדם בצאתך ויהודי באוהלך. The saying was coined by the Russian-Jewish poet Yehuda Leib Gordon in his celebrated 1863 poem "Awake, My People" [Hakitza ami].

3. This was a commonplace belief of most *maskilim*. For a summary of these beliefs and various references, see Klaus Hoedl, "Physical Characteristics of the Jews," http://web.ceu.hu/jewishstudies/pdf/01_hoedl.pdf. Echoes of this dynamic can be seen as late as 1999 in Karen Brodkin's famous book *How Jews Became White Folks and What That Says about Race in America* (New Brunswick, NJ: Rutgers University Press, 1998).

4. Various Jewish communities during the Hellenistic period also come to mind in this respect, although it is hard to determine the extent to which these communities were secular in ways that correspond to our understanding of the term today. For a historiosophical consideration, see Shaye Cohen, *The Beginnings of Jewishness: Boundaries, Varieties, Uncertainties* (Berkeley: University of California Press, 2001).

5. For a consideration of the Jewish character of the Yishuv, especially the so-called Sabbath Wars in Tel Aviv, see Maoz Azaryahu, *Tel Aviv: Mythography of a City* (Syracuse, NY: Syracuse University Press, 2007), 79–84.

6. For the persistence of this designation and labeling in Israeli culture, see Dana Kachtan, "The Construction of Ethnic Identity in the Military: From the Bottom Up," *Israel Studies* 17, no. 3 (2012): 150–175.

7. See Nissim Leon, *Harediyut raka: Hitchadshut datit bayahadut hamizrachit* [Soft orthodoxy: Religious renewal in Mizrahi Judaism] (Jerusalem: Yad Ben-Tzvi, 2010).

8. In the late 1940s and early 1950s several cases of "secular coercion" have taken place at various immigrant transit camps (*ma'abarot*) where Yemeni children were forced by camp counselors to cut off their earlocks. A commission was appointed to investigate these allegations, which were found to be true. See Tzvi Tzameret, "The Frumkin Commission" [Va'adat Frumkin], *Iyunim bitkumat Yisrael* 1 (1991): 405–439.

9. For a revealing example of early Ashkenazi attitudes toward Jewish immigrants from Muslim countries, see Arye Gelblum's infamous article in *Ha'aretz* from April 22, 1949. Gelblum, a reporter for *Ha'aretz*, spent a few weeks in a transit camp for newcomers in order to report about them to readers. His accounts are full of harsh racial language about the immigrants. For a history of early immigration into Israel, see Tom Segev, *1949: The First Israelis* (New York: Henry Holt, 1988; Hebrew, 1984).

10. The film has received so much critical attention that it will be discussed here

only with respect to religiosity. See Yaron Peleg, "From Black to White: The Changing Image of Mizrahim in Israeli Cinema, 1960–2000," *Journal of Israel Studies* 13, no. 2 (Summer 2008): 122–145.

11. For a review of Topol's performance of Tevye on the London stage, see S. J. Goldsmith, "Tevye and Professor Higgins," *Jewish Quarterly* 15, nos. 1–2 (1967): 16.

12. See Uri Klein's review article on Topol's career, which refers to this binary portrayal: "Between Shtetl and Immigration Transit Camp" [Beyn hashtetl lama'abara], *Ha'aretz*, April 8, 2015, http://www.haaretz.co.il/gallery/cinema/klein/.premium-1.2609399.

13. See Shohat, http://www.amalnet.k12.il/sites/commun/library/cinema/comi0378.htm.

14. As Sallah lies in bed one night in his leaking cabin in the transit camp, he is asked by one of his children why they have to live in such squalor. He replies that this is the fate of all immigrants and that one day, when they have moved out to a nice apartment, someone else will be suffering in their stead.

15. The derogatory association between pajamas and Mizrahim was made in the 1950s when Iraqi Jews imported their custom of wearing pajamas at home as a sign of domesticity, comfort, and respect toward guests. The custom was interpreted as backward and impolite by Ashkenazi culture. The belittling phrase "Iraqi pajama" was immortalized by the poet Ronny Somek in his poem "Patriotic Poem" [Shir patriyoti], in which he makes fun of ethnic stereotypes that circulate in Israeli culture. The poem begins with these lines: "I'm a pajama Iraqi, my wife's a Romanian gal / and our daughter is the thief of Baghdad." For a Hebrew copy of the poem and a short discussion of some of the stereotypes it contains, see the blog entry by the writer and critic Ran Yagil at http://www.nrg.co.il/app/index.php?do=blog&encr_id=7b710fc4596b25648b44472262adc013&id=3967.

16. According to Nissim Leon, Mizrahim themselves wished to preserve their religious traditions as a way to grapple with the vicissitudes of immigration and in order to shield themselves from the alienating influence of Israeli statist secularism. See Leon, *Harediyut raka*, 93–97.

17. Television broadcasts began in Israel in 1968 on one public channel and one educational channel. Commercial TV began operating in Israel in 1992.

18. See Yaron Shemer, *Identity, Place, and Subversion in Contemporary Mizrahi Cinema in Israel* (Ann Arbor: University of Michigan Press, 2013), 100; Leon, *Harediyut raka*, 85–86.

19. See Baruch Kimmerling, "Between Hegemony and Dormant Kulturkampf in Israel," in *In Search of Identity: Jewish Aspects in Israeli Culture*, ed. Dan Urian and Efraim Karsh (London: Frank Cass, 1999), 62–64.

20. The rapprochement between Arabs and Jews, both inside and outside Israel, characterized the years immediately after Oslo. One expression of it was the many collaborations between Arab and Jewish-Israeli artists. For an overall assessment of these relations, see Mahmoud Kayyal, "A Hesitant Dialogue with 'The Other': The Interactions of Arab Intellectuals with the Israeli Culture," *Israel Studies* 11, no. 2 (Summer 2006): 54–74. It is perhaps worth noting the brevity of this episode in the annals of Israeli culture, which retracted into a deeper form of insular tribalism after the suicide bombings of the late 1990s and the Second Intifada in 2000. See Rebecca Lunna Stein's article about the so-called cleansing of Israeli imaginative spaces of Arab/Palestinian presence: "Spatial Fantasies: Israeli Popular Culture after Oslo," *Middle East Report* no. 216 (Autumn 2000): 36–38.

21. See Itamar Rabinowitz, *Waging Peace: Israel and the Arabs, 1948–1993* (Princeton, NJ: Princeton University Press, 2004).

22. See Ben-Porat, *Between State and Synagogue*. See also "Israeli Secular-Religious Dialectics," special issue, *Israeli Studies* 13, no. 3 (Fall 2008). The ethnic tensions between Ashkenazim and Mizrahim that animated Bourekas films were among the chief reasons that brought Likud to power in 1977. Once in power, Likud's energized development of the territories preempted these tensions, first by improving the socioeconomic status of the lower middle classes, Mizrahim included, and providing cheap housing in the territories, and second by shifting attention from what remained of Ashkenazi-Mizrahi tensions and raising instead—inadvertently—the tribal-religious aspect of the conflict with the Arabs. See Kenneth Brown, "Iron and a King: The Likud and Oriental Jews," *MERIP Reports* no. 114, "Israel Divided" (May 1983): 3–13.

23. See Baruch Kimmerling, *The Invention and Decline of Israeliness: State, Society, and the Military* (Berkeley: University of California Press, 2005).

24. In his 2012 novel *Biz'er anpin* [Minutiae], Yirmi Pinkus paints a droll picture of the Israeli petit bourgeoisie on the eve of the country's capitalist revolution in the 1980s. The middle-class Ashkenazi characters in the novel are poised between the waning influence of the Labor establishment and the yet unfulfilled promise of the new liberal Likud establishment. While they are not ashamed to express their naked thirst for luxuries, marked in the novel by their annual pilgrimage to the Austrian village of Seefeld, the still socialist economy necessitates working long, hard, and not always honestly to obtain them.

25. Asaf Inbari provides a lively description of this dynamic in his 2009 novel *Habayta* [Home]. Although fictional, the novel is closely based on the history of Inbari's native kibbutz of Afikim and follows the fervor with which its founders fashioned a new society and new communal traditions based on older diasporic traditions, even as they ostensibly rebelled against them.

26. Yaron Shemer is wary of "essentialist" Mizrahi critiques of the kind I provide here and calls for a more nuanced consideration of the film's aesthetics. This is a legitimate demand that does not take away from the consideration of *Sh'chur* in the context of this historical study about perceptions of Jewish religiosity in Israel. See Yaron Shemer, "The Burden of Self-Representation: Reflections on *Sh'chur* and Its Legacy for Contemporary Mizrahi Films in Israel," *Journal of Levantine Studies* 2, no. 2 (Winter 2013): 39–62.

27. The national Bible proficiency competition began in 1958 and for several years was an extremely popular and venerated event that was broadcast live on national radio, expressing Zionism's preoccupation with modern Israel's ancient origins. It was immortalized in various satirical skits and is part of Israeli national lore.

28. The prominent place given to Moroccan Jewish culture in Israel stems not only from the substantial size of that community but also from its relative political awareness and visibility, primarily on account of the community's historical reluctance to accept uncritically the acculturating tenets of statism. The issue has been researched extensively. For a seminal study, see Eliezer Ben-Rafael and Stephen Sharot, *Ethnicity, Religion and Class in Israeli Society* (Cambridge: Cambridge University Press, 1991).

29. The so-called postmodern politics of representation does have value, of course, even if initially it may only affect awareness or consciousness. For a reevaluation of postmodernism and a critique of its critique, see Linda Hutcheon, *The Politics of Postmodernism* (London: Routledge, 2003).

30. When worn by Mizrahi men, the jacket denoted Levantinism, especially when it was worn over a long gown, a white *jellabiya*. The mixing of Eastern and Western clothing items was considered sartorially uninformed and inappropriate according to the ascetic and quasi-military fashion during the early decades of statehood. When worn by Ashkenazi men, mainly German Jews, the jacket was seen as too formal and thus un-Israeli as well. Some claim that the derogatory term for German Jews, "Yekke," comes from the word "Jacke," which means "jacket" in German (*j* being pronounced as *y* in German). On the history of Israeli fashion, see Anat Helman, *A Coat of Many Colors: Dress Culture in the Young State of Israel* (Brighton, MA: Academic Studies Press, 2011).

31. See Leon, *Harediyut raka*.

32. Gabizon has a tendency to use crass humor in his films. This is probably most apparent in his first film, *Shuroo*, where the narrative features a series of humorous anecdotes.

33. For a summary, see Sami Shalom Chetrit, "Mizrahi Politics in Israel: Between Integration and Alternative," *Journal of Palestine Studies* (2000): 51–65.

34. In principle, this was not different from the way *ashkenaziyut*, ashkenaziness, developed as an inclusive category in Israel. Despite the different traditions of Jews who came to Israel from across Europe, especially from its eastern parts, they were quickly subsumed under the Ashkenazi label, irrespective of language, food, religious practices, and so forth. Mizrahim were subjected to the same homogenizing process, which resulted in their very label. The term "Mizrahi," meaning "Eastern," as opposed to "Sephardi," meaning "Spanish," was used to denote distance and direction from Europe rather than a connection to Spain after the 1492 expulsion. But what did distinguish Mizrahim from Ashkenazim early on was the incorporation of Jewish religious elements into their identity. As mentioned before, by the 1990s this so-called traditionalism had become an integral part of Mizrahi identity in Israel over and against its absence from the cinematic representation of non-Orthodox, nonsettler Ashkenazim.

35. See paintings by various Dutch masters (Frans Hals, for example). In many of the scenes in *Shiva*, the mise-en-scène appears to be consciously orchestrated to give an impression of poise, self-possession, and sometimes even haughtiness. The characters are often stationary or move slowly and rigidly. Dressed in black and framed against the background of big, fairly empty white rooms, they seem like moving pictures. Some of it comes from the unusual need to be quiet and respectful, and some of it comes from the animosity between the family members, who are stifled by their suppressed anger.

36. An evocative Ashkenazi contrast can be found in Orly Castel-Bloom's 2003 novel *Human Parts*, in the pathetic Shiva one of the protagonists, Adir, is organizing for his deceased sister, Liat. Since Adir lacks any kind of family, he treats the affair as a social function and focuses much more on the "guest list" and the catering challenges it poses. See Orly Castel-Bloom, *Human Parts* (Toronto: Key Porter Books, 2003), 84–87.

37. The Mizrahi family stands at the center of the other two films in the cinematic trilogy of the siblings Ronit and Shlomi Elkabetz: *And Thou Shalt Take a Wife* [Velakachta lecha isha] (2008) and *Divorce: The Trial of Viviane Amsalem* [Gett] (2014). All three films explore that trope and enrich our understanding of it far beyond its simplistic earlier perception. Another recent work that examines the Mizrahi family as a cultural symbol is *The Zagoury Empire* [Zagoury imperia] (HOT3 TV), a very successful television drama series that began in 2014. The series explores the tense relations be-

tween members of an extended Mizrahi family in the city of Beer Sheva and conclusively undermines Mizrahi familial wholesomeness. Intense hatreds and treason characterize the Zagoury family, making it seem like a Shakespearian royal family.

38. See Peleg, "From Black to White."

39. There is an interesting similarity here to American socializing models, which tolerate different ethnic traditions as long as they are left at home and do not become part of the official culture. Social acceptance is conferred only after allegiance to the republic has been demonstrated through language, dress, code of conduct, and all of the other spoken and unspoken ways that make up a culture. An American version of the old maskilic idiom about being a Jew at home and a human being outside: be ethnic at home and American outside. See Kathleen Neils Conzen, David A. Gerber, Ewa Morawska, George E. Pozzetta, and Rudolph J. Vecoli, "The Invention of Ethnicity: A Perspective from the USA," *Journal of American Ethnic History* 12 (1992): 3–41.

40. I make this point in *Israeli Culture between the Two Intifadas*.

41. Tribal in the sense that the war with the Arabs, especially the Palestinians, became more religious rather than political in nature, animated by the messianic tendencies of the settlers rather than by "cold" statist politics. Israel's operation in Gaza in the summer of 2014 is a telling case in point. See the afterword to this book.

42. A brief history of political campaigns in Israel in the 1990s and 2000s would suffice to illustrate this point, especially the visibility of SHAS in the 1990s and the rise of the new Jewish Home Party (Habayit Hayhudi) in the 2000s.

43. Avi appears to belong to what is popularly known as the NANACH (ננח) faction of the Breslov Hasidic sect, the most visible faction of the sect because of its members' habit of proselytizing by playing music and dancing in the streets. While the simple, working-class Avi fits the general Breslov emphasis on the simplicity of faith and its rejection of *pilpul*, his violence is less characteristic of the sect's history and profile.

44. Even if Avi's violence is a substitute for military violence, the fact that it is sublimated is important in and of itself and certainly an improvement over outright violence.

45. Hasidism, especially the renewed Breslov sect, generally keeps out of Israel politics. As such, it is a fitting framework for Avi's quest for meaning and purpose, which centers on religion and not on the state.

46. Television critic Moran Sharir touched on this dynamic in his review of a TV coffee commercial: "In the Elite Coffee commercial [actor] Aviv Aloush appears in the role of a coach who helps a geek to successfully pass a job interview. Aloush reminds the geek that the boss is a manly-man . . . and that if he wants to get the job he needs to act accordingly. Following this advice the geek grows bigger balls and drinks Turkish coffee. The boss is happy and so is Aloush. The subtext of this commercial says: 'don't be a geek, be manly.' But this subtext has an under-subtext. Aloush's role as a coach in folksiness tells the geek in the commercial as well as viewers: 'don't be Ashkenazi, don't be a dead Friedman, be a little more Mizrahi and you'll have it easier in life.' At the end of the commercial the geek mends his ways and is rewarded. 'You've been accepted' Aloush tells him. Where? To Israeli society." Moran Sharir, "Kartis haknisa lachevra hayisre'elit" [The entry ticket into Israeli society], *Ha'aretz*, May 18, 2015, http://www.haaretz.co.il/gallery/television/tv-review/.premium-1.2225504.

1. Tom Segev, *1967: Israel, the War and the Year That Transformed the Middle East* (New York: Henry Holt, 2007; Hebrew edition, 2005).

2. See Idith Zertal and Akiva Eldar, *Lords of the Land: The War over Israel's Settlements in the Occupied Territories, 1967–2007* (New York: Nation Books, 2007), as well as Gideon Aran, *Kookism* (Tel Aviv: Carmel, 2013), about the origins of Gush Emunim, the Block of the Faithful.

3. Gideon Shimoni, *The Zionist Ideology* (Hanover, NH: University Press of New England, 1995).

4. Jehuda Reinarz, "Jewish Nationalism and Jewish Identity in Central Europe," *Leo Baeck Institute Yearbook* 37, no. 1 (1992): 147–167.

5. The name has nothing to do with the later designation of Mizrahim. On the origins of Hamizrahi, see Shimoni, *Zionist Ideology*, 127–165.

6. The most telling expression of these emotions was the plethora of popular songs composed in the wake of the war, which evocatively expressed the national giddiness. Ehud Asheri provides an excellent summary of these songs and the phenomenon of Israeli war songs in general. Asheri counts twenty-three popular songs that were written in the wake of the 1967 war, the same number that were written after the War of Independence in 1948. He notes the sharp decline in composers' zeal from the 1980s on and makes the connection between the sense of national emergency and relief after victory, which accounts for the musical effervescence. One of the most telling aspects Asheri notes is the participation of secular, left-leaning artists in the musical party, including the poet Dahlia Ravikovitch, who penned the song "Emek Dotan" [Dotan valley], which celebrates the pastoral beauty of Samaria after it was captured in the war. The song makes no mention of Palestinian inhabitants. A few years later Ravikovitch became one of the harshest critics of the 1982 Lebanon War, against which she penned extremely pointed poems. See Ehud Asheri, "Chazrnu elayich shenit" [We returned to you again], *Ha'aretz*, May 16, 2015, http://www.haaretz.co.il/misc/1.1411743. See also two articles by Dalia Gavriely-Nuri, "The Social Construction of 'Jerusalem of Gold' as Israel's Unofficial National Anthem," *Israel Studies* 12, no. 2 (Summer 2007): 104–120, and "Saying 'War,' Thinking 'Victory': The Mythmaking Surrounding Israel's 1967 Victory," *Israel Studies* 15, no. 1 (Spring 2010): 95–114.

I personally remember my Bible teacher, Ada Lekach, telling us at one of our Bible classes in my kibbutz high school in the mid-1970s that if someone were to write a history of Israel's spectacular military victories in the twentieth century, they would sound just as miraculous as the great military victories described in the Hebrew Bible.

7. For an overview of Lerski's cinematic work in Israel, see Jan-Christopher Horak, "Helmar Lerski in Israel," in *Israeli Cinema: Identities in Motion*, ed. Miri Talmon and Yaron Peleg (Austin: University of Texas Press, 2011).

8. See George Mosse, *Confronting the Nation: Jewish and Western Nationalism* (Hanover, NH: Brandeis University Press, 1993).

9. For a retrospective review of an exhibition of Lerski's photography, see Vince Aleti, *New Yorker*, May 3, 2007, http://www.newyorker.com/culture/photo-booth/critics-notebook-helmar-lerski.

10. For a study of the erotic aspects of Zionist pioneers' attachment to the land of Israel, see Boaz Neumann, *Land and Desire in Early Zionism* (Hanover, NH: Brandeis University Press, 2011).

11. A lot of the poetry that was written at the time suggested this quasi-religious fervor—for example, Uri Zvi Greenberg's "With My God, the Smith" [Im elly hanapach]. The first stanza reads as follows: "The revelations of my days burn like chapters of prophecy / My body pressed between them like a block of metal that shall soon be melted / Over me, like a smith, stands my god and beats down mightily / Every wound, which time has gashed in me, opens up / Emitting pent-up fire in spark-like moments." Avraham Shlonsky's poem "Labor" [Amal] is another example: "Dress me, good mother, in a beautiful coat of many colors / And at dawn, lead me to work / My land is wrapped in light like a prayer shawl / Houses stand like frontlets / And roads laid out by hands stretch out like tefillin." Both poems use biblical metaphors as well as Jewish rituals and ritualistic objects in a new, secular, Zionist context. For a synoptic study of this phenomenon, see Oz Almog, *The Sabra: The Creation of the New Jew* (Berkeley: University of California Press, 2000).

12. In yet another curious and ironic reversal of this trend, it is worth noting the increasing calls of religious Zionists in recent years to restore the actual temple in Jerusalem. See the afterword for more on this.

13. For some of these new "rituals," see Yael Zerubavel, *Recovered Roots: Collective Memory and the Making of Israeli National Tradition* (Chicago: University of Chicago Press, 1995).

14. For an exception to this, see Shmuel Almog, Jehuda Reinharz, and Anita Shapira, eds., *Zionism and Religion* (Hanover, NH: University Press of New England, 1998).

15. Sigmund Freud, *Moses and Monotheism* (London: Vintage, 1955); Jan Assmann, *Moses the Egyptian: The Memory of Egypt in Western Monotheism* (Cambridge, MA: Harvard University Press, 2007).

16. For the Zionist reinterpretation of traditional Jewish holidays, see Francois Guisnet, "Chanukkah and Its Function in the Invention of a Jewish-Heroic Tradition in Early Zionism, 1880–1900," in *Nationalism, Zionism and Ethnic Mobilization of the Jews in 1900 and Beyond*, ed. Michael Berkowitz (Leiden: Brill, 2004). For the reinterpretation of the Passover Haggadah, see Mookie Tzoor, ed., *Yotz'im bechodesh ha'aviv, Pesach eretz yisre'eli Haggadah kibbutzit* [The kibbutz Haggadah] (Jerusalem: Yad Ben Tzvi Press, 2004). For a contemporary consideration of the biblicism of modern Hebrew, see Alain Dieckhoff, "Hebrew, the Language of the Nation," in *The Invention of a Nation: Zionist Thought and the Making of Modern Israel*, trans. Jonathan Derrick (London: Hurst, 2003).

17. For an evocative anecdote about this historical confusion that records Theodore Herzl's actual meeting with these proto-Zionists during his 1899 visit to Palestine and the reaction of both parties to the meeting from two different perspectives, see Yaron Peleg, *Orientalism and the Hebrew Imagination* (Ithaca, NY: Cornell University Press, 2005), 1–2.

18. Shohat focuses on the relations between Jews and Arabs in the film as an Israeli version of the white supremacism of European settlers toward Native Americans. My interest here is focused more on their Jewish legacy and not so much on their relations with their Arab neighbors. See Ella Shohat, *Israeli Cinema: East/West and the Politics of Representation* (Austin: University of Texas Press, 1989).

19. Michael Coyne, *The Crowded Prairie: American National Identity in the Hollywood Western* (London: I. B. Tauris, 1998).

20. One is reminded here especially of the first Hebrew novel, Abraham Mapu's 1853 biblical romance, *The Love of Zion* [Ahavat Tziyon].

21. As the popular songs quoted above make clear (note 6), this notion became widespread immediately after the war.

22. In the last three years of Labor's rule, between 1974 and the election of Likud in 1977, early settlement activities by Gush Emunim were by and large supported by Labor coalitions. In fact, the dynamics that characterize the settlement project in the territories to this day, whereby the settlers initiate illegal action, which is supported by the authorities ex post facto, was established during those years. See Zertal and Eldar, *Lords of the Land*.

23. Numerous studies have been dedicated to Israel's so-called settlers and their impact on Israeli politics, society, and history. In addition to the studies mentioned in the introduction, see David Newman, "From Hitnachalut to Hitnatkut: The Impact of Gush Emunim and the Settlement Movement on Israeli Politics and Society," *Israel Studies* 10, no. 3 (2005): 192–224, and Ehud Sprinzak, "From Messianic Pioneering to Vigilante Terrorism: The Case of the Gush Emunim Underground," *Journal of Strategic Studies* 10, no. 4 (1987): 194–216.

24. See the introduction to Aran's *Kookism*.

25. The literature on both Kooks, father and son, is plentiful. For a good overview of Abraham Yitzhak Hacohen Kook, see Benjamin Ish-Shalom, *Rav Avraham Itzhak HaCohen Kook: Between Rationalism and Mysticism* (New York: SUNY Press, 2012).

26. On the controversies surrounding the legacy of the senior Kook, see Eliezer Don-Yihya, "Orthodox Jewry in Israel and in North America," *Israel Studies* 10, no. 1 (2005): 157–187. On the Merkaz Harav Yeshiva, where this legacy was developed, see Moshe Hellinger, "Political Theology in the Thought of 'Merkaz HaRav' Yeshiva and Its Profound Influence on Israeli Politics and Society since 1967," *Totalitarian Movements and Political Religions* 9, no. 4 (2008): 533–550.

27. The homily is well known and has a dedicated Wikipedia entry. For the full version of the flowery Hebrew text, see http://www.yeshiva.org.il/midrash/2022.

28. This is what the popular song writer and composer Yoram Tehar-lev wrote about the composition of his popular 1969 song "Al kapav yavi" (Delivered by his hands), which describes various artisans in Jerusalem who dream about performing simple services for Elijah the Prophet: "After the Six-Day War the country was awash with songs of triumph and glory. But under the surface there were mystical stirrings of faith because of the miracles that happened to us. I wrote this song two years after the war, but I think it is imbued with the spirit of Jewish tradition . . . for Elijah is considered a herald of the Messiah." The song ends with these words: "[and the builder] dreams that just as he helped build the city / he shall lay the foundation stone to the Temple / He shall deliver it by his own hands / to Elijah the Prophet." See http://www.taharlev.com/songs_selection_song.asp?id=71.

29. One is reminded here of Haim Hazaz's well-known short story "The Sermon" [Hadrasha]. See the end of chapter 4 for a discussion of it.

30. Amos Oz, *In the Land of Israel* (London: Chatto and Windus, 1983).

31. The lacuna was primarily in cinema and to some extent in literature; the press was fully engaged.

32. Yaron Peleg, *Israeli Culture between the Two Intifadas: A Brief Romance* (Austin: University of Texas Press, 2008).

33. Things are more complicated than that, of course. Israeli literature continued to evolve and innovate. Poetry especially saw a revival in the 2000s after years of relative stagnation. But the significant improvement of the quality of Israeli cinema and

television programs during those years shifted attention from the written word to the visual image, which became more politically relevant also because of global trends.

34. I am referring here to various criminal, violent acts by radical elements in the settler community against Arabs, including damage to property and people. Such acts began shortly after the settlement of the West Bank but became more extreme with the passage of time and the more established the settlement project became. The latest iteration of these ugly acts is the anti-Arab violence called "*tag mechir*" (price tag). These actions by radical settlers aim to exact a "price" from Arabs not just for their war against Israel but for their very existence within the confines of the Holy Land. Despite the general low-level animosity toward Arabs in Israel, such acts are usually universally condemned.

35. Yeshivat Hesder is a Jewish seminary that combines advanced Torah study with military service. It originated in the 1950s as a way to enable religious youth to maintain their strict religious lifestyle while completing their military duty and to thus become fully integrated into Israeli society. In 1999 the ad hoc custom was fixed legally and popularized the service among religious youth, who have since raised their military profile and credentials, supplanting those of soldiers affiliated with the Labor movement, such as kibbutz members.

36. By "settlers" here and elsewhere in the book, I am not referring to every Jewish Israeli who resides behind the Green Line in territories captured after 1967. "Settler" here designates primarily the ideological core of a much wider sector of Israeli society, which may not always agree with the policies and actions of the sector's ideologues.

37. The reference here is to Shaul Tchernichovsky's poem "Facing the Statue of Apollo" [Lenochach pesel apolo], in which the poet laments how diasporic Judaism has taken the ancient, free, and mighty Jewish spirit (ויאסרוהו ברצועות של תפילין) and bound it with straps of phylacteries. See *Kol Kitvey Shaul Tchernichovsky* (Tel Aviv: Am Oved), 85–87.

38. For a historical consideration of this future, see the reflections of veteran historian Yehuda Bauer, who muses about one of the most malevolent and dangerous intellectual products to have come out of the settler community to date, the 2009 pseudo-halakhic book *Torat hamelech* [The Laws of the King], in which the authors, so-called rabbis Yitzhak Shapira and Yosef Elitzur, sanction the killing of non-Jews. In chapter 6 of their book, the authors go further to authorize the killing of Jews who disagree with their ruling and refuse to pursue non-Jews who endanger Jews. Bauer cites the venomous book as an example of the dangerous trends that have increased in Israel since the late 2000s. See Yehuda Bauer, *Ha'am Hamechutzaf* [The Chutzpadik nation] (Tel Aviv: Nahar Books, 2013).

39. The story is based on the actual experiences of several soldiers, distilled into a 2005 best-selling novel by the journalist Ron Leshem and titled *Im yesh gan eden* [If there's a heaven]. The novel was translated into English as *Beaufort*. The equally successful film of the same title was released two years later in 2007; it is not an adaptation of the novel, but was developed concurrently with it and in cooperation with its author, Leshem. The film competed unsuccessfully for the foreign Oscar in 2008.

40. For changes in the public perception of Israeli soldiers over a period of about thirty years, from the 1980s to the beginning of the 2000s, see Tzipi Yisra'eli and Elisheva Rosman-Stolman, "Milochem le ben shel ima? Hachayal hayisre'eli bir'i ha'itonut" [From Fighter to 'Momma's Boy'? Images of Israeli Soldiers in the Press], *Iyunim bitkumat Yisrael* 24 (2014): 185–219. The article charts a change from a public

perception of soldiers as brave heroes in the 1980s, to sacrificial pawns in the 1990s, and back again to heroes (albeit slightly more vulnerable) in the 2000s.

41. S. Yizhar, *Hirbet Hizah* (Jerusalem: Ibis Editions, 2008), 103–106.

42. This is the full quotation: "We can forgive the Arabs for killing our children. We cannot forgive them for making us kill their children. We will have peace with the Arabs only once they love their children more than they hate us." It is widely quoted, though I was not able to find a specific place and time for it. See Golda Meir's Wikipedia entry, http://he.wikipedia.org/wiki/%D7%92%D7%95%D7%9C%D7%93%D7%94_%D7%9E%D7%90%D7%99%D7%A8.

43. See Raya Morag, *Waltzing with Bashir: Perpetrator Trauma and Cinema* (London: I. B. Tauris, 2013).

CHAPTER 4: JEWISH AND POPULAR

1. Recent developments in television programming, especially changes in HBO's programming in the 1990s, have complicated these simplistic divisions between film and television. In some respects, television programs have become very complex, introducing multiple plotlines and thematic meanings that stretch over extended time, requiring an ever-growing viewing sophistication. Films have not changed to the same degree since the golden age of Hollywood cinema. However, because Israeli commercial television is relatively new—it began in 1992—the Israeli television industry in the 2010s has not yet reached the complexity levels of some contemporaneous US shows. On some of the differences between film and TV in this respect, see Kristin Thompson, *Storytelling in Film and Television* (Cambridge, MA: Harvard University Press, 2003).

2. Jonathan Cohen, "What I Watch and Who I Am: National Pride and the Viewing of Local and Foreign Television in Israel," *Journal of Communication* 58, no. 1 (2008): 149–167.

3. There were other, earlier shows that incorporated various aspects of religion into their stories. The successful series *Me'orav Yerushalmi* [Jerusalem mix], which revolves around the lives of a traditional Mizrahi family and which ran intermittently from 2004 to 2011 (Keshet TV), comes readily to mind. But I would like to suggest that *A Touch Away* is the first show to have been created specifically to address the issue of religiosity within the Israeli social context. On the Avi Chai Foundation, see Galeet Dardashti, "Televised Agendas: How Global Funders Make Israeli TV More 'Jewish,'" *Jewish Film and New Media* 3, no. 1 (Spring 2015): 77–103.

4. The series garnered a remarkable viewership record of 35.9 percent for its eighth and last chapter, and won numerous "best" awards in 2007. See this report: http://www.globes.co.il/news/article.aspx?did=1000195237.

5. "Those of us born in, say, the '60s were trained by television to look where it pointed, usually at versions of 'real life' made prettier, sweeter, livelier by succumbing to a product or temptation." David Foster Wallace, "E Unibus Pluram: Television and U.S. Fiction," in *A Supposedly Fun Thing I'll Never Do Again: Essays and Arguments* (Boston: Little, Brown, 1997), 86.

6. *Srugim* literally means "knitted" and refers to the kind of knitted yarmulkes the men of the national religious community in Israel wear and that differ from the black yarmulkes of the Orthodox, for instance.

7. Ruta Kupfer actually called it so in a news item announcing the production of the show. See http://www.haaretz.co.il/gallery/1.1444772.

8. Uri Ram describes this peculiar dichotomy between capital and politics, between the bourgeoisification of society and its growing disconnection from politics in his book *The Globalization of Israel: McWorld in Tel Aviv, Jihad in Jerusalem* (London: Routledge, 2013). My previous book, *Israeli Culture between the Two Intifadas: A Brief Romance* (Austin: University of Texas Press, 2008), is also predicated on the premise that after the First Intifada in 1987, young secular Israelis were fed up with the old political way of doing business and disconnected from politics almost completely in protest. Conversely, many members of the national religious community became even more involved with politics, since they opposed the Oslo accords, which threatened the settlement project.

9. See an interview with one of the show's creators, Hava Divon, at http://www.itu.org.il/?CategoryID=1691&ArticleID=16350.

10. There are numerous articles on this. For an article that summarizes and reflects on the three seasons, see Shushan, "Srugim: Tzarat rabim, chatzi nechama" [Srugim: A sorrow shared is a sorrow halved], *Y-Net*, October 24, 2011, http://www.ynet.co.il/articles/0,7340,L-4138028,00.html. After watching the beginning of the third and final season, Shushan congratulates the creators of the show for focusing once again on issues of personal intimacy rather than "bigger" issues, which rendered the second season false for him.

11. Although Israeli films have other strictures, commercial viability is not one of them. Because the market in Israel is so small, very few Israeli films can hope to make money. That is why most films produced in Israel are supported by public funds, which are dispersed by committees or boards that are elected democratically on a rotating basis.

12. See, for example, a review article on the show *Shtisel*, about a Haredi family in the Me'ah She'arim Orthodox neighborhood in Jerusalem. The article is tellingly entitled "When the Religious Disappear and Real People Appear behind Them" [Keshehadosim ne'elamin vetzafim bimkomam anahshim], emphasizing precisely the humanizing aspect of the show. The show is not a religious safari, writes the reviewer, who extols it specifically for this reason—its abandonment of politics in favor of the politics of representation. See Moran Sharir, *Ha'aretz*, August 11, 2013, http://www.haaretz.co.il/gallery/television/tv-review/.premium-1.2094035.

13. The show won best TV drama in 2013, http://www.haaretz.co.il/gallery/television/1.2225813.

14. This can also be said about *Srugim*, of course, even though it was not supported by the Avi Chai Foundation.

15. On some of the changes undergone by Heredi society in Israel, see Yohai Hakak, "Haredi Male Bodies in the Public Sphere: Negotiating with the Religious Text and Secular Israeli Men," *Journal of Men, Masculinities and Spirituality* 3, no. 2 (2009): 100.

16. The involvement of the Avi Chai Foundation in the show's production should be borne in mind; it must have influenced the writing of the script.

17. See Daniel Boyarin, *Unheroic Conduct: The Rise of Heterosexuality and the Invention of the Jewish Man* (Berkeley: University of California Press, 1997). The models of Jewish masculinity Boyarin wrote about in the early 1990s were part of a general spirit of postmodern and post-Zionist critique. They comprised part of the critical wave that had emerged in Israel during the 1980s against calcified notions about Zion-

ism, its history, and its legacy in what began to be called then the postmodern era. Boyarin's promotion of alternative ideas of Jewish masculinity was motivated also by a desire to undermine regnant notions of Jewish-Israeli masculinity that had gone awry by that time. See Yaron Peleg, "Re-Orientalizing the Jew: Zionist and Contemporary Israeli Masculinities," in *Orientalism, Gender, and the Jews*, ed. Ulrike Brunotte, Anna-Dorothea Ludwig, and Axel Stahler (Oldenbourge: De Gruyter, 2015). See also the award-winning 2012 Israeli documentary *The Gatekeepers* (dir. Dror Moreh), in which former Israeli heads of Mossad exemplify the masculine ideals of the Zionist revolution while at the same time attesting to their limits.

18. See Susan M. Alexander, "Stylish Hard Bodies: Branded Masculinity in *Men's Health* Magazine," *Sociological Perspectives* 46, no. 4 (Winter 2003): 535–554, and Victor J. Seidler, *Unreasonable Men: Masculinity and Social Theory* (London: Routledge, 2013).

19. As mentioned in the previous chapter, one result of this hypermasculinity was that sections of Israeli society, primarily Ashkenazim, the descendants of pioneers who eventually made up the Israeli upper middle class, began to disassociate themselves from this kind of abusive masculinity. What they adopted instead was not necessarily Boyarin's older forms of Jewish masculinity. Those were not so relevant anymore in a capitalist, cosmopolitan Israel that had abandoned Zionism's anti-diasporism and its old animosity toward manifestations of Jewish religiosity. Instead, they opted for milder Western models of masculinity that were modified primarily by the feminist revolution of the mid-twentieth century, by the long peace and prosperity since the end of the Second World War, and the spread of human rights in the wake of that war and because of its legacy.

20. Leger Grindon, *The Hollywood Romantic Comedy: Conventions, History, Controversies* (Malden, MA: Wiley, 2011).

21. The show presents other models, the most prominent of which is the older model represented by Akiva's widowed father, Sholem, who is busy looking for a helpmate as well—a helpmate and not a lover. This is an important distinction that reflects not only Sholem's age but also an Orthodox reality. So while Akiva's image is more of a secular construct, Sholem is closer to more prevalent Orthodox patriarchal masculine models. In addition to those two, the show also includes other members of the Shtisel clan, including the older brother, Tzvi Aryeh (Sar'el Pitterman), and Lippeh, the son-in-law and Giti's husband (Zohar Shtrauss). Tzvi Aryeh, who is a little fat, pinkish, and soft, is probably closest to the stereotype of the yeshiva student, not only in his appearance but also in his profession, which is literally a seminary student who hopes to become a rabbi. Lippeh, who is married to Akiva's sister, Giti, is yet another masculine model, closer to secular Israeli models perhaps. His decision to use his overseas assignment as a kosher observer in a slaughterhouse in Argentina to remain away from home for a while moves him closer to post-army Israeli men, many of whom spend a year or so abroad traveling in far-flung corners of the globe. His defiance and abandonment not only of his family but also of his community render him less "religious." On the other hand, by abandoning the smaller Orthodox community, he is getting closer to the masculine models of the national, secular community, which complicates the show.

22. *Urim Vetumim* refers to the twelve precious stones that adorned the *choshen*, the breastplate worn by the high priest in the temple and through which he communicated with God. The term is not exactly clear but is understood to mean "guiding lights." It is first mentioned in Exodus 28:30.

23. The *cheyder*, or "room," in Hebrew, was a religious day class to which most Jewish boys were sent to study from age three to thirteen. The *melamed*, or "teacher," was the religious instructor in the *cheyder*, who taught the Hebrew alphabet and the Yiddish translation of the Pentateuch, the so-called *ivry-teitsh*.

24. The information is based on a telephone interview with one of the show's creators, Shuki ben Na'im, on August 18, 2013.

25. For a recent study of the genre, see Lana A. Whited, ed., *The Ivory Tower and Harry Potter: Perspectives on a Literary Phenomenon* (St. Louis: University of Missouri Press, 2004).

26. Julia Briggs, Dennis Butts, and Matthew Orville Grenby, eds., *Popular Children's Literature in Britain* (London: Ashgate, 2008).

27. Gershon Shaked has demonstrated this well in his seminal 1970 study *Gal chadash basiporet ha'ivrit: Masot al siporet yisre'elit tze'irah* [New wave in Hebrew fiction] (Tel Aviv: Sifriyat Poalim, 1970–1971).

28. Ibid.

29. Dror Burstein articulates a similar indictment in his brilliant 2003 novel *Avner Brenner*. One of the characters in the novel, Ovadia Shemtov, a Hebrew Bible teacher in a national religious high school, commits suicide by jumping from a roof after finding out that his daughter has been dating an Arab: "[Ovadia] didn't try to think why the fact that his daughter was seeing an Arab shocked him so. Actually, he couldn't even think about it, the very thought was anathema to him, he just could not say to himself, your daughter is touching an Arab, from reasons that Ovadia did not even consider as racist at all. He didn't hate Arabs, he really didn't. He just felt a deep apathy toward them, which was in fact a total demand that they disappear from his life completely" (89–90).

30. Bob Dixon, "The Nice, the Naughty and the Nasty: The Tiny World of Enid Blyton," *Children's Literature in Education* 5, no. 3 (1974): 43–61.

31. For detailed information on Hasamba and Israeli popular textual culture in general, see Ellie Eshed's informative blog at http://no666.wordpress.com. See also Ellie Eshed, *Mitarzan ve'ad zbeng: Hasipur shel hasifrut hapopularit ha'ivrit* [From Tarzan to Zbang: The history of popular Israeli literature] (Tel Aviv: Bavel, 2002). For a review of the book, see Eitan Bar-Yosef, "Uriel Ofek mehagehenom" [Uriel Ofek from hell], *Ha'aretz*, May 19, 2015, http://www.haaretz.co.il/misc/1.824782.

32. The bad guys in this book are not ordinary grave robbers, but powerful Arab agents—an Egyptian millionaire by the name of Democlitos and his agent, George Mansour.

33. On the role of archeology in Zionist culture, see Rachel S. Hallote and Alexander H. Joffe, "The Politics of Israeli Archaeology: Between 'Nationalism' and 'Science' in the Age of the Second Republic," *Israel Studies* 7, no. 3 (2002): 84–116.

34. Yael Zerubavel has written quite forcefully about this in her seminal study *Recovered Roots: Collective Memory and the Making of Israeli National Tradition* (Chicago: University of Chicago Press, 1995).

35. Fans of the Indiana Jones film series will remember the first film, titled *Indiana Jones and the Raiders of the Lost Ark* (dir. Stephen Spielberg, 1981), in which archeologists unearth the winged chest containing the tablets of the Ten Commandments. The second season of *Hasamba* is inspired by that film, in which Nazis vie for control of the ark and are ultimately thwarted by the very god of Israel, who obliterates them when they try to open the ark and get to the sacred tablets. Note also the musical score

during the opening episode, a mischievous reference to John Williams's famous wind ensemble score for the Indiana Jones film series.

36. Revach was frequently cast in Bourekas and other films as an overtly Mizrahi character, which he played with exaggerated gestures and speech. With the decline of the genre and with older age, Revach's more versatile acting talents became better known and appreciated. In 2011 he won the Ophir Lifetime Achievement Award for his contribution to Israeli cinema.

37. The phenomenon has been widely parodied in Israeli culture, most prominently perhaps by the character called the Babah Buba, played by actor Moni Moshonov in the popular television comedy series *Zehu ze!* [That's it!] (1978–1998).

38. Renen is the name of Yigal Mossensohn's daughter. "Igi" is short for "Yigal" in Hebrew.

39. The show's production values seem to be deliberately low and resemble those of similar cult shows like the British *Dr. Who.*

40. This is not unusual in the context of modern nationalism, which regards the state as the official guardian of national culture, heritage, past, and so forth. As a representative of these values, both symbolically and practically, the state is expected to epitomize such interests and act on its citizens' behalf to protect and preserve them. Both Greece and Egypt, for instance, have demanded in the last few decades that various archeological artifacts that were taken out of those countries during the colonial era be returned to them, repatriated as it were. And while there is little direct connection between the modern nations of either Greece or Egypt and the ancient cultures that once thrived in their current territories, their demands are not dismissed lightly and are accorded increasing weight. See Brian M. Fagan, *The Rape of the Nile: Tomb Robbers, Tourists, and Archaeologists in Egypt* (New York: Basic Books, 2004).

41. In the show, the museum is a private institution established with money donated by Zerach Zorkin. The museum is probably inspired by a real private museum in Israel called Machon Hamikdash, the Temple Institute. The institute promotes the rebuilding of the third temple in Jerusalem and displays reconstructed artifacts from the temple and information on the temple worship services. Its aspirations are regarded by most as bizarre. See Nadav Sharagai, "Me'avnet ve'ad michnasayim, hakol bigdey shesh" [From belt to trousers, fineries all], *Ha'aretz*, July 8, 2008, http://www.haaretz.co.il/misc/1.1335943, as well as the afterword to this book.

42. Adat Hayachad is identified by many scholars as part of the Essenes, the ascetic Jewish sect that flourished around the Dead Sea in the second and third centuries BCE and that composed the famous Dead Sea scrolls. In the cable show, the name is given to a group of kabbalists who reside in the Galilean town of Safed and who have key information about the whereabouts of the *choshen*.

43. The name Microwave is probably a direct parody of the real rabbi Yeshayahu Pinto, who is called "the X-Ray" for his alleged ability to see through people and events. In 2014 Rabbi Pinto was indicted for wide-scale corruption involving banking tycoons, politicians, and high-ranking police officers. In the spring of 2015, he was found guilty of these crimes, *Ha'aretz*, May 12, 2015, http://www.haaretz.co.il/news/law/1.2634518.

44. At one point he vividly describes his vision of the future as a triangle whose base is non-Jews, above whom are Chinese and blacks, above whom are animals, above whom are religious Jews, and above whom is Zerach, topping the pyramid.

45. Etta Bick, "The Shas Phenomenon and Religious Parties in the 1999 Elections," *Israel Affairs* 7, nos. 2–3 (2000): 55–100; Yoav Peled, "Towards a Redefinition of Jewish

Nationalism in Israel? The Enigma of Shas," *Ethnic and Racial Studies* 21, no. 4 (1998): 703–727.

46. Ashkenazi religious parties, which have taken part in Israeli politics longer than Mizrahi religious parties, consult their own religious leaders as well. But since they do not officially recognize the state they do not usually get involved in matters that do not concern their communities directly, especially foreign or military relations. Their main concerns are financial subsidies for their constituents.

47. The most notorious election campaign to have involved kabbalist rabbis and politicians was the 1996 campaign in which several prominent politicians sought the support of the Babah Baruch, heir to the Babah Sali, in the hope of appealing to traditional Mizrahi voters. See Uri Ram, "Bechirot '96: Tadmiyot vekme'ot" [The '96 election campaign: Images and mascots], *Teoria Uvikoret* 9 (1999): 199–207.

48. His use of gutturals has become comic if not campy because it no longer follows the traditional, received pronunciation of official Hebrew. In a shift that has come to characterize comedians who create overtly Mizrahi characters in the media, he freely uses ayin and chet (ע/ח) even for consonants that are not pronounced that way, like alef and chaf (א/כ). Other comedians, like Ilan Peled for instance, use the same technique in creating exaggerated images of Mizrahim. See Peled's cult TV shows *Ahad Ha'am 1* (2003) and *Ahad Ha'am 101* (2010), readily available on YouTube.

49. This dynamic has actually begun to change slowly since the 2000s with the increased nationalization or Israelization of the Orthodox community. For an unusual manifestation of these trends, see this article about the Orthodox film industry: Yael Feldman and Yohai Hakak, "Jewish Revenge (Yehuda Grovais, 2003–2010): Haredi Action in the Zionist Sphere," *Jewish Film and New Media* 3, no. 1 (Spring 2015): 48–76.

50. This is essentially what Guy Ben-Porat says in his book *Between State and Synagogue: The Secularization of Contemporary Israel* (Cambridge: Cambridge University Press, 2013).

51. Tali Artman, "The Newer Jews of Hasamba 3rd Generation," *Jewish Film and New Media* 3, no. 1 (Spring 2015): 104–112.

52. Yitzhak Laor, "Hadrasha achar chamishim shana" [The "Sermon" after fifty years], *Ha'aretz*, September 9, 1993.

53. Artman, "The Newer Jews."

AFTERWORD

1. For a report on both events, see http://www.ynet.co.il/articles/0,7340,L-4530676,00.html.

2. Moran Sharir, "Return Our Boys from Channel 1" [Hachziru et habanim shelanu michannel 1], http://www.haaretz.co.il/gallery/television/tv-review/.premium-1.2350946.

3. Uri Misgav, "First Results of the Ground Offensive: Israel Was Conquered. By Prayers" [Totza'ot rishonot lape'ula hakarka'it: Yisrael nichbesha bitfilot], *Ha'aretz*, July 18, 2014, http://www.haaretz.co.il/blogs/misgav/.premium-1.2380690. On July 4, 2014, Colonel Offer Vinter concluded his letter to his soldiers thus: "I raise my eyes up to the heavens and call together with you, hear O Israel, the Lord is our God, the Lord is one. Lord, God of Israel, make us successful in our endeavors to fight for your people of Israel against an enemy that vilifies thy name. In the name of soldiers of the IDF and

especially the soldiers and officers of our division, make these words come true, 'for the LORD your God is He that goeth with you, to fight for you against your enemies, to save you' [Deuteronomy 20:4], amen," http://www.haaretz.co.il/news/politics/1.2373864.

4. Stuart A. Cohen, "From Integration to Segregation: The Role of Religion in the IDF," *Armed Forces and Society* 25, no. 3 (1999): 387–405, as well as "Towards a New Portrait of the (New) Israeli Soldier," *Israel Affairs* 3, nos. 3–4 (1997): 77–114.

5. On the religification of the IDF as a long-term phenomenon, see Kobi Ben-Simhon, "When and How Has the Army Become So Religious?" [Matay velama hafach hatzava hayisre'eli ledati kol kach?], *Ha'aretz*, November 1, 2014, http://www.haaretz.co.il/magazine/.premium-1.2472342.

6. The passage of the Cinema Law in 1999, which increased funding for and imposed regulation on independent filmmaking in Israel, helped tremendously as well and is responsible in large part for the impressive international success Israeli films have been enjoying since then. The Israeli films that made it internationally during the 2000s and beyond, films like *Late Marriage* [Chatuna me'ucheret] (2001, dir. Dover Kosashvili), *Walk on Water* (2004, dir. Eytan Fox), *Ushpizin* [The guests] (2003, dir. Gidi Dar), *Beaufort* [Bufor] (2007, dir. Joseph Cedar), *Waltz with Bashir* [Vals im bashir] (2008, dir. Ari Folman), to name a few, did well internationally because they marketed Israeliana, so to speak. Each of them dealt in depth and unabashedly with core issues that are unique to Israel and identify it in the world, like the war in Lebanon, the religious-secular divide, Jihadist terrorism, and Holocaust trauma. Yet many of these issues resonated internationally as well because they were part of Western culture in the global era. The Israeli context provided a greater degree of involvement in issues that were not as sharply focused in a bigger and more peaceful West.

7. One indication of it is the increasing number of Israeli TV shows that are being bought by foreign cable producers around the world, especially in the US. Many of the Israeli TV shows that were sold to foreign markets in the past decade attracted international attention because of their universality. A show like *Betipul*, renamed *In Treatment*, which was the first major television show to be sold abroad, dealt with the traumas which years of combat service left on an Israeli air force pilot, who is undergoing psychoanalysis on the show. Another Israeli show that was sold to a US cable company was *Hatufim*, meaning "Kidnapped" in Hebrew and renamed *Homeland* in its English version. The show follows the re-acclimation of two Israeli soldiers who were held captive for seventeen years in a Syrian prison and have become heroes in Israel during that time. Both shows have been very successful in Israel and the US.

8. Arianna Melamed, "*Katmandu*: Stopping at Chabad House on the Way to Nepal" [Katmandu: Baderech lenepal otzrim bevet chabad], *YNet*, July 17, 2012, http://www.ynet.co.il/articles/0,7340,L-4230435,00.html. *Katmandu* is the name of an Avi Chai–supported TV show that follows Chabad missionaries in Nepal.

9. Arjun Appadurai, "Grassroots Globalization and the Research Imagination," *Public Culture* 12, no. 1 (Winter 2000): 17.

10. Jeffrey Gettleman, "Americans' Role Seen in Uganda Anti-Gay Push," *New York Times* 3 (2010).

11. Appadurai, "Grassroots Globalization and the Research Imagination," 8.

12. Andreas Huysson, "Present Pasts: Media Politics, Amnesia," in *Globalization*, ed. Arjun Appadurai (Durham, NC: Duke University Press, 2001).

13. Ibid., 70.

14. See also Uri Ram's discussion of nationalism in the postmodern age and the

"ebbing of the nationality tide," as he puts it. "In the era of the ascendancy of nationalism, historicist memory functioned as a major progenitor of constructed collective identities, or the uniting of nations. In the era of the ascendancy of the global social formation and post-modern culture, post-historicist memory functions as a progenitor of the deconstruction, the dissolution and the fragmentation of collective identities, or the disuniting of nations"; see Uri Ram, "From Nation-State to Nation-----State," in *The Challenge of Post-Zionism: Alternatives to Israeli Fundamentalist Politics*, ed. Ephraim Nimni (London: Zed Books, 2003), 21–22.

15. This hankering for a greater Jewish meaning and context to life in Israel, without an accompanying religiosity, has been expressed by various public figures, mainly writers. See Gideon Katz, *Le'etzem hachiloniyut* [On secularism: A philosophic analysis of secularity in its Israeli context] (Jerusalem: Yad Yitzchal Ben Tzvi, 2011), 195–206.

16. Carlo Strenger, "Israel Is Unraveling" [Yisrael mitpareket], *Ha'aretz*, March 7, 2014, http://www.haaretz.co.il/opinions/.premium-1.2262459.

17. In the 2015 election campaign, Burg joined the Arab-Israeli party, Chadash.

18. Avraham Burg, "Jewish and Democratic: Nitro and Glycerin" [Yehudit vedemokratit: Nitro veglitzerin], *Ha'aretz*, May 19, 2015, http://blogs.haaretz.co.il/avrum burg/45/.

19. Cedar probably based this part of the plot on the example of the so-called Jewish underground, a small group of religious Zionists who planned to blow up the mosque on Temple Mount in order to ignite an apocalyptic holy war with the Muslim world that will hasten the arrival of the messiah and the rebuilding of a third temple. The plot was uncovered and members of the underground were arrested in 1984, tried, and sent to prison.

20. The original prohibition against entering the Temple Mount complex arose soon after the temple was destroyed in the second century CE, probably for fear that Jews entering the ruins of the temple might accidentally step into the area of the Holy of Holies, the exact location of which became unknown after the destruction. Some rabbis permitted the entry in certain instances and after various cleansing rituals were performed.

21. Moshe Glantz, "His Life's Battle: Temple Mount Is My Life" [Krav chayav: Har habayit ze mamash hachayim sheli], *YNet*, October 30, 2014, http://www.ynet.co.il /articles/0,7340,L-4586163,00.html.

22. See Yaacov Golomb's review of a collection of articles by Rotenstreich: "The Man Who Dared to Speak against the Statist Messianism of Ben-Gurion" [Ha'ish shehe'ez latzet neged hamshichiyut hamamlachtit shel Ben Gurion], *Ha'aretz*, December 26, 2014, http://www.haaretz.co.il/literature/study/.premium-1.2522383.

23. Noted in Tomer Persiko, "Why Is Everyone Clamoring Suddenly to Go Up to Temple Mount?" [Lama kulam rotzim la'alot lehar habayit pit'om?], *Ha'aretz*, November 14, 2014, http://www.haaretz.co.il/magazine/the-edge/.premium-1.2483964. See also a similar discussion of the famous letter in Katz, *Le'etzem hachiloniyut*, 202.

24. Persiko, "Why Is Everyone Clamoring Suddenly to Go up to Temple Mount?"

25. Ibid. Although the revisionist poet Uri Zvi Greenberg was among the most articulate about this kind of secular "messianism," the messianic undercurrent in secular, pioneering Zionism was not confined to revisionism. In her book about the figure of Jesus in twentieth-century Jewish literature, Neta Stahl shows that it pervaded the writings of labor Zionists as well, who found in the messianic figure of Jesus "a transcendent figure that will provide both meaning and inspiration" (24); see Stahl, *Other*

and Brother: Jesus in the 20th-Century Jewish Literary Landscape (Oxford: Oxford University Press, 2013).

26. Tomer Persiko, "Temple Mount as the Starting Point and the Endpoint of Zionism" [Har habayit ketchilata vesofa shel hatziyonut], *Ha'aretz*, November 19, 2015, http://www.haaretz.co.il/magazine/the-edge/.premium-1.2490280.

27. Quoted in ibid.

28. One of the readers of Persiko's article left this droll yet poignant response: "What pains me the most [about such efforts], though, is the ignominy to which they subject the Jewish people—a people that has always been considered wise even by its detractors—which has sunk so low as to attempt to go back to its distant childhood with an infantile eagerness, like a baby who plays with its own poo." Ibid., response number 1.

29. The two instances in history when similar conditions existed, the so-called Golden Age of Jews in medieval Iberia and the golden age of Jews in the Polish-Lithuanian Commonwealth during the sixteenth and eighteenth centuries, produced some of the most enduring Jewish cultural and, in the Polish case, even political innovations. The poetic and intellectual legacy of Spanish Jewry is among the highlights of Jewish genius, while the Polish-Jewish Council of Four Lands (Va'ad arba Ha'aratzot) remains one of the most impressive communal institutions in Jewish history.

30. See Samuel C. Heilman, *Portrait of American Jews: The Last Half of the Twentieth Century* (Seattle: University of Washington Press, 1995), as well as a republication of Mordechai M. Kaplan's seminal study, *Judaism as a Civilization: Toward a Reconstruction of American-Jewish Life* (Philadelphia: Jewish Publication Society, 2010). On a more popular and contemporary note, which is telling nevertheless, see an opinion piece by the American Jewish pundit, Peter Beinart, "Hot Pastrami and the Decline of Secular, Jewish-American Identity: How Deli Stopped Being an Essential Part of the Jewish-American Story," *Ha'aretz*, January 24, 2015, http://www.haaretz.com/opinion/.premium-1.638249. Beinart notes how contemporary Jewish communities in the US are defined more by their religious affiliation than by secular habits, such as a distinct cuisine. In this respect, American Jews are different from other US minorities, most notably Italian Americans, who only hold to a few vague culinary traditions, but who are otherwise not organized communally.

31. Ephraim Nimni offers a fascinating analysis of the Jewish nature of Israeli society and its relationship to and with diasporic Jewish communities since the emergence of Zionism, but especially in the post-Zionist era. "The unexpected, and perhaps unintended, result of the Zionist settlement and the creation of a Jewish state, was a remarkable process of ethnogenesis, a kind of ethnic engineering that has few parallels in contemporary nation building" (140), writes Nimni, who considers secular Israelis, especially though not exclusively of Ashkenazi background, to be a distinct Jewish ethnic group, Israeli Hebrews, who are defined primarily by their Hebrew language and their relationship to the Israeli state. See Ephraim Nimni, "Post-Zionist and Jewish Diasporas," in Nimni, *Challenge of Post-Zionism*.

32. On the role of Christianity in European democracies, see Jonathan Fox and Shmuel Sandler, "Separation of Religion and State in the Twenty-First Century: Comparing the Middle East and Western Democracies," *Comparative Politics* (2005): 317–335. On Borgen in particular, see Birgit Eriksson, "Pure and Public, Popular and Personal—and the Inclusiveness of *Borgen* as a Public Service Blockbuster," *Akademisk kvarter* 7 (2013): 80–92.

BIBLIOGRAPHY

Alexander, Susan M. "Stylish Hard Bodies: Branded Masculinity in *Men's Health* Magazine." *Sociological Perspectives* 46, no. 4 (Winter 2003): 535–554.

Almog, Shmuel, Jehuda Reinharz, and Anita Shapira, eds. *Zionism and Religion*. Hanover, NH: University Press of New England, 1998.

Appadurai, Arjun, ed. *Globalization*. Durham, NC: Duke University Press, 2001.

———. "Grassroots Globalization and the Research Imagination." *Public Culture* 12, no. 1 (Winter 2000): 1–19.

Aran, Gideon. *Kookism*. Tel Aviv: Carmel, 2013.

Artman, Tali. "The Newer Jews of Hasamba 3rd Generation." *Jewish Film and New Media* 3, no. 1 (Spring 2015): 104–112.

Assmann, Jan. *Moses the Egyptian: The Memory of Egypt in Western Monotheism*. Cambridge, MA: Harvard University Press, 2007.

Avineri, Shlomo. *The Making of Modern Zionism: The Intellectual Origins of the Jewish State*. New York: Basic Books, 1981.

Azaryahu, Maoz. *Tel Aviv: Mythography of a City*. Syracuse, NY: Syracuse University Press, 2007.

Bar-Levav, Avriel, Ron Margolin, and Shmuel Feiner, eds. *Tahalichey chilun batarbut hayehudit* [Secularization in Jewish culture]. Tel Aviv: Open University Press, 2012.

Bauer, Yehuda. *Ha'am Hamechutzaf* [The Chutzpadik nation]. Tel Aviv: Nahar Books, 2013.

Ben-Porat, Guy. *Between State and Synagogue: The Secularization of Contemporary Israel*. Cambridge: Cambridge University Press, 2013.

Ben-Rafael, Eliezer, and Stephen Sharot. *Ethnicity, Religion and Class in Israeli Society*. Cambridge: Cambridge University Press, 1991.

Berkowitz, Michael. *Zionist Culture and West European Jewry before the First World War*. Cambridge: Cambridge University Press, 1996.

Bick, Etta. "The Shas Phenomenon and Religious Parties in the 1999 Elections." *Israel Affairs* 7, nos. 2–3 (2000): 55–100.

Bilu, Yoram, and E. Y. A. L. Ben-Ari. "The Making of Modern Saints: Manufactured Charisma and the Abu-Hatzeiras of Israel." *American Ethnologist* 19, no. 4 (1992): 672–687.

Boyarin, Daniel. *Unheroic Conduct: The Rise of Heterosexuality and the Invention of the Jewish Man*. Berkeley: University of California Press, 1997.

Briggs, Julia, Dennis Butts, and Matthew Grenby Orville, eds. *Popular Children's Literature in Britain*. London: Ashgate, 2008.
Brodkin, Karen. *How Jews Became White Folks and What That Says about Race in America*. New Brunswick, NJ: Rutgers University Press, 1998.
Brown, Kenneth. "Iron and a King: The Likud and Oriental Jews." *MERIP Reports* no. 114, "Israel Divided" (May 1983): 3–13.
Brunotte, Ulrike, Anna-Dorothea Ludwig, and Axel Stahler, eds. *Orientalism, Gender, and the Jews*. Berlin: De Gruyter Oldenbourg, 2015.
Chetrit, Sami Shalom. "Mizrahi Politics in Israel: Between Integration and Alternative." *Journal of Palestine Studies* (2000): 51–65.
Chyutin, Dan. "'Lifting the Veil': Judaic-Themed Israeli Cinema and Spiritual Aesthetics." *Jewish Film and New Media* 3, no. 1 (Spring 2005): 25–47.
Cohen, Jonathan. "What I Watch and Who I Am: National Pride and the Viewing of Local and Foreign Television in Israel." *Journal of Communication* 58, no. 1 (2008): 149–167.
Cohen, Shaye. *The Beginnings of Jewishness: Boundaries, Varieties, Uncertainties*. Berkeley: University of California Press, 2001.
Cohen, Stuart A. "From Integration to Segregation: The Role of Religion in the IDF." *Armed Forces and Society* 25, no. 3 (1999): 387–405.
———. "Towards a New Portrait of the (New) Israeli Soldier." *Israel Affairs* 3, nos. 3–4 (1997): 77–114.
Coyne, Michael. *The Crowded Prairie: American National Identity in the Hollywood Western*. London: I. B. Tauris, 1998.
Dardashti, Galeet. "Televised Agendas: How Global Funders Make Israeli TV More 'Jewish.'" *Jewish Film and New Media* 3, no. 1 (Spring 2015): 77–103.
Deshen, Shlomo, Charles S. Leibman, and Moshe Shokeid, eds. *Israeli Judaism: The Sociology of Religion in Israel*. Schnitzer Studies in Israeli Society, vol. 7. New Brunswick, NJ: Transaction, 1995.
Dieckhoff, Alain. "Hebrew, the Language of the Nation." In *Zionist Thought and the Making of Modern Israel*, 98–127. London: Hurst, 2003.
———. *The Invention of a Nation: Zionist Thought and the Invention of Modern Israel*. Translated by Jonathan Derrick. New York: Columbia University Press, 2002.
Dixon, Bob. "The Nice, the Naughty and the Nasty: The Tiny World of Enid Blyton." *Children's Literature in Education* 5, no. 3 (1974): 43–61.
Don-Yihya, Eliezer. "Orthodox Jewry in Israel and in North America." *Israel Studies* 10, no. 1 (2005): 157–187.
Eriksson, Birgit. "Pure and Public, Popular and Personal—and the Inclusiveness of *Borgen* as a Public Service Blockbuster." *Akademisk kvarter* 7 (2013): 80–92.
Eshed, Ellie. *Mitarzan ve'ad zbeng: Hasipur shel hasifrut hapopularit Ha'ivrit* [From Tarzan to Zbang: The history of popular Israeli literature]. Tel Aviv: Bavel, 2002.
Fagan, Brian M. *The Rape of the Nile: Tomb Robbers, Tourists, and Archaeologists in Egypt*. New York: Basic Books, 2004.
Feldman, Yael, and Yohai Hakak. "Jewish Revenge (Yehuda Grovais, 2003–2010): Haredi Action in the Zionist Sphere." *Jewish Film and New Media* 3, no. 1 (Spring 2015): 48–76.
Flapan, Simha. *The Birth of Israel: Myths and Realities*. New York: Pantheon Books, 1987.
Fox, Jonathan, and Shmuel Sandler. "Separation of Religion and State in the Twenty-

First Century: Comparing the Middle East and Western Democracies." *Comparative Politics* (2005): 317–335.

Friedman, Menachem. *The Haredi Ultra-Orthodox Society: Sources, Trends and Processes*. Jerusalem: Jerusalem Institute for Israel Studies, 1991.

Friedman, Yael, and Yuval Hakak. "Jewish Revenge (Yehuda Grovais, 2003–2010): Haredi Action in the Zionist Sphere." *Jewish Film and New Media* 3, no. 1 (2015): 48–76.

Freud, Sigmund. *Moses and Monotheism*. London: Vintage, 1955.

Gavriely-Nuri, Dalia. "Saying 'War,' Thinking 'Victory': The Mythmaking Surrounding Israel's 1967 Victory." *Israel Studies* 15, no. 1 (Spring 2010): 95–114.

———. "The Social Construction of 'Jerusalem of Gold' as Israel's Unofficial National Anthem." *Israel Studies* 12, no. 2 (Summer 2007): 104–120.

Gertz, Nurit, Orly Lubin, and Judd Ne'eman, eds. *Mabatim fiktiviyim al kolnoa yisre'eli* [Fictive takes on Israeli cinema]. Tel Aviv: Open University Press, 1991.

Glazer, Nathan. *American Judaism*. 2nd ed. Chicago: University of Chicago Press, 1972.

Gluzman, Michael. *The Zionist Body: Nationality, Gender and Sexuality in Modern Hebrew Literature*. Tel Aviv: Hakibbutz Hame'uhad, 2007.

Goldberg, Yaniv. "Ephraim Kishon's 'Lefi Ratzon'—'As Much as You Like': The Metamorphosis of a Skit across Languages and Cultures." *Israeli Journal of Humor Research* 1, no. 2 (2012): 52–62.

Goldsmith, S. J. "Tevye and Professor Higgins." *Jewish Quarterly* 15, nos. 1–2 (1967): 16.

Grindon, Leger. *The Hollywood Romantic Comedy: Conventions, History, Controversies*. Malden, MA: Wiley, 2011.

Guisnet, Francois. "Chanukkah and Its Function in the Invention of a Jewish-Heroic Tradition in Early Zionism, 1880–1900." In *Nationalism, Zionism and Ethnic Mobilization of the Jews in 1900 and Beyond*, edited by Michael Berkowitz, 227–245. Leiden, Boston: Brill, 2004.

Hakak, Yohai. "Haredi Male Bodies in the Public Sphere: Negotiating with the Religious Text and Secular Israeli Men." *Journal of Men, Masculinities and Spirituality* 3, no. 2 (2009): 100–122.

———. *Young Men in Israeli Haredi Yeshiva Education: The Scholar's Enclave in Unrest*. Leiden: Brill, 2012.

Halkin, Simon. *Modern Hebrew Literature*. New York: Schocken Books, 1970.

Hall, Mathew. "Analysing Discursive Constructions of 'Metrosexual' Masculinity Online: 'What Does It Matter, Anyway?'" *GEXcel Work in Progress Report* 6 (2009): 111–117.

Hallote Rachel S., and Alexander H. Joffe. "The Politics of Israeli Archaeology: Between 'Nationalism' and 'Science' in the Age of the Second Republic." *Israel Studies* 7, no. 3 (2002): 84–116.

Heilman, Samuel C. *Portrait of American Jews: The Last Half of the Twentieth Century*. Seattle: University of Washington Press, 1995.

Hellinger, Moshe. "Political Theology in the Thought of 'Merkaz HaRav' Yeshiva and Its Profound Influence on Israeli Politics and Society since 1967." *Totalitarian Movements and Political Religions* 9, no. 4 (2008): 533–550.

Helman, Anat. *A Coat of Many Colors: Dress Culture in the Young State of Israel*. Brighton, MA: Academic Studies Press, 2011.

Herberg, Will. *Protestant-Catholic-Jew: An Essay in American Religious Sociology*. Garden City, NY: Doubleday, 1955.

Hockings, Paul, ed. *Principles of Visual Anthropology*. Berlin: Mouton de Gruyter, 1995.

Horak, Jan-Christopher. "Helmar Lerski in Israel." In *Israeli Cinema: Identities in Motion*, edited by Miri Talmon and Yaron Peleg, 16–29. Austin: University of Texas Press, 2011.

Hutcheon, Linda. *The Politics of Postmodernism*. London: Routledge, 2003.

Huysson, Andreas. "Present Pasts: Media Politics, Amnesia." In *Globalization*, edited by Arjun Appadurai, 57–77. Durham, NC: Duke University Press, 2001.

Ish-Shalom, Benjamin. *Rav Avraham Itzhak HaCohen Kook: Between Rationalism and Mysticism*. New York: SUNY Press, 2012.

Kachtan, Dana. "The Construction of Ethnic Identity in the Military: From the Bottom Up." *Israel Studies* 17, no. 3 (2012): 150–175.

Kahana-Carmon, Amalia. "The Song of the Bats in Flight." In *Gender and Text in Modern Hebrew and Yiddish Literature*, edited by Naomi B. Sokoloff, Anne Lapidus Lerner, and Anita Norich, 235–245. New York: Jewish Theological Seminary of America, 1992.

Kaplan, Mordechai. *Judaism as a Civilization: Toward a Reconstruction of American-Jewish Life*. Philadelphia: Jewish Publication Society, 2010.

Katz, Gideon. *Le'etzem hachiloniyut* [On secularism: A philosophic analysis of secularity in its Israeli context]. Jerusalem: Yad Yitzchal Ben Tzvi, 2011.

Kayyal, Mahmoud. "A Hesitant Dialogue with 'The Other': The Interactions of Arab Intellectuals with the Israeli Culture." *Israel Studies* 11, no. 2 (Summer 2006): 54–74.

Kedar, Nir. "Ben-Gurion's Mamlachtiyut: Etymological and Theoretical Roots." *Israel Studies* 7, no. 3 (2003): 117–133.

Keren, Michael. *The Pen and the Sword: Israeli Intellectuals and the Making of the Nation-State*. Boulder, CO: Westview, 1989.

Kimmerling, Baruch. "Between Hegemony and Dormant Kulturkampf in Israel." In *In Search of Identity: Jewish Aspects in Israeli Culture*, edited by Dan Urian and Efraim Karsh, 49–72. London: Frank Cass, 1999.

———. *The Invention and Decline of Israeliness: State, Society, and the Military*. Berkeley: University of California Press, 2001.

———. *Palestinians: The Making of a People*. New York: Free Press, 1993.

Kouts, Gideon. "The Representation of the Foreigner in Israeli Films (1966–1976)." *European Journal of Hebrew Studies* 2 (1999): 80–108.

Lehmann, David, and Batia Siebzehner. *Remaking Israeli Judaism: The Challenge of Shas*. London: Hurst, 2006.

Leibowitz, Yeshayahu. *Judaism, the Jewish People and the State of Israel* [Yahadut, am yehudi umedinat Yisra'el]. Jerusalem: Schocken, 1975.

Leon, Nissim. "Dat vechiloniyut" [Religion and secularity: What shall we call this mysterious phenomenon? Concerning the development of Mizrahi orthodoxy in Israel]. *Iyunim bitkumat Yisrael* 16 (2006): 85–107.

———. *Charediyut raka: Hitchadshut datit bayahadut hamizrachit* [Soft orthodoxy: Religious renewal in Mizrahi Judaism]. Jerusalem: Yad Ben-Tzvi, 2010.

Levy, Emanuel. "Art Critics and Art Publics: A Study in the Sociology and Politics of Taste." *Empirical Studies of the Arts* 6, no. 2 (1988): 127–148.

Liebman, Charles S., and Eliezer Don-Yihya. *Civil Religion in Israel: Traditional Judaism and Political Culture in the Jewish State*. Berkeley: University of California Press, 1983.

Loshitzky, Yosefa. *Identity Politics on the Israeli Screen*. Austin: University of Texas Press, 2001.

Mintz, Alan, ed. *The Boom in Contemporary Israeli Fiction*. Hanover, NH: Brandeis University Press, 1997.

Morag, Raya. *Waltzing with Bashir: Perpetrator Trauma and Cinema*. London: I. B. Tauris, 2013.

Morris, Benny. *The Birth of the Palestinian Refugee Problem, 1947–1949*. Cambridge: Cambridge University Press, 1988.

Mosse, George. *Confronting the Nation: Jewish and Western Nationalism*. Hanover, NH: Brandeis University Press, 1993.

Neils Conzen, Kathleen, David A. Gerber, Ewa Morawska, George E. Pozzetta, and Rudolph J. Vecoli. "The Invention of Ethnicity: A Perspective from the USA." *Journal of American Ethnic History* 12 (1992): 3–41.

Neumann, Boaz. *Land and Desire in Early Zionism*. Hanover, NH: Brandeis University Press, 2011.

Newman, David. "From Hitnachalut to Hitnatkut: The Impact of Gush Emunim and the Settlement Movement on Israeli Politics and Society." *Israel Studies* 10, no. 3 (2005): 192–224.

Nimni, Ephraim, ed. *The Challenge of Post-Zionism: Alternatives to Israeli Fundamentalist Politics*. London: Zed Books, 2003.

———. "Post-Zionist and Jewish Diasporas." In *The Challenge of Post-Zionism: Alternatives to Israeli Fundamentalist Politics*, edited by Ephraim Nimni, 117–152. London: Zed Books, 2003.

Oz, Almog. *Preda misrulik, shinuy arachim ba'elita hayisre'elit* [Changing values in the Israeli elite]. Haifa: Haifa University Press/Zmora-Bitan, 2004.

———. *The Sabra: The Creation of the New Jew*. Berkeley: University of California Press, 2000.

Oz, Amos. *In the Land of Israel*. London: Chatto and Windus, 1983.

Pak-Shiraz, Nacim. *Shi'i Islam in Iranian Cinema: Religion and Spirituality in Film*. London: I. B. Tauris, 2011.

Parchek, Roni. "Haregesh hadati bakolnoa hayisre'eli" [The religious sentiment in Israeli cinema]. In *Mabatim fiktiviyim al kolnoa yisre'eli*, edited by Nurit Gertz, Orly Lubin, and Judd Ne'eman, 328–341. Tel Aviv: Open University Press, 1991.

Peled, Yoav. "Towards a Redefinition of Jewish Nationalism in Israel? The Enigma of Shas." *Ethnic and Racial Studies* 21, no. 4 (1998): 703–727.

Peleg, Yaron. "Ecce Homo: The Transfiguration of Israeli Manhood in Israeli Films." In *Israeli Cinema: Identities in Motion*, edited by Miri Talmon and Yaron Peleg, 30–40. Austin: University of Texas Press, 2011.

———. "From Black to White: The Changing Image of Mizrahim in Israeli Cinema, 1960–2000." *Journal of Israel Studies* 13, no. 2 (Summer 2008): 122–145.

———. *Israeli Culture between the Two Intifadas: A Brief Romance*. Austin: University of Texas Press, 2008.

———. *Orientalism and the Hebrew Imagination*. Ithaca, NY: Cornell University Press, 2005.

———. "Re-Orientalizing the Jew: Zionist and Contemporary Israeli Masculinities." In *Orientalism, Gender, and the Jews*, edited by Ulrike Brunotte, Anna-Dorothea Ludwig, and Axel Stahler, 176–194. Oldenbourge: De Gruyter, 2015.

Rabinowitz, Itamar. *Waging Peace: Israel and the Arabs, 1948–1993*. Princeton, NJ: Princeton University Press, 2004.

Ram, Uri. "Bechirot '96: Tadmiyot vekme'ot" [The '96 election campaign: Images and mascots]. *Teoria Uvikoret* 9 (1999): 199–207.

———. "From Nation-State to Nation-----State." In *The Challenge of Post-Zionism*, edited by Ephraim Nimni, 20–41. London: Zed Books, 2003.

———. *The Globalization of Israel: McWorld in Tel Aviv, Jihad in Jerusalem*. London: Routledge, 2013.

Ravitzky, Aviezer. *Is a Halakhic State Possible?* [Ha'im titachen medinat halacha? Haparadoks shel hate'okratya hayehudit]. Jerusalem: Israel Democracy Institute, 2004.

———. *Messianism, Zionism, and Jewish Religious Radicalism*. Chicago: University of Chicago Press, 1996.

———. *Religious and Secular Jews in Israel: A Kulturkampf?* [Datiyim vechilonim beyisrael: Milchemet tarbut?]. Jerusalem: Israel Democracy Institute, 2000.

———. *Religion and State in Jewish Thought* [Dat umedinah bemachshevet Yisrael]. Jerusalem: Israel Democracy Institute, 1998.

Rebhun, Uzi, and Chaim I. Waxman, eds. *Jews in Israel: Contemporary Social and Cultural Patterns*. Hanover, NH: Brandeis University Press, 2004.

Regev, Motti, and Edwin Seroussi. *Popular Music and National Culture in Israel*. Berkeley: University of California Press, 2004.

Reinarz, Jehuda. "Jewish Nationalism and Jewish Identity in Central Europe." *Leo Baeck Institute Yearbook* 37, no. 1 (1992): 147–167.

Rubinstein, Amnon. *From Herzl to Rabin: The Changing Image of Zionism*. New York: Holmes and Meier, 2000.

Schweid, Eliezer. "Lev'ayat hamkorot bemishnato shel A. D. Gordon." *Proceedings of the Fifth World Congress of Jewish Studies* 3 (1969): 345–351.

———. "Rejection of the Diaspora in Zionist Thought." In *Essential Papers on Zionism*, edited by Yehuda Reinhartz and Anita Shapira, 133–160. London: Cassell, 1996.

Segev, Tom. "Between the Orthodox and the Secular." In *1949: The First Israelis*, 195–262. New York: Henry Holt, 1986.

———. *1949: The First Israelis*. New York: Henry Holt, 1988. Hebrew edition, 1984.

———. *1967: Israel, the War and the Year That Transformed the Middle East*. New York: Henry Holt, 2007. Hebrew edition, 2005.

———. *One Palestine, Complete: Jews and Arabs under the British Mandate*. New York: Metropolitan Books, 2000. Hebrew edition, 1999.

———. *The Seventh Million: Israelis and the Holocaust*. New York: Hill and Wang, 1993. Hebrew edition, 1991.

Seidler, Victor J. *Unreasonable Men: Masculinity and Social Theory*. London: Routledge, 2013.

Shaked, Gershon. *Gal chadash basiporet ha'ivrit: Masot al siporet Yisre'elit tze'irah* [New wave in Hebrew fiction]. Tel Aviv: Sifriyat Poalim, 1970–1971.

———. *Modern Hebrew Fiction*. New Milford, CT: Toby, 2008.

Shamir, Michal, and Asher Arian. "Collective Identity and Electoral Competition in Israel." *American Political Science Review* 93, no. 2 (June 1999): 265–277.

Shapira, Anita, Yehuda Reinharz, and Yaacov Harris, eds. *Idan hatziyonut* [The Zionist era]. Jerusalem: Zalman Shazar Center for Jewish History, 2000.

Shapira, Avraham. *Or hachayim be-or ktanot: Mishnat A. D. Gordon umekoroteha bakabala uvachasidut* [The Jewish sources of A. D. Gordon]. Tel Aviv: Am Oved, 1996.

Shemer, Yaron. "The Burden of Self-Representation: Reflections on *Shchur* and Its Legacy for Contemporary Mizrahi Films in Israel." *Journal of Levantine Studies* 2, no. 2 (Winter 2013): 39–62.
———. *Identity, Place, and Subversion in Contemporary Mizrahi Cinema in Israel*. Ann Arbor: University of Michigan Press, 2013.
Shimoni, Gideon. *The Zionist Ideology*. Hanover, London: University Press of New England, 1995.
Shlaim, Avi. "The Likud in Power: The Historiography of Revisionist Zionism." *Israel Studies* 1, no. 2 (Fall 1996): 278–293.
Shohat, Ella. *Israeli Cinema: East/West and the Politics of Representation*. Austin: University of Texas Press, 1989.
Shokeid, Moshe. "The Religiosity of Middle Eastern Jews." In *Israeli Judaism: The Sociology of Religion in Israel*, edited by Shlomo Deshen, Charles S. Leibman, and Moshe Shokeid, 213–239. Schnitzer Studies in Israeli Society, vol. 7. New Brunswick, NJ: Transaction, 1995.
Silberstein, Laurence. *The Postzionist Debates: Knowledge and Power in Israeli Culture*. New York: Routledge, 1999.
Sokoloff, Naomi B., Ann Lapidus Lerner, and Anita Norich, eds. *Gender and Text in Modern Hebrew and Yiddish Literature*. New York: Jewish Theological Seminary of America, 1992.
Sprinzak, Ehud. "From Messianic Pioneering to Vigilante Terrorism: The Case of the Gush Emunim Underground." *Journal of Strategic Studies* 10, no. 4 (1987): 194–216.
Stahl, Neta. *Other and Brother: Jesus in the 20th-Century Jewish Literary Landscape*. Oxford, New York: Oxford University Press, 2013.
Stein, Rebecca Lunna. "Spatial Fantasies: Israeli Popular Culture after Oslo." *Middle East Report* no. 216 (Autumn 2000): 36–38.
Talmon, Miri. *Israeli Graffiti: Nostalgia, Groups, and Collective Identity in Israeli Cinema*. Tel Aviv: Open University Press, 2001.
Talmon, Miri, and Yaron Peleg, eds. *Israeli Cinema: Identities in Motion*. Austin: University of Texas Press, 2011.
Taylor, Dov. *Joseph Perl's Revealer of Secrets: The First Hebrew Novel*. Boulder, CO: Westview, 1996.
Thompson, Kristin. *Storytelling in Film and Television*. Cambridge, MA: Harvard University Press, 2003.
Tzameret, Tzvi. "The Frumkin Commission" [Va'adat Frumkin]. *Iyunim bitkumat Yisrael* 1 (1991): 405–439.
Tzoor, Mookie, ed. *Yotz'im bechodesh ha'aviv, Pesach eretz yisre'eli Haggadah kibbutzit* [The kibbutz Haggadah]. Jerusalem: Yad Ben Tzvi Press, 2004.
Urian, Dan, and Efraim Karsh, eds. *In Search of Identity: Jewish Aspects in Israeli Culture*. Israeli History, Politics, and Society, book 7. London: Frank Cass, 1999.
Vinig, Marylin. *Orthodox Cinema* [Hakolno'a hacharedi]. Tel Aviv: Resling, 2011.
Wallace, David Foster. *A Supposedly Fun Thing I'll Never Do Again: Essays and Arguments*. Boston: Little, Brown, 1997.
Weakland, John H. "Feature Films as Cultural Documents." In *Principles of Visual Anthropology*, edited by Paul Hockings, 45–67. Berlin: Mouton de Gruyter, 1995.
Whited, Lana A., ed. *The Ivory Tower and Harry Potter: Perspectives on a Literary Phenomenon*. St. Louis: University of Missouri Press, 2004.

Yerushalmi, Yosef Hayim. *Zakhor: Jewish History and Jewish Memory*. Seattle: University of Washington Press, 1996.

Yisra'eli, Tzipi, and Elisheva Rosman-Stolman. "Milochem le ben shel ima? Hachayal hayisre'eli bir'i ha'itonut [From fighter to 'momma's boy'? Images of Israeli soldiers in the press]. *Iyunim bitkumat Yisrael* 24 (2014): 185–219.

Yizhar, S. *Khirbet Khizeh*. Jerusalem: Ibis Editions, 2008.

Zertal, Idith, and Akiva Eldar. *Lords of the Land: The War over Israel's Settlements in the Occupied Territories, 1967–2007*. New York: Nation Books, 2007.

Zerubavel, Yael. *Recovered Roots: Collective Memory and the Making of Israeli National Tradition*. Chicago: University of Chicago Press, 1995.

FILMOGRAPHY

The Appointed [Hameyu'ad]. Dir. Daniel Wachsmann. 1990.
Avodah. Dir. Helmar Lerski. 1935.
Beaufort [Bufor]. Dir. Joseph Cedar. 2007.
Campfire [Medurat hashevet]. Dir. Joseph Cedar. 2004.
Eyes Wide Open [Einayim petuchoth]. Dir. Haim Tabakman. 2009.
God's Neighbors [Ha'mashgichim]. Dir. Meny Yaesh. 2012.
I Love You, Rosa [Ani ohev otach, Rosa]. Dir. Moshe Mizrahi. 1972.
Kadosh. Dir. Amos Gitai. 1999.
Kuni Leml in Cairo [Kuni Leml beKahir]. Dir. Joel Silberg. 1983.
Kuni Leml in Tel Aviv [Kuni Leml beTel Aviv]. Dir. Joel Silberg. 1976.
Lovesick on Nana Street [Chole ahava Beshikun gimel]. Dir. Savi Gabizon. 1995.
The Policeman [Ha'shoter Azulai]. Dir. Ephraim Kishon. 1970.
Sallah Shabati. Dir. Ephraim Kishon. 1964.
Salomonico. Dir. Alfred Steinhardt. 1974.
Sh'chur [Black magic]. Dir. Shmuel Hasfari. 1993.
Shiva [Seven days]. Dir. Ronit Elkabetz and Shlomi Elkabetz. 2008.
Shuroo. Dir. Savi Gabizon. 1990.
They Were Ten [Hem hayu asarah]. Dir. Baruch Dienar. 1960.
Time of Favor [Ha-hesder]. Dir. Joseph Cedar. 2000.
Two Kuni Leml [Shnei Kuni Leml]. Dir. Israel Becker. 1966.
Ushpizin [The guests]. Dir. Gidi Dar. 2003.
Waltz with Bashir [Vals im bashir]. Dir. Ari Folman. 2008.

TV PROGRAMS

A Touch Away [Merchak negi'a]. 2007.
Srugim [Knitted]. 2008–2012.
Shtisel. 2013.
Shuli's Guy [Habachur shel Shuli]. Dir. Doron Tzabari. 1997.
Hasamba 3rd Generation [Hasamba dor shalosh]. 2010–2013.
Urim Vetumim [Guiding lights]. 2011.

INDEX

Ahad Ha'am (Asher Ginsberg), 2, 143, 145, 170
Appointed, The (film), 31–34
Avi Chai Foundation, 19–20, 106–108, 111–112, 115, 137–138, 142, 165n6, 166n14
Avodah (film), 84–89, 96

Babahs, 33, 127, 130–131, 154n25, 169n37, 170n47
Beaufort (film), 18, 20, 100, 104, 164n39, 171n6
Ben-Gurion, David, 1, 3, 83, 139–140, 145n1, 145n3
Bialik, Haim Nahman, 2, 3, 143, 145n3
Boyarin, Daniel, 11, 115–116, 166n17
Burstein, Mike, 18, 25–26, 31, 44, 153n12, 154n24
Burstein, Rama, 18, 44, 155nn36–37

Campfire (film), 17, 20, 75, 94–99
Cedar, Joseph, 17–18, 20, 40, 44, 75–76, 94–111, 123, 139, 171n6, 172n19
choshen, 126–130, 167n22, 169n42

Eyes Wide Open (film), 19, 45, 47–48, 50

Fiddler on the Roof (film), 25, 55
Fill the Void (film), 18, 44, 63
Frankenstein, 95, 97, 99

gefilte fish, 24–25, 152n10
God's Neighbors (film), 18, 20, 44, 73–74, 76, 78, 155n31
Gordon, A. D., 3
Gordon, Y. L., 156n2
Gush Emunim (Block of the Faithful), 8, 89, 92, 140, 161n2, 163nn22–23

halakha, 5–6, 26, 36, 82–83, 86–87, 120
Hasamba 3rd Generation (TV series), 20, 106, 111, 128, 132–134, 168n31, 168n35
Haskala, the, 23, 53, 118, 151n4
Hazaz, Haim, 133, 163
homosexuality, 47–50, 121

I Love You, Rosa (film), 19, 31
Indiana Jones films, 126, 129, 168n35
Intifadas, 93–95, 166n8

Jewishness as identity, 1

Kadosh (film), 19, 34–40, 45, 47, 51, 108
Kishon, Ephraim, 20, 54–55, 58, 152n7
Kook, Itzhak Hacohen, 5, 82, 91–92, 163n25
Kook, Zvi Yehuda, 90–92, 141, 163n25
Kuni Leml in Tel Aviv (film), 18, 24, 26

Leibowitz, Yeshayahu, 5–6, 146n9
Lerski, Helmar, 84–85, 87, 89, 161n7
Lovesick on Nana Street (film), 20, 61, 68

Ma'aleh School, 94, 111
mamlachtiyut (statism), 4, 146n5
masortiyut (tradionalism), 4, 20, 70, 72–73, 131
metrosexuality, 50, 73, 156n39

Mivtza Yonatan (film), 31
Mossensohn, Yigal, 61, 124, 169n38
My Father, My Lord (film), 17

negation of exile, 11, 23, 149n30
New Jew, 11, 23, 133

Oslo Accords, 60, 64, 73, 93, 95, 141, 157n20, 166n8
Oz, Amos, 7, 93–94, 120, 122, 124

Policeman, The (film), 58–59

Rand, Shuli, 17, 32, 40, 42, 44, 155n34, 155n36
Ravitzky, Avi, 5–6

Sallah (character), 54–56, 65, 67–68, 157n14
Sallah Shabati (film), 24, 54, 56, 61, 70
Salomonico (film), 57–58, 63, 65
Scholem, Gershon, 140, 141
Segev, Tom, 14, 81, 83, 92, 151n4
SHAS, 8, 33, 38–39, 68, 127, 131–132, 148n23, 155n29, 160n42
Sh'chur (film), 20, 61, 64–67, 70, 158n26
Shiva (film), 20, 45, 70–72, 159n35
Shohat, Ella, 88, 162n18
shtetls, 11, 24–26, 114, 118, 153n12
Shtisel (TV series), 20, 106, 111–113, 115–117, 137–138, 166n12, 167n21
Shuli's Guy (film), 68–70
Shuroo (film), 20, 61–63, 73, 159n32
Siege (film), 30, 154n19
Srugim (TV series), 18, 20, 106, 109–111, 119, 138, 165n6, 166n7, 166n10, 166n14

Temple Mount, 41, 95, 97, 139–141, 172n19
They Were Ten (film), 87–89
Time of Favor (film), 17, 20, 40, 75, 94–98
Topol, Haim, 54–55, 157n11
Touch Away, A (TV series), 18, 20, 106–109, 111, 137, 165n3

Urim Vetumim (TV series), 20, 106, 111, 117–120, 122–123, 138, 167n22
Ushpizin (film), 17, 19, 33, 40–47, 78, 155nn31–34, 171n6

Waltz with Bashir (film), 18, 20, 100–104, 171n6

Yaesh, Meny, 18, 44, 73, 76, 155n36
Yehoshua, A. B., 94, 120, 122, 124
Yizhar, S., 94, 102

Zohar, Uri, 44

אתלחתא הלואגד (beginning of redemption), 82, 91